OXFORD ENGLISH MONOGRAPHS

CONRAD AND HISTORY

RICHARD NILAND

OXFORD

UNIVERSITY PRESS

Great Clarendon Street, Oxford OX2 6DP

Oxford University Press is a department of the University of Oxford.
It furthers the University's objective of excellence in research, scholarship,
and education by publishing worldwide in

Oxford New York

Auckland Cape Town Dar es Salaam Hong Kong Karachi
Kuala Lumpur Madrid Melbourne Mexico City Nairobi
New Delhi Shanghai Taipei Toronto

With offices in

Argentina Austria Brazil Chile Czech Republic France Greece
Guatemala Hungary Italy Japan Poland Portugal Singapore
South Korea Switzerland Thailand Turkey Ukraine Vietnam

Oxford is a registered trade mark of Oxford University Press
in the UK and in certain other countries

Published in the United States
by Oxford University Press Inc., New York

© Richard Niland 2010

The moral rights of the author have been asserted
Database right Oxford University Press (maker)

First published 2010

British Library Cataloguing in Publication Data

Data available

Library of Congress Cataloging in Publication Data
Library of Congress Control Number: 2009938807

Typeset by SPI Publisher Services, Pondicherry, India
Printed in Great Britain
on acid-free paper by the
MPG Books Group, Bodmin and King's Lynn

ISBN 978-0-19-958034-7

3 5 7 9 10 8 6 4 2

Abstract

This work examines the philosophy of history and the subject of the nation in the literature of Joseph Conrad. It explores the importance of nineteenth-century Polish Romantic philosophy in Conrad's literary development, arguing that the Polish response to Hegelian traditions of historiography in nineteenth-century Europe influenced Conrad's interpretation of history. After investigating Conrad's early career in the context of the philosophy of history, the book analyses *Nostromo* (1904), *The Secret Agent* (1907), and *Under Western Eyes* (1911) in light of Conrad's writing about Poland and his sustained interest in the subject of national identity. These novels treat the question of the nation and history, with Conrad juxtaposing his belief in an inherited Polish national identity, derived from Herder and Rousseau, with a sceptical questioning of modern nationalism in European and Latin American contexts. *Nostromo* presents the creation of the modern nation state of Sulaco; *The Secret Agent* explores the subject of 'foreigners' and nationality in England; while *Under Western Eyes* constitutes a systematic attempt to undermine Russian national identity. Conrad emerges as an author who examines critically the forces of nationalism and national identity that troubled Europe throughout the nineteenth century and in the period before the First World War. This leads to a consideration of Conrad's work during the Great War. In his fiction and newspaper articles, Conrad found a way of dealing with a conflict that made him acutely aware of being sidelined at a turning point in both modern Polish and modern European history. Finally, this book re-evaluates Conrad's late novels *The Rover* (1923) and *Suspense* (1925), a long-neglected part of his career, investigating Conrad's sustained treatment of French history in his last years alongside his life-long fascination with the cult of Napoleon Bonaparte.

To Elizabeth

Contents

Acknowledgements

This study was written over a four-year period at Corpus Christi College, University of Oxford, during which time I received invaluable support and encouragement from my supervisor Dr Susan Jones at St Hilda's College. I was assisted throughout by the *Joseph Conrad Society UK*, and special thanks are owed to J.H. Stape, Allan H. Simmons, Laurence Davies, Keith Carabine, and Owen Knowles. Dr Charles Kraszewski at *The Polish Review* in New York agreed to publish parts of the first chapter, while a short section of chapter 4 appeared in *Joseph Conrad in Context* (Cambridge University Press, 2009). Many former and recent academic mentors and colleagues also helped, including: Andrew Carpenter, J.C.C. Mays, Sylvère Monod (1921–2006), Jakob Lothe, and Dominique Kalifa. I thank the staff of the Bodleian Library; Corpus Christi College Library; the University of Oxford English, History, and Philosophy Faculty libraries; the British Library; and the Bibliothèque de la Sorbonne for providing access to the resources used in this book.

Unfailing moral and financial support from my parents afforded me the means to complete a doctoral degree at Oxford. I also obtained monetary backing from the following sources: two travel grants from the Meyerstein Fund at the Oxford English Faculty; a travel grant from Corpus Christi College; a substantial award from the University of Oxford Vice-Chancellors' Fund; two generous donations from the University of Oxford Prendergast Bequest; and a particularly munificent and welcome endowment from the Jenkins Memorial Scholarship, which allowed me the opportunity to carry out research at the Université de Paris I-Panthéon-Sorbonne.

My special thanks to Jacqueline Baker, Ariane Petit, Claire Thompson, Sara Barnes, and James Eaton at Oxford University Press.

Abbreviations

All references to Conrad's writings are to the Collected Dent Edition (1946–55) of the works, with the exceptions of *Almayer's Folly*, *The Secret Agent*, and *Notes on Life and Letters*, in which instances the Cambridge Edition is cited. All references to Conrad's correspondence are to *The Collected Letters of Joseph Conrad* (9 vols), edited by Frederick R. Karl and Laurence Davies (Cambridge: Cambridge University Press, 1983–2008). Secondary works are documented in footnotes throughout, with the exception of Zdzisław Najder's *Conrad Under Familial Eyes*, translated by Halina Carroll-Najder (Cambridge: Cambridge University Press, 1983), which contains texts from Conrad's Polish background. References to this volume and all Conrad's works and letters appear in parentheses after the citation, using the following abbreviations:

Almayer's Folly (AF)	*The Nigger of the 'Narcissus' (NN)*
Tales of Unrest (TU)	*Lord Jim (LJ)*
Youth (Y)	*Typhoon (T)*
Nostromo (N)	*The Mirror of the Sea (MS)*
The Secret Agent (SA)	*A Set of Six (SS)*
Under Western Eyes (UWE)	*A Personal Record (PR)*
Victory (V)	*Chance (C)*
Within the Tides (WT)	*The Shadow-Line (SL)*
The Arrow of Gold (AG)	*Notes on Life and Letters (NLL)*
The Rover (R)	*Suspense (S)*
Tales of Hearsay (TH)	*Last Essays (LE)*

Karl and Davies eds., *Collected Letters of Joseph Conrad (CL)*
Najder ed., *Under Familial Eyes (UFE)*

Illustrations

Images courtesy of Kujawsko-Pomorska Digital Library and Biblioteka Uniwersytetu Kazimierza Wielkiego w Bydgoszczyf, Poland.

Introduction

In 1884, ten years before Joseph Conrad's final settlement in London, W.R. Morfill, Oxford Professor of Slavonic Languages and Literature, published the first Polish grammar in English. Along with his later lectures on Slavonic literature at Oxford in 1890, Morfill sought to enable English readers to enjoy the nineteenth-century Polish Romantic poets 'Mickiewicz and Krasiński in the original,'[1] as he believed 'Polish literature has been almost entirely neglected among us.'[2] In the 1890 lectures Morfill called for more faithful translations of Mickiewicz, noting that the Polish national experience was captured in the poet's work: 'the genius of the country may be seen faithfully mirrored, its aspirations and struggles, its popular beliefs and traditions.'[3] Morfill's efforts to give Mickiewicz a wider audience in England occurred at a time when Conrad was working on the manuscript of *Almayer's Folly* (1895). The novel launched a literary career that created some of the finest fiction in English literature, and, as seminal studies by Zdzisław Najder and Andrzej Busza have shown, a corpus of writing greatly informed by the Polish literary culture of Conrad's youth.[4]

---

[1] W.R. Morfill, *A Simplified Grammar of the Polish Language* (London: Trübner & Co., 1884), vii.

[2] W.R. Morfill, *An Essay on the Importance of the Study of Slavonic Languages* (London: Henry Frowde, 1890), 11. In 1885, Morfill had corresponded with Stefan Buszczyński, Conrad's first guardian after the death of his father, Apollo Korzeniowski, in 1869.

[3] Morfill, *Essay*, 21.

[4] See Zdzisław Najder ed., *Conrad's Polish Background: Letters to and from Polish Friends*, translated by Halina Carroll (London: Oxford University Press, 1964); *Joseph Conrad: A Chronicle* (Cambridge: Cambridge University Press, 1983); ed., *Conrad Under Familial Eyes*, translated by Halina Carroll-Najder (Cambridge: Cambridge University Press, 1983); *Conrad in Perspective: Essays on Art and Fidelity* (Cambridge: Cambridge University Press, 1997). See also Andrzej Busza, 'Conrad's Polish Literary

According to Najder, the 'most powerful element' of Conrad's Polish inheritance 'was the work of the great Romantic poets, Adam Mickiewicz (1798–1855), Juliusz Słowacki (1809–49), and Zygmunt Krasiński (1812–59). Their Romanticism was of the continental kind, saturated with the spirit of communal and especially national responsibilities.'[5] Conrad's major biographers, Jocelyn Baines, Najder, and Frederick Karl, have acknowledged the importance of Poland's historical and literary heritage for Conrad's parents, Apollo Korzeniowski and Ewa Korzeniowska, his guardian Tadeusz Bobrowski, and for Conrad.[6] In his epic poem *Dziady* [*Forefathers' Eve*] (1832), Adam Mickiewicz represented Polish Romanticism in the voice of an 'old man,' capturing many of the images and motifs associated with Conrad's life and writing:

> Since that day, ah! I've sailed to distant strands
> And passed by all known isles and all known lands.
> All our hereditary treasures here
> In the abyss of time thus disappear,
> And so, what can your faces ever be,
> Or voices, or the grasp of hands to me?
> The faces, which I grew to love from youth,
> The hands that used to fondle, voice to soothe,
> Where have they vanished? They are all changed, erased,
> Or faded, or gone out – ah, I am dazed,
> And know not whether I'm amid the dead
> Corpses, or have died myself instead.
> One world I knew, a different world I quit:
> Unhappy who grows graveward bit by bit![7]

Background and Some Illustrations of the Influence of Polish Literature on his Work,' *Antemurale* 10 (1966): 109–255.

[5] Zdzisław Najder, 'Polish Inheritance,' *Oxford Reader's Companion to Conrad*, edited by Owen Knowles and Gene M. Moore (Oxford: Oxford University Press, 2000), 320.

[6] Jocelyn Baines, *Joseph Conrad: A Critical Biography* (London: Weidenfeld & Nicholson, 1960); F.R. Karl, *Joseph Conrad: The Three Lives* (London: Faber, 1979); Najder, *Conrad: A Chronicle.*

[7] Adam Mickiewicz, *Forefathers*, translated into English verse by Count Potocki of Montalk (Draguignan: The Royal Polish Cultural Foundation, 1968), 113.

Mickiewicz's old man, who has sailed to distant strands, contemplates the disappearance of the past and the land of his youth. The poem expresses a marked awareness of time, as 'hereditary treasures here/In the abyss of time thus disappear.' In addition to the transience of youth and the loss of familial bonds, in a Polish context the most regretted vanishing hereditary treasure was the Polish nation. The dispossession of Poland's political identity between 1795 and 1918 by Prussia, Russia, and the Austrian Habsburg Empire was the overriding concern of nationally conscious Poles in the nineteenth century, and the dismemberment of Poland by strategic imperial expansion represented a barbaric political crime in the diplomatic rhetoric of contemporary Europe. Conrad's ancestors had fought in the Napoleonic Wars under the promise of the restoration of the boundaries of the Polish-Lithuanian Commonwealth (1569–1795), the historical apex of Poland's political, geographical, and cultural prestige, and Conrad's family actively sought the return of the Polish state during his childhood by supporting periodic insurrections (1830, 1846, 1863) against Russian and Austrian rule. Conrad accompanied his parents when they were exiled north of Moscow for subversive political activity in 1862, and by 1869, at the age of eleven, Conrad was orphaned by the vicissitudes of Polish history. According to Najder, this 'sense of an inherited catastrophe, both personal and communal, was also part of [Conrad's] mental background,'[8] ensuring that the narrative of Conrad's life was bound early to the fortunes of Polish and European history.

In 1894, after twenty years of intermittent life at sea and travel to the outposts of European imperialism, Conrad wrote to Marguerite Poradowska (1848–1937) on the eve of his transition from seaman to author, sceptically reflecting concerns about time and history analogous to those of Mickiewicz: 'I well understand this yearning for the past which vanishes little by little, marking its route in tombs and regrets. Only that goes on forever' (*CL* 1, 162). Conrad's correspondence with Poradowska from the period of his literary apprenticeship reveals the writer's thought to be infused with the historical and temporal divisions of past, present, and future: 'I am forming some vague plans for the future, very vague! Besides what is the good of planning, since the

---

[8] Najder, 'Polish Inheritance,' 321.

unforeseen always occurs' (*CL* 1, 83).[9] The present exists only as a destroyer of the past as it 'vanishes little by little.' Conrad's ambiguity about the future leads to an embracing of the past in the early correspondence. In language echoing the Polish Romantic tradition of Mickiewicz, 'a friend's voice turns the current of thought into a more fruitful valley in the seamed land of the past' (*CL* 1, 347). In 1885, Conrad wrote from Calcutta: 'I live mostly in the past and the future. The present has, you easily understand, but few charms for me. I look with the serenity of despair and the indifference of contempt on passing events' (*CL* 1, 17). Conrad's nostalgic yearning is rooted in the Polish national experience with its refusal to accept the present as the fulfilment of history, looking to a lost past while revealing an uncertain faith in the future. Conrad's most characteristic writing, the retrospective narratives of 'Youth' (1898), 'Heart of Darkness' (1899), *Lord Jim* (1900), 'Freya of the Seven Isles' (1912), 'A Smile of Fortune' (1912), and *The Shadow-Line* (1917), contemplates individual history and meditates deeply on time, while the major political works *Nostromo* (1904), *The Secret Agent* (1907), and *Under Western Eyes* (1911) treat the effect of conflicting political ideologies on the unfolding national histories of Costaguana, England, and Russia.

This book examines the origins and development of Conrad's representation of history, exploring Conrad's life and work in the context of European history and philosophy of the late nineteenth and early twentieth centuries. It employs a historicist methodology, investigating principally the philosophical and historical influences to which Conrad may have been exposed during his life. In an attempt to properly understand Conrad's writing within the context of the years leading up to the Great War, the thesis draws predominantly on the history and thought of the nineteenth century. The work begins by looking behind the Romantic literature that Conrad read in his youth, examining Polish Romantic philosophy. Polish Romantic historicism, the treatment of the philosophy of history by patriotic Polish writers, flourished in the 1830s and 1840s, and essential to its development was its conflict or

---

[9] Poradowska was a writer of romantic historical novels, becoming a close friend of Conrad in the years before his marriage to Jessie George in 1896. For her role in Conrad's literary development, see Susan Jones, *Conrad and Women* (Oxford: Clarendon Press, 1999).

consensus with the work of G.W.F. Hegel, which dominated historical debate in Poland and Europe.[10] According to Andrzej Walicki, 'the controversy about Hegel was especially intense in partitioned Poland and [it] gave birth to a number of quite interesting philosophical systems.'[11] Conrad's exposure to such systems, as advocated by philosophers August Cieszkowski (1814–94), Edward Dembowski (1822–46), Bronisław Trentowski (1808–69) and Henryk Kamieński (1813–66), came through the Romantic writings of Mickiewicz, Słowacki, and Krasiński, and the more immediate influence of his family.

The approaches to history of Apollo Korzeniowski, Conrad's first guardian Stefan Buszczyński, and of his later custodian Tadeusz Bobrowski, all contributed to Conrad's engagement with time and history. Outlining the importance of Hegelian historical ideas in Poland in the nineteenth century, Chapter 1 explores the central text of Polish Romantic philosophy, August Cieszkowski's *Prolegomena zur Historiosophie* [*A Prologue to a Historiosophy*] (1838), and its relationship to the literature of the Polish Romantic poets. The absence of any previous study of Polish Romantic historiography in Conrad criticism is especially surprising given that August Cieszkowski's work has been understood as one of the most original offshoots of Hegelianism in European philosophy, and, more significantly, as an important forerunner of, and perhaps shaping influence on, the thought of Hegel's most wayward disciple, Karl Marx.[12] In 1969, the philosopher and historian Shlomo Avineri explained that 'Cieszkowski, a Polish aristocrat from the Posen area educated at Berlin University is one of the more original – and somewhat bizarre – thinkers on the margin of the Hegelian school. After having been neglected for almost a century, he is only recently being

---

[10] Georg Wilhelm Friedrich Hegel (1770–1831), one of the foremost German Idealist philosophers, along with Kant, Fichte, and Schelling. His philosophy of history posited that history is guided by a 'Geist,' or 'Spirit,' ensuring its logical, although not necessarily smooth, progress towards freedom, which Hegel saw manifesting itself in the coming of the 'State.' For a contextual positioning of Hegel in nineteenth-century Prussian society and politics, see Christopher Clark, *Iron Kingdom: The Rise and Downfall of Prussia 1600–1947* (London: Penguin, 2007), 431–35.

[11] Andrzej Walicki, *Philosophy and Romantic Nationalism: The Case of Poland* (Oxford: Clarendon Press, 1982), 2.

[12] See Nikolaus Lobkowicz, 'Eschatology and the Young Hegelians,' *Review of Politics* 27.3 (1965): 437.

slowly rescued from obscurity and oblivion.'[13] This study brings Cieszkowski and the Polish response to Hegelian philosophy into Conrad studies for the first time, drawing attention to a once central figure in nineteenth-century Polish literature. Chapter 1 also examines the writings of Stefan Buszczyński, particularly his long work on history and politics *La Décadence de l'Europe* (1867), in the context of earlier Polish Romantic thought such as that represented in Cieszkowski's *Prolegomena*, demonstrating that Cieszkowski's philosophy continued to occupy a prominent position in Polish literary and political culture.

While the historiography of Polish Romanticism constitutes a new context for Conrad, it is important to regard this writing alongside previously treated aspects of Polish history. Conrad's biographers have relied extensively on the letters of Tadeusz Bobrowski, who opposed Polish Romantic idealism and supported the Polish Positivists after the defeat of the 1863 insurrection. Positivism, including, incidentally, the later ideas of August Cieszkowski, argued against the militant tradition, promoting a pragmatic approach to Poland's national identity, in which political independence would be forsaken in favour of strengthening the economic power and cultural bonds of the nation. Conrad was strongly aware of the clash between Romanticism and Positivism, but inextricably bound to both these opposing traditions, attempting to reconcile them in his fiction. In an 'Author's Note' to *Almayer's Folly*, which remained unpublished until the Sun-Dial Edition of 1921, Conrad wrote that it was the fate of all humanity to 'endure [. . .] the curse of facts and the blessing of illusions, the bitterness of our wisdom and the deceptive consolation of our folly' (*AF*, 4).[14] Conrad lived at a turning point in Polish history; from 1863 until 1874, when Conrad travelled to Marseilles to begin his career as a seaman, Poland experienced the bitterness of wisdom in admitting the folly and failure of the 1863 insurrection, but an uneasy parting from the deceptive consolation of Romanticism. The manifestation of these conflicting traditions of Polish historical thought in *The Nigger of the 'Narcissus'* (1897)

---

[13] Shlomo Avineri, *The Social and Political Thought of Karl Marx* (Cambridge: Cambridge University Press, 1969), 124.

[14] For details on the piece, see David Leon Higdon, 'The Text and Context of Conrad's First Critical Essay,' *Polish Review* 20 (1975), 97–105.

illustrates how Conrad balances the complex polarities of his philosophical inheritance.

The Nigger of the 'Narcissus,' Conrad's first 'English' novel, also celebrates the British maritime tradition, eulogising a generation of seamen who worked the trade routes of the British Empire. Edward Garnett, Conrad's unofficial literary adviser, had suggested in 1896 that Conrad would have greater success with the public if he bound his literary style to his experiences at sea. In March 1896, Conrad wrote to Garnett: 'You have driven home the conviction and I *shall* write the sea-story' (*CL* 2, 268). It is important, then, in interpreting Conrad's early fiction, to balance an appreciation of his Polish inheritance with Conrad's determination to adapt to English literature. Chapter 2 assesses Conrad's artistic aims as he left the sea behind and became a writer. According to Allan H. Simmons, Conrad's 'rich inheritance yielded fictions that combine the authenticity of first-hand experience with the insights of profound meditation.'[15] Naturally infused with a melancholic and nostalgic disposition – torn between what biographer Frederick Karl has labelled his 'Three Lives,' as Pole, Seaman, and Writer – Conrad reflected on the boundaries that shaped his life, directing his attention to the contemplation of history in a Britain at the height of its imperial power. Chapter 2, therefore, surveys the philosophical and literary culture of late nineteenth- and early twentieth-century Britain, arguing that Conrad engaged with British literary forerunners and contemporaries expressly concerned with time and history, the foundation of his cultural education in Poland.

Conrad was drawn to the work of writers such as William Hazlitt and Thomas Carlyle, and Chapter 2 looks at the correspondences between British and Polish thought in 'Youth' and 'Heart of Darkness,' examining British currents of historical investigation. While Conrad's elegiac view of the past emerges from the Polish tradition, it also borrows from the lyrical English Romanticism of William Hazlitt's essays, with their focus on the subjective power of memory, and follows the historical treatments of Thomas Carlyle. Carlyle's writing, particularly his quasi-Hegelian satire *Sartor Resartus* (1838), was instrumental in bringing German philosophy into English literary culture in the nineteenth

---

[15] Allan H. Simmons, *Critical Issues: Joseph Conrad* (London: Palgrave, 2006), 1.

century, and Carlyle's work explored questions of history and representation that characterised the Polish response to German Idealism.[16]
Chapter 2 also evaluates the relationship between Conrad's early fiction
and the work of Conrad's immediate contemporaries, especially neo-
Hegelians such as F.H. Bradley, analysing Conrad's stories in magazines
such as *Blackwood's* in the 1890s alongside philosophical discussions
then appearing in the journal *Mind*. While Conrad had grown up in a
Polish culture negotiating its reception of Hegelianism, neo-Hegelian
Idealism, preoccupied with the philosophy of time, problems of truth in
history, and the interdependence of individual and society, was the
dominant philosophical school in turn-of-the-century Britain. From
Conrad's individual concern with time and ageing in 'Youth,' to rumi-
nations on the nature of experience and historical judgement in 'Heart
of Darkness' and *Lord Jim*, retrospective subjectivity and historical
indeterminacy shape Conrad's literary style. For Conrad, the 'whole
of the truth lies in the presentation' (*CL* 2, 200), and Conrad's narratives in 'Youth,' 'Heart of Darkness,' and *Lord Jim*, with their overt
focus on the boundaries between oral and written histories, disclose the
fluid and equivocal nature of recollection. The chapter concludes by
exploring Conrad's narrative technique in *Lord Jim*, locating a source
for the novel in the *Histories* of Herodotus, thereby connecting Conrad
to a long tradition of European historiography.

Conrad, however, remained an author of Polish origin writing in
English. He felt that contemporary reviewers presented him as 'a sort of
freak, an amazing bloody foreigner writing in English' (*CL* 3, 488). As
the short story 'Amy Foster' (1901) reveals, Conrad's position as an
outsider negotiating a position within a new national environment
made him sensitive to the issue of national identity, something com-
pounded by his education in a Polish culture dominated by the national
quest. According to Conrad, 'Amy Foster' treated the 'essential difference of the races' (*CL* 2, 402). Still, by the time he wrote his autobiographical account *Some Reminiscences*, later *A Personal Record*, for the
English Review in 1908, Conrad accepted that his national background
and its pervasive focus on historical tradition had moulded the 'fine
edge of my conscience':

---

[16] See Rosemary Ashton, *The German Idea: Four English Writers and the Reception of
German Thought, 1800–1860* (Cambridge: Cambridge University Press, 1980).

that heirloom of the ages, of the race, of the group, of the family, colourable and plastic, fashioned by the words, the looks, the acts, and even by the silences and abstentions surrounding one's childhood; tinged in a complete scheme of delicate shades and crude colours by the inherited traditions, beliefs, or prejudices – unaccountable, despotic, persuasive, and often, in its texture, Romantic. (*PR*, 94)

Conrad's political novels concentrate on nationalism and national identity, with the author returning to the overriding 'inherited traditions' (*PR*, 94) of his youth in his major works. Nationalism in nineteenth-century European history represents a subject treated at length in Conrad's political essays, and the politics of nineteenth-century Latin America, then experiencing global prominence after the Spanish-American War (1898) over Cuba, dominate *Nostromo*. Conrad's interest in South America came from his own historical reading, exposure to contemporary accounts of opposition to rising US imperialism, and through Robert Cunninghame Graham, who had a wealth of experience and historical knowledge of the tumultuous continent. The central conflict of *Nostromo*, between the materialistic Europeanised elite of Sulaco and the violent internal dictatorships of Costaguana, recalls one of the seminal works of nineteenth-century Latin American literature, *Facundo, civilización y barbarie* (1845), by Argentine president Domingo F. Sarmiento. *Nostromo* also resonates with contemporary voices on national identity in South America, such as the poetry of Nicaragua's Rubén Darío and the political writings of Uruguay's José E. Rodó, which addressed the awakening of a modern Latin American historical consciousness.

Chapter 3 details how *Nostromo* (1904), *The Secret Agent* (1907), and *Under Western Eyes* (1911) are indebted to the Polish Romantic view of the nation and broader concepts of nationhood in nineteenth-century Europe and Latin America. Polish Romantics such as Mickiewicz and Cieszkowski drew from the philosophy of Jean-Jacques Rousseau and Johann Gottfried von Herder, regarding national identity as an inherited spiritual bond founded on shared cultural traditions, historical memory, and a stable political structure. As Conrad's perspective on Rousseau and Herder comes through the prism of his Polish background, it is important to acknowledge that Polish thought of the mid-nineteenth century was bound to trends in European philosophy. Polish culture responded to the overwhelming authority of Hegelianism in Europe, and Polish philosophers, reacting against the teleology of the Hegelian narrative of world history, adopted the philosophy of Herder and Rousseau, which supported independent national and cultural identities. Conrad's view of the nation is evaluated in light of the author's belief in a spiritual Polish national identity, unambiguously expressed in his writings on Poland, and his position in *Nostromo*, where Conrad observes nations being created by the force of modern industrial capitalism. *Nostromo* borrows from Rousseau and Herder's Romantic philosophies of nationalism in presenting the cultural diversity and plurality of Costaguana. Complete with folk legends, festivals, and characters from various racial and ethnic origins, Conrad encountered 'ever-enlarging vistas opening before me as I progressed deeper into my knowledge of the country' (*N*, xviii). Yet, Conrad anticipates later theoretical work on national identity, such as that of Ernest Geller, Eric Hobsbawm, and Benedict Anderson, in his focus on the invention of the Republic of Sulaco.

In *The Secret Agent*, Conrad questioned the threat of Anarchism and its associations with foreign groups in late nineteenth-century London. Conrad undermined historical and theoretical systems, juxtaposing the philosophical assertions of self-proclaimed anarchists with the artistic endeavours of young Stevie, whose 'coruscations of innumerable circles' suggesting 'chaos and eternity' (*SA*, 179) better reflected Conrad's understanding of history. Conrad's position as a Polish immigrant in England ensured the novel also treated race and national identity. Chapter 3 contends that Conrad presented a London in which distinctions of national difference are rendered obsolete by the materiality of the city, with Conrad's characters becoming 'denationalised' (*SA*, 115) and unidentifiable by national origin. One important exception remains Mr Vladimir, the official from a foreign embassy, who, while his nation remains undefined, is 'racially, nationally and individually' (*SA*, 169) marked by the structures of Russian autocratic power.

Conrad's efforts to efface the exclusive marks of national identity in *The Secret Agent* did not prevent reviewers from persistently labelling Conrad someone whose writing could never be integrated into English literary tradition. In an unsigned review of *The Secret Agent* in the *Glasgow News* in 1907, Conrad's novel was praised for possessing something 'entirely alien to our national genius.'[17] Nevertheless, while the complexities of national identity seemed to pursue him, Conrad also invited such judgement of his work in his own treatment of nationhood. Writing in 1926, Thomas Mann discussed Conrad's delineation of Mr Vladimir in *The Secret Agent*, believing the novel unveiled Conrad's Polish Russophobia 'expressing itself in British.'[18] This argument can best be understood through an examination of *Under Western Eyes*, Conrad's 'most deeply meditated novel' (*CL* 5, 695), and the author's fictional foray into the Russian nation that loomed over politically dispossessed Poland. In pursuing 'the very soul of things Russian' (*CL* 4, 8), a fragile and illusory concept that Conrad saw as inseparable from the power of Russian autocracy, Conrad attempted to subvert Russian claims to inheritance of Western traditions of nationhood, particularly those represented by Herder and Rousseau. *Under Western Eyes* promotes Conrad's claim to a historical consciousness derived from the main currents of European thought. Writing in 1924 of Poland and Russian political power, Conrad insisted:

Polish temperament, at any rate, is far removed from Byzantine and Asiatic associations. Poland has absorbed Western ideas, adopted Western culture, sympathized with Western ideals and tendencies as much as it was possible, across the great distances and in the special conditions of its national and political life, whose main task was the struggle for life against Asiatic despotism at its door. (*CL* 8, 291)

Conrad's resolute positioning of Polish civilisation against Russian barbarism guaranteed that 'the formative forces acting on me, at the most plastic and impressionable age, were purely Western: that is French and English: and that, as far as I can remember, those forces found in me no resistance, no vague, deep-seated antagonism, either racial or temperamental' (*CL* 8, 291). This chapter also reveals how Conrad revisited Polish Romantic and Positivist philosophies to acquire an authentic discourse of nationhood for Razumov and Haldin, the ideologically opposed Russian students of *Under Western Eyes*.

---

[17] Norman Sherry ed., *Conrad: The Critical Heritage* (London: Routledge & Kegan Paul, 1973), 195.
[18] Ian Watt ed., *Conrad, The Secret Agent: A Casebook* (Basingstoke: Macmillan, 1973), 102.

Conrad, of course, was not a systematic thinker. It would be disingenuous to hold that Conrad subscribed to any given philosophy of
history. Conrad cultivated a career-long interest in history, both individual and collective. In *Almayer's Folly*, the assertive Nina rejects her
'feeble and traditionless' (*AF*, 35) father Almayer, turning to the past to
construct a coherent present. In an essay entitled 'Legends,' left unfinished at his death and later published in *Last Essays* (1926), Conrad
wrote: 'I have nothing against a legend twining its tendrils fancifully
about the facts of history' (*LE*, 44). History and representation contin-
ually inspired Conrad's literature. Yet, Conrad's conception of history
can only be isolated, if at all, as he described it in *A Personal Record*:
'I have come to suspect that the aim of creation cannot be ethical at all.
I would fondly believe that its object is purely spectacular' (*PR*, 92).
Consequently, this study does not impose a rigid framework upon an
author whose most pronounced philosophical standpoint was that of
sceptic. In a letter to John Galsworthy, Conrad wrote: 'Scepticism is the
tonic of minds, the tonic of life, the agent of truth – the way of art and
salvation' (*CL* 2, 359). While his Polish background established the
foundation of his understanding, Conrad's thought, 'colourable and
plastic' (*PR*, 94) as he admitted in *A Personal Record*, revealed its
willingness to adapt to the cultural influences in France and England,
while also responding to contemporary developments in European and
world history.

A central text in any political and philosophical discussion of history
in Conrad's work must be the 1905 essay 'Autocracy and War,' in which
Conrad elaborated on contemporary politics, Russian despotism, and
Polish nationality, while holding Napoleon to be the central figure in
European history. Conrad's essay presciently foresees the causes of the
First World War, but owing to its publication in 1905 as mutual Anglo-
German naval and military rivalry escalated, it also forms part of a web
of anti-German writing that dominated Conrad's adopted culture.
'Autocracy and War' is analysed in the context of European and British
political and literary culture in Chapter 4, which initially concentrates
on Conrad's position during the Great War. In his fiction and newspa-
per articles, Conrad found a way of dealing with a conflict that made
him sharply aware of being sidelined at a turning point in both modern
Polish and modern European history. 'Poland Revisited' (1915) *The
Shadow-Line* (1917), 'The Warrior's Soul' (1916) and 'The Tale'

(1917), register consciousness of a sudden dividing line between past and present, and these works also address the charges of a younger generation of writers and soldiers, such as Siegfried Sassoon, who accused Conrad's generation of sending them off to die at the front. As Laurence Davies has noted, Conrad's writing is 'not an escape from contemporary horrors so much as a way of thinking about them.'[19] If Conrad had been educated at the crossroads of two philosophical movements in Poland, and attempted throughout his life to balance Polish, French, and English traditions, then during the First World War he recognised that history had placed him on the wrong side in the contemporary battle of the Ancients and the Moderns.

Conrad's attitude to history, however, can only be completely scrutinised through a thorough appreciation of the cultural climates of Poland, England, and France. This becomes paramount in Conrad's last years, when the author returned to the subject that had been a major reference point in his understanding of history: Napoleon and French historical and literary culture. From his correspondence and the memoirs of his literary acquaintances, it is clear that Conrad, as his long-standing friend R.B. Cunninghame Graham observed, had a mind 'steeped in the modern literature of Europe, especially in that of France' (*TH*, ix). In *A Personal Record*, Conrad recalled the work of Gustave Flaubert and Victor Hugo, claiming that his father's translation of Hugo's *Les Travailleurs de la mer* (1866) had instigated his desire to go to sea. Conrad's later admiration for Maupassant and Stendhal, and French literature more generally, supports his recollection that, in his youth, if his 'mind took a tinge from anything it was from French romanticism perhaps' (*CL* 7, 616). Conrad's early encounters with French culture and history included tales of his ancestors' exploits in the Napoleonic wars, and in his introduction to Conrad's last, unfinished, and posthumously published novel *Suspense*, Richard Curle wrote: 'All his life Conrad was a student of the Napoleonic era. He had absorbed the history, the memoirs, the campaigns of that period with immense assiduity and unflagging interest' (*S*, vi). Throughout his career, Conrad's interest in Napoleon saw him often undertake to write

[19] Laurence Davies, introduction, *The Collected Letters of Joseph Conrad 5*, edited by Frederick Karl and Laurence Davies (Cambridge: Cambridge University Press, 1996), xxxiii.

a great historical novel set during the Napoleonic era. Chapter 4 re-evaluates Conrad's late novels *The Rover* (1923) and *Suspense* (1925), redirecting attention to Conrad's sustained treatment of French history in his last years and his life-long fascination with Napoleon and the early nineteenth century. In his first published essay, 'Tales of the Sea' (1898), Conrad wrote an appraisal of the maritime adventure writer Frederick Marryat (1792–1848), idealising the nineteenth century. Conrad associated literature with the importance of a coherent national history, epistemological tradition, and questions of historical investigation:

> It [Marryat's work] is absolutely amazing to us, as the disclosure of the spirit animating the stirring time when the nineteenth century was young. There is an air of fable about it. Its loss would be irreparable, like the curtailment of national story or the loss of an historical document. It is the beginning and the embodiment of an inspiring tradition. (*NLL*, 46)

Conrad's concern in 1898 with historical authenticity, documentary evidence, the national story, tradition, and a romantic appreciation of history, represents what would be recurring concerns of his writing. In the years from the Treaty of Versailles to his death in 1924, Conrad returned to the shaping influences of the Europe of the Congress of Vienna (1815) as a means of immersing himself in the Romantic past, but also of examining the Europe of the post-Great War settlement. In *The Rover* and *Suspense*, Conrad captured the spirit of the Napoleonic era and renegotiated his relationship with Napoleon Bonaparte, an historical figure encapsulating the vicissitudes of history in its glory, cruelty, and irony. In doing so, Conrad borrowed widely from French Romantic literature, particularly from Balzac, Stendhal, Alexandre Dumas, and the poetry of Victor Hugo. Conrad's fascination with the period of the Napoleonic wars and the legend of the Emperor, first evident in *The Mirror of the Sea* (1906) and 'The Duel' (1908), has important correlations with Conrad's inheritance of Polish Romantic historiography and Poland's complex relationship with Napoleon. In *The Rover* and *Suspense*, Conrad strove to reconcile his own past with the representation of time and history that concerned him throughout his life and works.

1

Conrad and the Philosophy of History: Youth, Poland, and the Romantic Past

In the manuscript of *Almayer's Folly*, the story of the inexorable decline of Dutch trader Kaspar Almayer in Borneo, Conrad offered an early expression of his historical scepticism: 'The well known, shrill voice started Almayer from the waking dream of past – and, perhaps, of future splendour.'[1] In the published novel, Conrad altered the narrative voice, with the trader now contemplating 'the wreckage of his past in the dawn of new hopes' (*AF*, 11). Almayer's shifting perspective sees the past as both inspiration and as discredited history. In the published novel, Almayer's anticipated future splendour with his daughter Nina in Europe never materialises, as Conrad's Dutch protagonist misjudges the resources and wealth of the adventurer Tom Lingard in his projected escape from his colonial demise. If Almayer's intolerable present between a lost past and an uncertain future should not be read as a direct allegory of the condition of Poland, then the language with which it is presented is certainly characteristic of Polish concerns with statehood and history in the nineteenth century. For Almayer, the present is a 'complete silence,' and he 'looked vainly westward, for a ray of light, out of the gloom of his shattered hopes. - Years passed' (*AF*, 23). An inert present and a westward glance for assistance signify major themes in Polish history between 1795 and 1918. Further, considering Conrad's dedication of the novel to his guardian Tadeusz Bobrowski – 'To the

---

[1] *Almayer's Folly* manuscript, quoted in Laura L. Davis, preface, *Conrad's Century: The Past and Future Splendour*, edited by Laura L. Davis, *Conrad: Eastern and Western Perspectives* 7 (Lublin: Marie Curie-Skłodowska University; Boulder, CO: East European Monographs, 1998), 1.

memory of T.B.' (*AF*, 2) – it is evident that, from the outset, Poland significantly shaped Conrad's early Modernist literary identity.

PARTITIONED POLAND AND THE
PHILOSOPHY OF HISTORY

On 12 January 1796, a tripartite convention between Russia, Austria, and Prussia in St Petersburg decreed 'the need to abolish everything which can recall the memory of the existence of the kingdom of Poland.'[2] Poland had succumbed to the third and final of three partitions in 1795 and would not become an independent state again until 1918. In the face of the loss of the Polish state and the suppression of the national culture, 'Romanticising Polish customs, history, songs and sights, although deeply rooted in the past, became tantamount to patriotic duties at the time of the partition.'[3] In 'The Crime of Partition,' written in December 1918 when the political landscape of post-First World War Europe was being redrawn, and first published in the *Fortnightly Review* in May 1919, Conrad insisted that the disappearance of the Polish state in 1795 had not constituted the death of the nation: 'But the spirit of the nation refused to rest therein. It haunted the territories of the Old Republic in the manner of a ghost haunting its ancestral mansion [...]. Poland deprived of its independence, of its historical continuity, and with its religion and language persecuted and repressed, became a mere geographical expression. [...] [T]he nation stabbed to the heart refused to grow insensible and cold' (*NLL*, 96).[4] Such a discourse reveals Conrad's exposure to the language of Polish patriotism. In his *Księgi narodu polskiego i pielgrzymstwa polskiego* [*Books of the Polish Nation and the Polish Pilgrimage*] (1830), the bible of Polish Messianism and the seminal expression of the immortality of the nation, Adam Mickiewicz wrote that 'the Polish nation is not

[2] Jerzy Lukowski and Hubert Zawadzki, *A Concise History of Poland* (Cambridge: Cambridge University Press, 2001), 105.
[3] Stanisław Eile, *Literature and Nationalism in Partitioned Poland 1795–1918* (Basingstoke: Macmillan, 2000), 36.
[4] See J.H. Stape, '"The Crime of Partition": Conrad's Sources,' *Conradiana* 15 (1983): 219–26.

dead! Its body, indeed, is in the tomb, but its soul has ascended from the surface of the earth.'[5] In his only story to deal specifically with Poland, 'Prince Roman' (1910), Conrad wrote of 'Polish nationality, that nationality not so much alive as surviving, which persists in thinking, breathing, speaking, hoping, and suffering in its grave, railed in by a million of bayonets and triple-sealed with the seals of three great empires' (*TH*, 29).

Literature played a powerful role in keeping the 'spirit of the nation' alive. The poetry of Father Jan Pawel Woronicz (1757–1829) developed a cult of the national past later appropriated by philosophers and poets such as August Cieszkowski, Juliusz Słowacki, and Mickiewicz. As a precursor to the 'great Romantic poets' of the 1830s and 1840s, the effect of Woronicz's poetry can be demonstrated in the language used to appraise it by Polish philosopher and literary critic Maurycy Mochnacki (1804–34). Mochnacki called Woronicz 'the senior poet in the temple of national memory,' who 'did his service at the altar of the past and kept its flames alive.'[6] This veneration of the past appears in Conrad's two autobiographical pieces, *The Mirror of the Sea* (1906) and *A Personal Record* (1912), where Conrad advocates an 'unconscious response to the still voice of that inexorable past' (*PR*, 25) as the basis of his art. This sensitivity to the past runs throughout Conrad's work and is routinely expressed in Romantic language. In 'Poland Revisited' (1915), an evocative account of his journey to a still-partitioned Poland in 1914, Conrad wrote: 'My eyes were turned to the past, not to the future; the past that one cannot suspect and mistrust, the shadowy and unquestionable moral possession the darkest struggles of which wear a halo of glory and peace' (*NLL*, 116). The dark struggles to which Conrad refers formed the backdrop to his childhood in Poland, and couching the past in a veneer of idealism was a necessary feature of Polish Romantic writing that reacted to the Hegelian *telos* of history, which Poles believed validated partitioned Poland. The stateless present could not be dwelt upon, yet it was the indelible awareness of this present that caused the intensity of the engagement with history. As the future had yet to be determined, the past held inspiration for movement

---

[5] Adam Mickiewicz, *The Books and the Pilgrimage of the Polish Nation* (London: James Ridgeway, 1833), 20.
[6] Mochnacki quoted in Eile, *Literature and Nationalism*, 37.

into the future. According to Zdzisław Najder, for Polish Romantics in the culture of Conrad's youth, 'to accept the present as the basis for change would have meant to resign from the national dream, to renounce the dignity and the glories of the past.'[7] In this context, Hegel's work becomes problematic, as his philosophy of history, which influenced European historical debate from the thinker's death in 1831, saw the past as something that should not be revived. Hegel's philosophy concerned the movement of historical forces and the belief that time was always in motion, its dynamism carrying history forward in the development of 'Reason.' Hegel sought to clarify that 'it is not *in* time that everything comes to be and passes away, rather time itself is the *becoming*, this coming-to-be and passing away, the *actually existent abstraction, Chronos*, from whom everything is born and by whom its offspring is destroyed. The real is certainly distinct from time, but is also essentially identical with it.'[8] The employment of Hegel's language was pervasive, and Maurycy Mochnacki's influential volume *O literaturze polskiej w wieku dziewiętnastym* [*On Polish Literature in the Nineteenth Century*] (1830) concurred that 'movement was the very foundation of existence: everything was "becoming," and nothing simply "was."'[9] An awareness of temporal dynamism inspired conflicting views of the future, as Poles could see time conveying the nation away from its glorious past or forward to the renaissance of the Polish state. Mickiewicz strongly condemned 'the doctrines of Voltaire and Hegel, which are like poison,'[10] and for Polish philosophers the 'Hegelian conception

---

[7] Zdzisław Najder, 'Conrad and Rousseau: Concepts of Man and Society,' *Joseph Conrad: A Commemoration*, edited by Norman Sherry (Basingstoke: Macmillan, 1976), 88. However, not all Polish philosophers saw the past as something sacred. Bronisław Trentowski (1808–69) was a harsh critic of Poland's romanticised, aristocratic heritage. In his émigré journal *Teraźniejszość i Przyszłość* [*The Present and the Future*] (1844–45), published in Paris, he saw Poland's decline as the rightful judgement of history. Trentowski was a critic of the Polish Romantic tendency to idealise heroism, believing the 'eagerness for heroic action should be controlled by reason.' This has an obvious correlation with Jim's romantic literary education and desire for heroism in *Lord Jim*. See Walicki, *Philosophy and Romantic Nationalism*, 170.

[8] G.W.F. Hegel, *Philosophy of Nature*, translated and edited by A.V. Miller (Oxford: Clarendon Press, 1970), 35.

[9] Quoted in Brian Porter, *When Nationalism Began to Hate: Imagining Modern Politics in Nineteenth-Century Poland* (Oxford: Oxford University Press, 2000), 24.

[10] Mickiewicz, *The Books and the Pilgrimage of the Polish Nation*, 30.

according to which history had already achieved its goal was unacceptable for a nation which could not reconcile itself with the present.'[11]

In 1838, August Cieszkowski, a close friend of the poet Zygmunt Krasiński, published an important precursor of Marxist philosophy entitled *Prolegomena zur Historiosophie*.[12] Although highly indebted to Hegel's work, having studied at the University of Berlin where Hegel had taught before his death, Cieszkowski saw the master as flawed because of his refusal to consider the future in his synopsis of history. Hegel had postulated a tetrachotomy in his division of history into four epochs: the Eastern Period, Greek, Roman, and Germanic, culminating with his own Absolute knowledge of history. As knowledge is only possible *post factum*, Hegel regarded the study of the future as mere speculation and not philosophy. However, Cieszkowski proclaimed in the *Prolegomena* that 'the totality of history must consist of the past and of the future, of the road already travelled as well as of the road yet to be travelled.'[13] A Christian thinker and a member of Mickiewicz's literary circle in Paris in the 1830s, Cieszkowski nevertheless distanced himself from Messianic visions of Poland as the 'Christ of Nations,' a view that regarded Poland's sufferings as having redemptive qualities for humankind. 'The Hegelian dialectic remained the keystone of the Cieszkowskian system. This exasperated Mickiewicz whose admiration for the powerful mind of the author of the historiography did not keep him from calling him the slave of German thought.'[14] In place of the

---

[11] Walicki, *Philosophy and Romantic Nationalism*, 95.

[12] Cieszkowski's philosophical career can be divided into two parts, the contrasts of which capture the shifting perspectives of the Romantic and Positivist eras in Poland. The first constitutes the thought of the *Prolegomena*, and the second is expressed in his posthumously published work *Our Father*, which Cieszkowski began in the 1830s. In the latter work, Cieszkowski treated the Lord's Prayer as a vision of a coming Christian Utopia. Ultimately, Cieszkowski came to support 'organicism,' which believed that economic industriousness would shape Poland's future. In 1841, Cieszkowski 'cooperated in the founding the *Biblioteka Warszawska*, an enlightened general periodical which was blessed with extraordinary longevity and was soon to become the herald of Polish positivism.' See *Selected Writings of August Cieszkowski*, 34.

[13] August Cieszkowski, *Selected Writings of August Cieszkowski*, edited and translated with an introductory essay by André Liebach (Cambridge: Cambridge University Press, 1979), 51. See also, André Liebach, *Between Ideology and Utopia: The Politics and Philosophy of August Cieszkowski* (Dordrecht: Reidel, 1979), and Avineri, *The Social and Political Thought of Karl Marx*.

[14] Benoit P. Hepner, 'History and the Future: The Vision of August Cieszkowski,' *The Review of Politics* 15.3 (1953): 333.

histrionics of Polish literary Messianism, Cieszkowski soberly forwarded a trichotomic categorisation of history into past, present, and future, with each division part of a larger historical and temporal sequence; 'in every present we see the fusion of the past and the future.'[15] Cieszkowski believed the philosophy of history must transcend Hegel's idealism and enter the realm of the real. The philosophy of the *Prolegomena*, which can be described as a 'philosophy of action,' promoted the idea of a 'deed,' or *czyn*, as necessary to propulsion into the future, and this idea manifested itself in Polish Romantic literature. According to Brian Porter, 'the term "historiosophy" – which refers to the interpretation of time in a way that inscribes the past with meaning and offers predictions for the future – was of fundamental importance to Polish intellectuals in the 1830s and 1840s.'[16]

Cieszkowski used the past as a means of understanding the present, and he sought to make '*the wants of the past form the satisfactions of the future.*'[17] Such interpretations of the past and predictions for the future were infused with the Hegelian concept of dynamic time. As Cieszkowski put it, 'tradition is not shaped with one blow in an eternal form; it is ceaselessly shaping itself, it is transforming itself in the process of taking shape; it is progressing forward in accordance with the level of its development.'[18] As well as with his friend Krasiński, Cieszkowski's future-orientated history is discernible in the work of poet Juliusz Słowacki, who adhered to the Cieszkowskian vision. In *Genezis z Ducha* [*Genesis from the Spirit*] (1844), Słowacki endowed the past with significance only if it was useful in moving towards the future: 'But the teachings and experiences of the past ages were worthless if they did not give us the right directions for the future.'[19] Conrad's language too, derived from the Polish experience, is indebted to such philosophy. Conrad gave a distinctly Cieszkowskian elucidation of time in the aptly titled *The*

---

[15] Cieszkowski quoted in Marek N. Jakubowski, 'The Meaning of History in August Cieszkowski,' *Dialectics and Humanism* 8.3 (1981): 147. See also Jakubowski's 'On August Cieszkowski's "Philosophy of Action,"' *Dialectics and Humanism* 4.4 (1977): 95–104.

[16] Porter, *When Nationalism Began to Hate*, 23.

[17] Cieszkowski, *Selected Writings*, 57.

[18] Cieszkowski quoted in Porter, *When Nationalism Began to Hate*, 36.

[19] Juliusz Słowacki, *Genesis from the Spirit*, translated by Col. K. Chodkiewicz (1844; London: Col. K. Chodkiewicz, 1966), 26.

Inheritors (1901), on which he collaborated with Ford Madox Ford: 'It is permitted to no man to break with his past, with the past of his kind, and to throw away the treasure of his future.'[20] This attitude to history, with its Janus-faced gaze towards the past and the future, denotes an innate tenet of Polish Romantic historiographies before the 1863 insurrection.

In 'Heart of Darkness,' a journey to the underworld of imperial exploitation in Africa, first published in *Blackwood's Magazine* in 1899, Conrad's narrator, Marlow, oppressed by his experience of atrocity and madness in King Leopold's Congo, acknowledges that the exploration of time and history must adhere to Cieszkowski's *Prolegomena*. The need to create a clear version of the past, a prerequisite of a proper evaluation of the present, becomes a controlling force in Marlow's narrative, inspiring the temporal shifts in the story. Marlow outlines his historical inheritance and distinguishes himself from Africans by stressing his individual appreciation of time, the past, and the role history plays in shaping the future: 'I don't think a single one of them had any clear idea of time, as we at the end of countless ages have. They still belonged to the beginnings of time – had no inherited experience to teach them as it were' (*Y*, 103). For Marlow, history should be understood in the Cieszkowskian tradition, with inherited experience teaching the way to the future. In the most direct echo of Cieszkowskian language in Conrad's work, Marlow declares: 'The mind of man is capable of anything – because everything is in it, all the past as well as all the future' (*Y*, 96). This historical perspective supports the novella's scathing critique of imperialism and its sceptical demythologising of the insatiable power of Kurtz, drawing attention to the belated but ultimately inescapable encounter between historical judgement and European colonial rapacity. *Nostromo* (1904), a novel concerned with the forces of history and the development of a nation, in this case Conrad's brilliantly imagined Costaguana, unveils further evidence of Conrad's appropriation of the language of Polish Romantic philosophy. In her

---

[20] Joseph Conrad and Ford Madox Hueffer, *The Inheritors: An Extravagant Story* (New York: Doubleday, Page, 1925), 305. In a letter dated 2 August 1901, later published in the *New York Times* 'Saturday Review' on 24 August, Conrad wrote that the protagonist of *The Inheritors*, Etchingham Granger, is 'made to understand that no man is permitted "to throw away with impunity the treasure of his past – the past of his kind – whence springs the promise of his future"' (*CL* 2, 348).

consideration of history, Mrs Gould asserts that 'for life to be large and full, it must contain the care of the past and of the future in every passing moment of the present. Our daily work must be done to the glory of the dead, and for the good of those who come after' (*N*, 520).[21] In Costaguana, the national spirit is ultimately usurped by the rise of modern capitalism, yet history informs the present and represents a guide to the future. In Cieszkowski's words, 'what has been overcome is in no way destroyed. It exists both ideally, as a moment in the new, and really, taking refuge in a forgotten corner of existence, having placed itself there to serve as a direct witness of the past.'[22] According to Marek Jakubowski, this approach to history 'appears under many guises in the writings of almost all Polish philosophers between 1831 and 1863.'[23]

While Cieszkowski's *Prolegomena* did not support a militant interpretation of practical philosophy, its language was ambiguous enough to be applied to a range of patriotic ideas. Inevitably, there emerged those who desired a more radical application of a philosophy of action. Edward Dembowski (1822–46), born in Warsaw and later killed fighting Austrian troops during the 1846 Cracow Uprising, also developed a 'philosophy of creativity' that used the past to deduce the future. In Dembowski's thought, 'the present is the fruit of the past and it is for the present and the future that we investigate the past.'[24] Dembowski felt that the Polish national spirit and history were returning in the Romantic poetry of Mickiewicz, which would help create the rebirth of the Polish state. He wrote that 'before 1830 young people lived on "Ode to Youth" and "Wallenrod" as though they were their catechism, after 1830 "Dziady" (*Forefathers' Eve*) became the focal point of everybody's thought and feeling.'[25] In Mickiewicz's *Oda do młodości* ['Ode to Youth'] (1820), the poet had called on his fellow Poles to recapture past glories: 'We point thee a more lofty goal/Till, freed from mouldy

---

[21] Conrad also directly echoes here the traditional British conservative politics of Edmund Burke.
[22] Cieszkowski quoted in Jakubowski, 'Meaning of History in August Cieszkowski,' 146.
[23] Jakubowski, 'Meaning of History in August Cieskowski,' 150.
[24] Dembowski quoted in Stefan Morawski, 'Polish Theories of Art Between 1830 and 1850,' *The Journal of Aesthetics and Art Criticism* 16.2 (1957): 222.
[25] Dembowski quoted in Morawski, 217. See also Jan Cavanaugh, *Out Looking In: Early Modern Polish Art, 1890–1918* (London: University of California Press, 2000), 15.

bank, thy soul/Recall its long-lost, verdant day.'[26] Such writing discloses the intricate narrative web of historicism that existed in the literature of partitioned Poland in the run-up to 1863.

One of the most interesting philosophers of the period was Henryk Kamieński (1813–66), Dembowski's cousin, who saw the past filled with relative truths, looking to it as an inspiration for revolutionary action. Kamieński rejected Hegel's belief in Absolute knowledge of history and called for action in the face of the present political situation. He wrote a long work on guerrilla tactics in anticipation of insurrection.[27] In Kamieński's philosophy, facts 'are not something ready-made, "given"; they have to be selected and endowed with meaning, which presupposes a creative activity on the part of the knower. There are no "bare facts" in history because the so-called facts are inseparable from cognitive perspective which depends, in turn, on the desire to act in a certain direction.'[28] In his article *Filozofia ekonomii materialnej ludzkiego społeczeństwa z dodaniem mniejszych pism filozoficznych [A Few Words on the Philosophy of History]* (1844), the meaning of the past was waiting to be inscribed from the present. Conrad's perspective on history employs this method, from Marlow's highly subjective renderings of the past in 'Youth' and 'Heart of Darkness' to the autobiographical *A Personal Record*, composed of a retrospective narrative style that responds to the Hegelian philosophy of dynamic time. *A Personal Record* is 'concerned with the present and reflecting upon the past as the means of realizing this concern.'[29] The impression left by events – the subjective interpretation of their importance and meaning, as in Kamieński's thought – inspires Conrad's autobiographical writing. In *A Personal Record*, when discussing Poland and the culture of his youth, Conrad acknowledged that it was awareness of the increasing distance of the past that encouraged the act of retrospective narration. The past is imbued with significance by the passage of time as the memories recounted 'linger yet, dim but poignant, and awaiting the moment

---

[26] Adam Mickiewicz, *Selected Poetry and Prose*, edited with an introduction by Stanisław Helsztynski (Warsaw: Polonia Publishing House, 1955), 24.

[27] R.F. Leslie, *Reform and Insurrection in Russian Poland 1856–1865* (London: Athlone Press, 1963), 15.

[28] Walicki, *Philosophy and Romantic Nationalism*, 197–98.

[29] Noel Peacock, '"Undefaced Image": Autobiography and Vision in *A Personal Record*,' *Conrad's Century*, 152.

when their haunting reality, their last trace on earth, shall pass for ever with me out of the world' (*PR*, x). For Conrad, as long as the past can be recollected it continues to contain an element of reality. Conrad's childhood memories reveal the profound impact of Hegel's thought in partitioned Poland. In a letter to George T. Keating on 14 December 1922, Conrad remembered the role of German philosophy in his education: 'our historical studies were naturally tinted with Germanism, I know that all we boys, the six hundred of us, resisted that influence with all our might, while accepting the results of German research and thoroughness' (*CL* 7, 615). Polish acceptance of Hegelian thoroughness was tempered, as Conrad admitted in 'The Crime of Partition,' by a resistance to Hegelian determinism, because 'The Germanic tribes had told the whole world in all possible tones carrying conviction, the gently persuasive, the coldly logical; in tones Hegelian, Nietzschean, war-like, pious, cynical, inspired, what they were going to do to the inferior races of the earth, so full of sin and all unworthiness' (*NLL*, 101). Alongside the Germanism that shaped his learning, 'Polish Romantic poetry and patriotic literature were read and revered in the schools in Kraków and Lwów that Konrad Korzeniowski attended.'[30] Conrad's acknowledgement of the presence of Hegelian concepts of history is a reminder, in the words of Czesław Miłosz, of the 'fondness Polish Romantics displayed for the philosophy of history. Their themes were elaborated sometimes in opposition to, sometimes in agreement with, Hegelian thought. In any case Polish Romanticism was thoroughly imbued with historicism.'[31] Accordingly, Conrad's writing needs to be understood in relation to the historicism that informed the intellectual climate of his youth: 'Conrad's Polish biography has to be expanded from individual into collective, and from psychological into cultural. In a word, it has to be transcended and become a study of culture.'[32] The philosophy of Cieszkowski and his contemporaries represents a major aspect of this cultural world.

---

[30] Zdzisław Najder, 'Fidelity and Art: Joseph Conrad's Cultural Heritage and Literary Program,' *Conrad's Century*, 13.

[31] Czesław Miłosz, *The History of Polish Literature* (London: Macmillan, 1969), 202–03.

[32] Zdzisław Najder, *Conrad in Perspective: Essays on Art and Fidelity* (Cambridge: Cambridge University Press, 1997), 15.

APOLLO KORZENIOWSKI AND THE
FAILURE OF THE 1863 UPRISING

If nineteenth-century Polish culture was dominated by a discourse of historicism, then Conrad's individual relationships with his family and guardians directly exposed the future writer to the language of Polish Romantic historiography. Apollo Korzeniowski 'combined traditionalism, in the form of harking back to the time when Poland was an independent country, with radicalism in the form of linking the demands of national liberty with those of political equality.'[33] Polish Romantic philosophy informs Korzeniowski's awareness of the conflict involved in the historical process. In his memoir 'Poland and Muscovy,' written in exile after the failure of the 1863 insurrection, Korzeniowski doubted the outcome of the struggle: 'the present is so hard that the future may be even more frightful' (*UFE*, 91). However, he retained an inherent faith in the 'Polish spirit which shines just as brightly whether under a velvet cape or a peasant's coat' (*UFE*, 87).[34] The language of retrospection appeared in Korzeniowski's literary efforts, as in a poem he sent to Tadeusz Bobrowski in 1849: 'You steer towards the shores of fame!/And when you reach/Your journey's end,/The golden lands of bliss,/Please remember with a sigh/Those who perished in the storm!' (*UFE*, 23). The repose of the journey's end is tempered by a glance to the past to acknowledge its role in history, echoing Cieszkowski's philosophy.

The language of Cieszkowski's *Prolegomena*, the most accomplished Polish philosophical work of the period, is ubiquitous in the literature that formed Conrad's cultural education by Apollo. Conrad remembered being read the Romantic poetry of Słowacki, whose work he claimed contained the Polish soul. Słowacki was aware of the momentum and continuity of the historical process. In Cieszkowskian language, Słowacki 'saw clearly all these transitory forms and lives, and observed how my spirit had gone through them. In each form dwells the

---

[33] Najder, *Conrad in Perspective*, 28–29.
[34] For an extended discussion of Korzeniowski's 'Poland and Muscovy' and the extent of Korzeniowski's radicalism, see Addison Bross, 'Apollo Korzeniowski's Mythic Vision: *Poland and Muscovy*, "Note A,"' *The Conradian* 20.1 (1995): 77–102.

remembrance of past forms, and the revelation of future forms.'[35] Conrad recalled his encounter with this literature, believing that the influence of the great Romantics gave his own writing its inimitability: 'That is *Polishness*. Polishness which I took from Mickiewicz and Słowacki. My father read *Pan Tadeusz* aloud to me and made me read it aloud. Not just once or twice. I used to prefer *Konrad Wallenrod*, *Grażyna*. Later I liked Słowacki better. You know why Słowacki? *Il est l'âme de toute la Pologne, lui*' (*UFE*, 199). However, while in exile with his wife, the co-accused Ewa Korzeniowska, after their trial for subversive activism in 1862, Apollo Korzeniowski strayed from the *historiosophie* of Cieszkowski and Słowacki, and his scepticism increased in response to his surrounding conditions and the declining health of his wife and child. Like the early incarnation of Conrad's Almayer, Korzeniowski wrote: 'for us only the past exists, today falls into oblivion, of tomorrow we dare not dream. Even if – what use would there be for men creeping out of the grave' (*UFE*, 68). This reveals a Polish Romantic philosophy touched with pessimism from the failed political struggle. In a letter to family friends the Zagorskis, Korzeniowski lamented: 'Thanks to our present life I have got to know an illness new to me. I suffer from nostalgia – what is the Polish word for it? You can't imagine how tiring it is and yet I don't want to be cured. I would rather die from it' (*UFE*, 69). Korzeniowski was uncomfortable with his acquired pessimism, and a reluctant waning of his faith in the Romanticism of Mickiewicz emerges in his writing: 'I am afraid of falling back on memories, like people who refrain from touching the bones of the dead; and the present is such a huge nothing, it is awesome' (*UFE*, 71).

In a letter to R.B. Cunninghame Graham in 1899, as 'Heart of Darkness,' appeared in *Blackwood's Magazine*, Conrad wrote: 'For myself, I look at the future from the depths of a very dark past, and I find I am allowed nothing but fidelity to an absolutely lost cause, to an idea without a future' (*CL* 2, 161).[36] Conrad's immersion in the past as a means of encountering the future derives from the tradition of

[35] Słowacki, *Genesis from the Spirit*, 11.

[36] In an article in *Prawda* 21 (1909), while Conrad was working on *Under Western Eyes*, T. Miciński wrote: 'There is in Poland a fixed, eternal loyalty to the lost cause, unknown anywhere else in the world, an elevation of the rightful heart which can be seen only in a great act, unblemished honor, which in itself is nothing, and which feeds the soul with hunger in underground caves of the misery of existence.' See Rett R. Ludwikowski, *Continuity and*

Cieszkowski's reading of Hegel, but, critically, it has acquired pessimism from the failure of the deed, echoing the sombre tone of Korzeniowski's writing. The idea of an inherited but tenuously lucid history and an unpredictable future recurs in *Under Western Eyes* (1911). Razumov tells the bomb-throwing radical Victor Haldin: 'My tradition is historical. What have I to look back to but that national past from which you gentlemen want to wrench away your future' (*UWE*, 61). Haldin's mistaken belief that the conservative Razumov will support his revolutionary deed exemplifies the varying ideologies that dominate any historically conscious society. Razumov's political creed outlines these conflicting principals, accepting the logic of history and the futility of challenging time: 'History not Theory./Patriotism not Internationalism./Evolution not Revolution./Direction not Destruction./Unity not Disruption' (*UWE*, 66). The years before the 1863 uprising in Poland offered diverse views on the subjects of Razumov's doctrine. The Polish response to Hegel captured in Cieszkowski's work polarised history and theory, direction and destruction, evolution and revolution. The failed deed of 1863, however, undermined the insurrectionary offshoots of Cieszkowski's *Historiosophie*, and the 'defeat seemed to negate the ideals, beliefs, and hopes that had sustained so many for so long.'[37]

The shift in Polish culture can be seen in microcosm in the experience of Conrad's family. The effect of Ewa's death on Korzeniowski and on the young Conrad cannot be overestimated, and Conrad later wrote that his father felt 'the deadly blow of her loss' (*PR*, x). Apollo's distraught reaction to the death in a letter to Kazimierz Kaszewski expresses a sense of absolute desolation, directly evoking Conrad's later representation of the widowed Giorgio Viola in *Nostromo*:

And I am here so very much alone: no other company but this silent grave, bewitched in silence, deaf to prayers, unresponsive to tears, harder even than Adam's stone, for a tear will not seep through it. I spend the greatest part of my days by the grave, but what am I to do about it – how am I to rid myself of the remaining hours of vigil or of sleep? Tell me, my best friend. My deepest beliefs are shaken; doubts consume all my thoughts. When She is not here, when all I dream about is to see her again – this creature without a blemish, who

Change in Poland: Conservatism in Polish Political Thought (Washington: Catholic University of America Press, 1991), 177n.

[37] Porter, *When Nationalism Began to Hate*, 43.

constituted the entire delight of my existence – doubts overwhelm me and call me out: and if my faith is but deluded imagination? If my mother's teaching about another and better life for the soul was only her heart's mistake? If death does end everything? If I shall never see her, never?! Ah, my dear friend, what torments!   (*UFE*, 94–95)[38]

Korzeniowski's language, although rooted in personal tragedy, is also a thread in the larger narrative of loss of the nation. The Polish national language of retrospection darkens all the private correspondence amongst Conrad's family in the years of his childhood. Zdzisław Najder has described this language as the awareness of 'a great loss, of a world destroyed, of a cherished order of things smashed to pieces. There is a noticeable streak of morbidity expressed in terms sometimes despairing and nostalgic, sometimes caustic and bitter. It has little, or nothing, to do with the authors' personal attitudes – it is a reflection of national sentiment.'[39]

An instructive way of understanding Conrad's immersion in this world is to analyse Conrad's youth in the 1860s in conjunction with Polish art of the same period. Polish art of the nineteenth century visualises the loss of this cherished order and allows us to see into the world of 1863 Poland and the years that followed. According to Jan Cavanaugh, the period of the partitions 'abounded in pictures of fallen leaders,' as well as 'depictions of martyred or exiled insurgents, anonymous graves (of insurgents), funerals of heroes, and orphans. The lonely, parentless child, whether royal or peasant, embodies the fate of the nation or the Pole deprived of his motherland.'[40] In his series of drawings entitled *Polonia* (1863), the Polish artist Artur Grottger (1837–67) captured the misery of a family hearing of the defeat of the rising (Figures 1.1 and 1.2). *Polonia* depicts the world of Conrad's

---

[38] In his 'Author's Note' to *A Personal Record*, Conrad remembered his father as 'mortally weary – a vanquished man' (*PR*, viii). In *Nostromo*, Viola, on the death of his wife, almost 'called out to her by name; and the thought that no call from him would ever again evoke the answer of her voice, made him drop heavily into the chair with a loud groan, wrung out by the pain as of a keen blade piercing his breast.' Transformed by the death, 'The enthusiastic and severe soul of Giorgio Viola, sailor, champion of oppressed humanity, enemy of kings ... had descended into the open abyss of desolation amongst the shattered vestiges of his past' (*N*, 467).

[39] Najder, *Conrad in Perspective*, 16.

[40] Cavanaugh, *Out Looking In: Early Modern Polish Art*, 17.

Figure 1.1 'Żałobne wieści' (Mournful News), by Artur Grottger.

childhood known from his relatives' correspondence and extant photographs of his family; a monochrome world that must understand and accept failure.

Polonia 'begins with an allegorical figure of "Poland Unchained" and ends with heart-wrenching scenes of death and utter defeat,' and, as Cavanaugh notes, 'it received an enthusiastic response from the public at large, which regarded it as a form of reportage, almost a document of Polish history. [The historian] Stanisław Tarnowski, for example, wrote that Grottger had encompassed "in eight pictures the whole drama of '63, as it was reflected in private homes and attitudes. . . . They may not comprise the history of Poland, but it is the history of every Polish family, of every heart gripped in the most agonizing of sorrowful

Figure 1.2 'Po odejściu wroga' (After the Enemy's Retreat), by Artur Grottger.

moments.""[41] The defeat of the insurrection led to a resigned awareness that the past could not be returned to as the Romanticism of Mickiewicz believed. In 1867, Grottger completed his last cycle of drawings, entitled *Wojna* [*War*] (1866–67), an anti-war statement in which the violence and futility of conflict was portrayed, and where one can detect the crushing bitterness of the military failure. One of the drawings, 'Come with me through this Vale of Tears,' corresponds to the image of the grieving Korzeniowski (Figure 1.3) in its anguished portrayal of irreversible history.[42] It also anticipates the coming shift from Romanticism to Realism. This new approach to history, with its now altered

Figure 1.3 Pójdź ze mną przez ten padół płaczu (Come with me through this Vale of Tears), by Artur Grottger.

Janus-faced gaze towards an elegiac past and a barren present, saturates Conrad's writing. It is a consequence of his formative years at the most significant turning point in modern Polish history until the rebirth of the Polish state in 1918. As Zdzisław Najder has written, 'Conrad's early years can be looked on as almost symbolic in the combination of national and personal tragedy.'[43]

In 1921, in a poll conducted by *John O'London's Weekly* on 'The First Thing I Remember,' Conrad recalled a childhood memory of his mother in 1861 consistent with the silence and loss suffusing Grottger's drawings:

> I think my earliest memory is of my mother at the piano; of being let into a room which to this day seems to me the very largest room which I was ever in, of the music suddenly stopping, and my mother, with her hands on the keyboard, turning her head to look at me. This must have been early in 1861 [...]. I have a very convincing impression of details, such as the oval of her face, the peculiar suavity of her eyes, and of the sudden silence. That last is the most convincing as to the genuineness of its being an experience; for, as to the rest, I have to this day a photograph of her from that very time, which, of course, might have gone to the making up of the 'memory.'[44]

In assessing the literary influence of Apollo upon Conrad, Andrzej Busza has observed that 'although we can hardly expect to find direct borrowings, there are obvious points of likeness which may help us to get an idea of the kind of influence that Korzeniowski's thought and writing exerted on Conrad.'[45] Korzeniowski's lamentations recall Mickiewicz's *Forefathers*, echoing 'he who through his grief would save/ what's vanished in the past's dim grave.'[46] Although Korzeniowski did not die a broken man, he adapted his previous outlook to the realities of post-1863 Poland. His renewed activity in literary circles – 'the task of keeping the national spirit firm in the hope of an independent future, (*PR*, ix) – in Cracow before his death may highlight this change in

[43] Zdzisław Najder ed., *Conrad's Polish Background: Letters to and from Polish Friends*, translated by Halina Carroll (London: Oxford University Press, 1964), 5.

[44] Reprinted in Zdzisław Najder ed., *Congo Diary and Other Uncollected Pieces* (New York: Doubleday, 1978), 98–99.

[45] Andrzej Busza, 'Conrad's Polish Literary Background and Some Illustrations of the Influence of Polish Literature on his Work,' *Antemurale* 10 (1966): 132.

[46] Mickiewicz, *Forefathers*, 110.

attitude, as it divulges the growing dominance of the Positivist movement (see below) and its applied focus on work and cultural rejuvenation. The journal Korzeniowski helped to found, *Kraj* [*The Nation*],
later became a vocal organ of Positivism, but the language of Polish
Romanticism subdued by the failure of the insurrectionary deed colours
Korzeniowski's late correspondence.

The funeral procession of Apollo Korzeniowski in 1869 – 'a
manifestation of the national spirit' (*PR*, viii) – became a solemn
patriotic demonstration attended by thousands to honour the departed writer and activist, with the young Conrad, now a living embodiment of the artistic representation of the Polish orphan, walking at
the head of his father's cortege with Stefan Buszczyński.[47] *Kraj*
described the procession, as 'several thousand people followed in
silence' to 'pay their last respects to the prematurely departed poet
and Poland's noble son.'[48] Conrad later remembered the funeral in
'Poland Revisited':

In the moonlight-flooded silence of the old town of glorious tombs and
tragic memories I could see again the small boy of that day following a
hearse; a space kept clear in which I walked alone, conscious of an enormous following, the clumsy swaying of the tall black machine, the chanting
of the surpliced clergy at the head, the flames of tapers passing under the
low archway of the gate, the rows of bared heads on the pavements with
fixed, serious eyes. (*NLL*, 134)

In his description of the procession, Conrad related his father's beliefs to
Romantic philosophies of history, saluting 'the ardent fidelity of the
man whose life had been a fearless confession in word and deed of a
creed which the simplest heart in that crowd could feel and understand'
(*NLL*, 134). Korzeniowski's last letters to Stefan Buszczyński relate the
sympathy Buszczyński held for Apollo's political views. Buszczyński was
Korzeniowski's closest friend, and from May 1869 until August 1870
Conrad came under the guardianship of Buszczyński.

---

[47] While in 'Poland Revisited' Conrad recalled walking alone behind his father's
hearse, Teofila Bobrowska maintained that Buszczyński accompanied Conrad through
the streets of Cracow (*UFE*, 131).
[48] *Kraj* 70 (1869), cited in Najder, *Conrad: A Chronicle*, 28.

STEFAN BUSZCZYŃSKI AND LATE POLISH ROMANTICISM

A critic, journalist, poet, and historian, Stefan Buszczyński (1821–92) began his literary career with the novelette *Wymarzony kochanek* [*The Ideal Lover*] in 1848. He also published a brief biography of Korzeniowski upon his death, entitled *Mało znany poeta* [*A Little Known Poet*] (1870).[49] Buszczyński requires attention for the reason that 'after Apollo Korzeniowski's death Conrad remained under the influence of men similar to his father.'[50] According to Andrzej Busza, 'Buszczyński was probably the last outstanding representative of the so-called Polish romantic school of history and Apollo Korzeniowski has been called the "last [Polish] romantic dramatist."'[51] Both Korzeniowski and Buszczyński patently embraced Polish Romantic historicism.

One way of gauging Conrad's relationship with Buszczyński is through the only extant letter Conrad wrote to his former guardian, in 1883. Conrad states he has 'never forgotten either the country, the family, or those who were so kind to me – amongst whom I number you, dear Sir, my guardian when I was orphaned, and who amongst them must take the first place' (*CL* 1, 7). This reverence is coupled with the language of Polish Romanticism and an appeal to the ideology Buszczyński had espoused in his most famous work, *La Décadence de l'Europe* (1867): 'I always remember what you said when I was leaving Cracow: "Remember" – you said – "wherever you may sail you are sailing towards Poland!" That I have never forgotten, and never will forget' (*CL* 1, 7–8). Gustav Morf has understood this reference as an allusion to a verse by Juliusz Słowacki from a nostalgic song entitled

---

[49] The titles of Buszczyński's works written between 1860 and 1890 indicate the strength of his patriotism and his indebtedness to the *historiosophie* of Cieszkowski: *Przestroga historyi* [*The Warning of History*] (1882); *Znaczenie dziejów polski i walk o niepodległość* [*The Significance of Polish History and the Struggle for National Independence*] (1882); *Obrona spotwarzonego narodu* [*The Defence of a Slandered Nation*] (1888–90). See also Busza, 'Conrad's Polish Literary Background,' 140–41 and 144.

[50] Busza, 'Conrad's Polish Literary Background,' 143.

[51] Busza, 'Conrad's Polish Literary Background,' 144.

'Hymn' (1836).[52] It also recalls Mickiewicz's *Pan Tadeusz* (1834). In the 'Epilogue' to the poem, Mickiewicz reflected:

Today, for us, unbidden guests in the world, in all the past and in all the future – today there is but one region in which there is a crumb of happiness for a Pole: the land of his childhood! That land will ever remain holy and pure as first love; undisturbed by the remembrance of errors, not undermined by the deceitfulness of hopes, and unchanged by the stream of events.[53]

The stream of events, with its Hegelian acknowledgement of evolving history and the unending process of becoming, echoes Conrad's portrayal of the flow of time in 'A Familiar Preface' to *A Personal Record*, where 'the great stream carrying onward so many lives' (*PR*, xvii) winds its incessant course. Both Conrad in sailing towards the nation and Mickiewicz in his undisturbed remembrance of youth acknowledge Poland as a compass in the charting of 'all the past and all the future.'

Although Conrad never met Buszczyński again after leaving Poland, his former guardian remained a vital link in the chain connecting Conrad to his Polish past. Upon receiving requests for information about his family from John Galsworthy, Edward Garnett, and R.B. Cunninghame Graham, Conrad always referred to Buszczyński's biography of his father, which described Korzeniowski as a man who 'yearned for an ideal, and for him Poland and nothing but Poland was the eternal ideal' (*UFE*, 24). Buszczyński also features in the 'Author's Note' to *A Personal Record*, where Conrad alludes to both *A Little Known Poet* and the correspondence between Korzeniowski and Buszczyński in the University Library in Cracow.[54] Morf has decoded Conrad's letter to Buszczyński from 1883, observing that Conrad's writing whisks him back to childhood as he addresses a learned professor whose teaching he has not forgotten. Conrad's idea of Poland as a

---

[52] Gustav Morf, *The Polish Shades and Ghosts of Joseph Conrad* (New York: Astra Books, 1976), 84.

[53] Mickiewicz, *Selected Poetry and Prose*, 119.

[54] Conrad wrote in his 'Author's Note' to *A Personal Record* that Buszczyński's writing taught him most about his father: 'The political side of his life was being recalled too; for some men of his time, his co-workers in the task of keeping the national spirit firm in the hope of an independent future, had been in their old age publishing their memoirs, where the part he played was for the first time publicly disclosed to the world' (*PR*, ix).

reference point for all endeavours also strongly characterises Buszczyński's writing.

La Décadence de l'Europe, published in Paris in 1867, and praised by Victor Hugo and Jules Michelet, appeals to humanity to turn back from its road to decline and to nurture freedom and progress. In his introduction to *Décadence*, which Korzeniowski had confessed was 'a book, very close to my heart according to what I have understood' (*UFE*, 113), Buszczyński conceded that he would not focus on Poland – 'I leave aside my nationality as I write'[55] – but concentrate on the problems inherent in European society. However, Buszczyński's work gains its power through its silent reference to Poland, with the author borrowing from Alexis de Tocqueville's *Democracy in America* (1838). Speaking of *Democracy in America*, de Tocqueville had explained: 'In my work on America [...] though I seldom mention France, I did not write a page without thinking of her, and placing her as it were before me. [...] I believe that this perpetual silent reference to France was a principal cause of the book's success.'[56] Although he by no means preserved a studied silence on the subject of his homeland, Conrad's Polish background likewise takes shape in his writing in the adoption of the language of Polish Romantic philosophy and history. In 'First News' (1918), in which he wrote again of his return to Cracow before the Great War, Conrad felt his journey recalled 'the past, the great historical past in which lived the inextinguishable spark of national life' (*NLL*, 139). Zdzisław Najder has observed in his analysis of themes of guilt and betrayal in Conrad's work that 'what at first sight seems to be a peculiar Conradian obsession, apparently grounded in his personal experience, at a closer look turns out to be a literary stereotype, grounded in national history.'[57] In particular, Conrad's political essay 'Autocracy and War' (1905), written at the time of the Russo-Japanese War, benefits from being read alongside Buszczyński's *Décadence*, as it is heavily coloured by Polish historicism.

Conrad's analysis of Russia's defeat in the war anticipates the rise of German imperial power and is intensely sceptical about Europe's future.

[55] Stefan Buszczyński, *La Décadence de l'Europe* (Paris, 1867), xviii.

[56] Quoted in Harriet Martineau, *Society in America*, edited by Seymour Martin Lipset (New York: Anchor-Doubleday, 1962), 7.

[57] Najder, *Conrad in Perspective*, 13.

It confronts the issues that formed the central thesis of Buszczyński's book: the dominance of military spending and the rivalries and alliances of autocratic leaders in Europe. Conrad had first addressed the subject of 'Autocracy and War' in his early letters, which display the historical consciousness of Buszczyński and late Polish Romanticism. Buszczyński's original intention had been to affirm his faith in humanity misguided by political leaders, but he now regretted that historical progress had decreased to an imperceptible pace. The acceptance of Hegelian historicism had caused complacency in humankind's desire to implement the future: 'According to Hegel, world history is the development of the idea of liberty in the general element; that is, in humanity. Where, however, does he observe this development?'[58]

Buszczyński's proposal for reversing Europe's decline was the formation of a European Union-type association between nations, something then being thwarted by monarchs and their vast military budgets. 'Autocracy and War' recalls Buszczyński in this respect, as Conrad declares that '*Il n'y a plus d'Europe* – there is only an armed and trading continent, the home of slowly maturing economical contests for life and death and of loudly proclaimed world-wide ambitions' (*NLL*, 92). Conrad's survey of a changing Europe is a stylistic descendent of late Polish Romanticism. For Buszczyński, the present had become 'one of the gravest periods in history; behind us lies humanity's past, and before use arises a great question: which form will the future take?'[59] In the tradition of Cieszkowski, Buszczyński ironically criticised Hegel's willingness to abandon the future: 'Hegel was a profound thinker, but he was short-sighted.'[60] Buszczyński foregrounded the conflicting responses to Hegel's philosophy of history in Poland by writing that 'Several of his [Hegel's] most profound ideas have been understood recently in two contrary ways and have been applied to completely opposing methods.'[61] While Buszczyński refers directly here to the

---

[58] Buszczyński, *Décadence* (1867), 228.

[59] Buszczyński, *Décadence* (1867), 1.

[60] Buszczyński, *Décadence* (1867), 229.

[61] Buszczyński, *Décadence* (1867), 229. For a study of the opposing schools of Hegelian thought, see John Toews, *Hegelianism: The Path Towards Dialectical Humanism, 1805–1841* (Cambridge: Cambridge University Press, 1980), and Warren Breckman, *Marx, the Young Hegelians, and the Origins of Radical Social Theory: Dethroning of the Self* (Cambridge: Cambridge University Press, 1999).

split amongst Hegel's followers into left and right Hegelians, Buszczyński's own speculations on history and Conrad's later investigations of
history represent some of these divergent interpretations of Hegel's
philosophy. Conrad's historical consciousness emerges from the pages
of 'Autocracy and War' when Conrad considers Russia's decline and the
rise of Germany, revealing an entrenched aversion towards the historical
dividers of Poland: 'The common guilt of the two empires is defined
precisely by their frontier line running through the Polish provinces.
Without indulging in excessive feelings of indignation at that country's
partition [...]. Germany has been the evil counsellor of Russia on all
the questions of her Polish problem' (*NLL*, 79–80).

La Décadence de l'Europe and 'Autocracy and War' also use the
language of Polish Romantic philosophy in their defence of the cultural
foundations of the nation, locating the spirit of a nation in inherited
traditions. For Conrad, the 'true greatness' and 'inspiration' of any state
springs from the 'constructive instinct of the people,' and this instinct is
guided and 'governed by the strong hand of a collective conscience and
voiced in the wisdom and counsel of men who seldom reap the reward
of gratitude' (*NLL*, 77). Such wisdom and counsel can be construed as
the work of philosophers and poets, figures such as Cieszkowski, Słowacki, Mickiewicz, and Korzeniowski. Both Conrad and Buszczyński
crucially reject Pan-Slavism, promoting instead the individuality of
nations. Buszczyński believed the nation was a creation of nature and
that there could be no such thing as Pan-Slavism: 'Nothing remains [of
Pan-Slavism] but its descendants, who have long since formed themselves into *nations*, each with its own individuality.'[62] For Conrad,
Russian dominance throughout the nineteenth century and the denial
of Poland's individuality opened an 'abyss where the dreams of pansla-
vism, of universal conquest, mingled with the hate and contempt for
Western ideas drift impotently like shapes of mist' (*NLL*, 83).[63]

---

[62] Buszczyński, *Décadence* (1867), lxxiii.

[63] 'Autocracy and War' confronts many of the issues raised in Alexander Herzen's *The
Russian People and Socialism: An Open Letter to Jules Michelet* (1851). Herzen supported a
Pan-Slavism composed of autonomous nations: 'Once the Slav world has become
unified, and knit together into an association of free autonomous peoples, it will at last
be able to enter on its true historical existence.' See Alexander Herzen, *From the Other
Shore and The Russian People and Socialism: An Open Letter to Jules Michelet*, translated by
Richard Wollheim (London: Weidenfeld and Nicholson, 1956), 175. Herzen's *The*

Figure 1.4 Portrait of August Cieszkowski (1814–94) by Maksymilian Fajans (1827–90).

Conrad was particulary uncomfortable with Edward Garnett's attributing of the origins of his literary style to his 'Slav temperament,'
insisting it was the past experience of being uniquely Polish that contributed to his identity: 'You remember always that I am a Slav (it's your
idée fixe) but you seem to forget that I am a Pole' (*CL* 3, 492). Conrad
emphasised this point again during the Great War, when he wrote a
memorandum for the Foreign Office entitled 'A Note on the Polish
Problem' (1916), stating: 'The Poles whom superficial or ill-informed
theorists are trying to force into the social and psychological formula of
Slavonism are in truth not Slavonic at all. In temperament, in feeling, in
mind, and even in unreason, they are Western, with an absolute
comprehension of all the Western modes of thought, even of those
which are remote from their own historical experience' (*NLL*, 109). In
his 'Author's Note' to *A Personal Record*, Conrad reopened the issue in
relation to its manifestation in the literary world, explaining that his
opposition to Pan-Slavism originated in the culture of his youth: 'Nothing is more foreign than what in the literary world is called Sclavonism,
to the Polish temperament with its tradition of self-government,
its chivalrous view of moral restraints and an exaggerated respect for
individual rights: [...]. [This] was the dominant characteristic of the
mental and moral atmosphere of the houses which sheltered my hazard-
ous childhood' (*PR*, vi–vii).

In his last years, Conrad was still addressing this cornerstone of Polish
philosophical debate. In 1922, Conrad explained that he belonged 'to a
group which has historically a political past, with a Western Roman
culture derived at first from Italy and then from France; and a rather
Southern temperament; an outpost of Westernism with a Roman
tradition, situated between Slavo-Tartar Byzantine barbarism on one
side and the German tribes on the other' (*CL* 7, 615).[64] For Poles in the

---

Russian People and Socialism and Michelet's *Pologne et Russie* (1852), the work that
provoked Herzen's essay, are stylistic, philosophical, and political reference points for
Conrad's ideas on Russia. For further discussion on this point, see Chapter 3 below.

[64] In *The Polish Nation* (Paris: Boyveau et Chevillet, 1917), Polish philosopher
Wincenty Lutosławski (1863–1954) saw the 'Polish nation in its true light, as a civilising
power, much more akin to the Romans and to the British than to its present rulers'
(p. 19). Conrad had met Lutosławski in 1897, when the latter, an overly-mystic Polish
nationalist, failed to 'win Conrad for Polish literature.' As Laurence Davies notes, an
account of the meeting published in *Kraj* in 1899 'did some damage to Conrad's Polish

Romantic period, the individuality of the nation needed to be upheld. Conrad opposes Hegel's idea that in 'the same sense in which individuals are incorporated into the abstract concept of the person, the "individuals" that are independent nations will have to experience this fate as well: that is to say, their concrete form will be crushed by this universality.'[65] Conrad and Buszczyński resist being subsumed into a larger entity that will destroy individual identity. Indeed, for Buszczyński, the guarding of national identity contributes to the protection of the freedom of individuality: 'The protection of nationality, which is the unity of the individual properties of the nation, guaranties the protection of the rights of all humanity.'[66] Buszczyński's faith in the nation and his association of its preservation with the rights of the individual continues a long tradition of nineteenth-century Polish historiography reaching back to Prince Adam Czartoryski's *Essai sur la diplomatie* (1830). In 1899, Conrad wrote to R.B. Cunninghame Graham, explaining: 'I cannot admit the idea of a fraternity not so much because I believe it impracticable, but because its propaganda (the only thing really tangible about it) tends to weaken the national sentiment the preservation of which is my concern' (*CL* 2, 158). This privileging of national identity, which for Conrad comprises an inherited past, stands in agreement with Buszczyński, setting up an enduring correlation between the language of individual and national identity in Conrad's work.

It has been written that the Polishness of 'Autocracy and War' 'permeates its style: the whole piece reads like a literal translation from a late-romantic Polish writer.'[67] Józef Ujejski found it easy 'to succumb to the delusion that we are reading the prose of a Polish émigré of the Romantic period.'[68] Both Korzeniowski and Buszczyński were

---

reputation' (*CL* 4, 455n).' In a letter to Olivia Rayne Garnett in 1911, Conrad wrote: 'I don't understand him in the least' (*CL* 4, 490). For Lutosławski's version of the meeting, see *Blue Peter* 10 (1930), 638–40.

[65] G.W.F. Hegel, *Introduction to the Philosophy of History*, translated with an introduction by Leo Rauch (Indianapolis: Hackett, 1988), 96.

[66] Buszczyński, *Décadence* (1867), 204.

[67] Najder ed., *Conrad's Polish Background*, 25.

[68] Józef Ujejski, *O Konradzie Korzeniowskim* (Warszawa: Dom Książki Polskiej, 1936), 55. Quoted in Addison Bross, 'The January Rising and Its Aftermath: The Missing Theme in Conrad's Political Consciousness,' *Conrad and Poland*, edited by

critical influences on Conrad's historical scepticism. If Conrad writes that 'Nothing is certain except our ignorance of our future movements' (*CL* 1, 135) close to the publication of his first novel, then it is a consequence of the post-1863 transformation of Cieszkowski's *historiosophie* from optimism to scepticism.

TADEUSZ BOBROWSKI AND POLISH POSITIVISM

In 1870–71, when Conrad came under the guardianship of his uncle Tadeusz Bobrowski, the 'new realities within Poland and across Europe compelled many educated Poles to reassess critically their nation's predicament and its prospects for the future.'[69] The defeat of France in the Franco-Prussian War and the consolidation of German power in Europe ensured Poland's traditional westward glance for assistance would continue to be in vain. Tadeusz Bobrowski, while deeply attached to Polish culture and tradition, advocated an industrious acceptance of the political status quo. Bobrowski's traditionalist philosophy of history followed the Polish Positivists, who believed economic and cultural rejuvenation would restore Poland's honour. August Cieszkowski worked throughout these years on his posthumously published *Ojcze Nasz* [*Our Father*], which represents his later, Positivist thought, containing a organicist approach to the provision of Poland's spiritual and economic daily bread.[70]

One important point of continuity between Bobrowski and the Polish Romantic response to Hegel is that Bobrowski continued to align the plight of the nation with that of the individual. In his *Introduction to the Philosophy of History*, Hegel explained that the 'individual, as a single entity, goes through various stages of development and remains that individual. The same is true of a people: it, too, goes through a series of stages, until it reaches the one which is the universal stage of its Spirit.'[71] Conrad's immersion in this German

[69] Lukowski and Zawadzki, *Concise History of Poland*, 159.
[70] *Selected Writings of August Cieszkowski*, 32.
[71] Hegel, *Philosophy of History*, 81.

historiography may have led to an 'identification of the nation with the self.'[72] The Romantic critic and philosopher Maurycy Mochnacki advanced the notion that the development of the nation corresponded to the growth of the individual: 'One man, when he begins to think, moves towards a realization of himself, and in the same way an entire nation, in its thoughts, must have a self-recognition of its being. Just as the thoughts of one person contain within them, so to speak, the essence of his essence, so all thoughts gathered together into a whole represent the essence of a nation.'[73] In Poland, 'the interest in German idealism was not purely theoretical but "existential," stemming from a passionate search for meaning in individual and national life.'[74] History in its national context corresponded to the individual's own understanding of time, and this has since become a noted feature of much influential writing on national identity in various geographical contexts, such as Octavio Paz's *The Labyrinth of Solitude* (1950). Conrad's analogous reading of his individual experience of time with the Polish Romantic narrative of history led to an appropriation of the language of Polish Romantic retrospection. In 1885, Conrad wrote that in 'the presence of such national misfortune, personal happiness is impossible in its absolute form of general contentment and peace of heart' (*CL* 1, 12). The doubling of the national and individual quest for meaning can be found in a letter from Tadeusz Bobrowski to Conrad, where Bobrowski noted that if 'both Individuals and Nations were to establish as their aim "duty" instead of the ideal of greatness, the world would certainly be a better place.'[75] Decisively, the terms of reference have changed; the call word for the post-1863 period is not the deed, but duty.

The Polish shift from Romanticism to Positivism stands revealed in the oscillating influences of Conrad's guardians.[76] Under Stefan Buszc-zyński, Conrad first encountered Positivism, because the 'subject was

---

[72] Eloise Knapp Hay, *The Political Novels of Joseph Conrad* (Chicago: University of Chicago Press, 1972), 20.

[73] Mochnacki quoted in Porter, *When Nationalism Began to Hate*, 21.

[74] Walicki, *Philosophy and Romantic Nationalism*, 106.

[75] Bobrowski quoted in Busza, 'Conrad's Polish Literary Background,' 159.

[76] See Addison Bross, 'The January Rising and its Aftermath: The Missing Theme in Conrad's Political Consciousness,' *Conrad and Poland*, 61–87. Bross gives good examples of the shift from Romanticism to Positivism in Polish periodicals. Also relevant is Stephen G.W. Brodsky, 'Conrad's Two Polish Pasts: A History of Thirty Years of Critical Misrule,' *Conrad and Poland*, 9–31.

discussed at the Buszczyńskis.'[77] Positivism represented the 'first and most vigorous intellectual and historical condemnation of the futility of political Romanticism and of the tradition of armed insurrections.' It emerged 'in 1869 from a group of erstwhile freedom fighters, now prominent intellectuals in Krakow: the historian Jan Szujski and the literary historian Stanisław Tarnowski.'[78] In *Kilka prawd z dziejów naszych. Ku rozważeniu w chwili obecnej* ['Several Truths from Our History'], published in Cracow in 1867, Szujski argued against the idealisation of Poland's past. The most prominent Positivists, the journalist Aleksander Świętochowski, the novelists Bolesław Prus and Eliza Orzeszkowa, and the poet Adam Asnyk, advocated a less mystical dedication to history and the nation.[79]

Pivotal in setting out the contrast between the pre- and post-1863 worlds was the new belief that the pursuit of Poland's past was no longer necessary. 'The new version of Polish history was at bottom a critique of the myth formed by romantic historiography.'[80] If the nation existed without statehood for Poles of Cieszkowski and Korzeniowski's generation, then it only did so by aiming at a goal – the past – that needed to be recaptured. The new Positivism rejected this, making the present, previously an unbearable contrast to the past, an acceptable juncture to begin practical preparation for the coming of the Polish state. Adam Wiślicki's *Przegląd Tygodniowy* [*The Weekly Review*] was founded in 1866, attracting writers such as Świętochowski and Bolesław Limanowski. The conflict between the old world of Romanticism and the new Positivism marks the pages of Polish journals of the time. In 1871, Świętochowski wrote an article entitled *My i Wy* ['We and You'] in which the idealism of the Romantics was questioned and discredited. The Positivists wanted to 'replace what they saw as the characteristics of the old Poland – traditionalism, particularism, chauvinism, mysticism,

---

[77] Najder, *Conrad: A Chronicle*, 34.
[78] Lukowski and Zawadzki, *Concise History of Poland*, 159.
[79] See Porter, *When Nationalism Began to Hate*, 54. The most direct example of Conrad's relationship with the Positivist movement is Eliza Orzeszkowa's essay 'The Emigration of Talent,' published in *Kraj* in Warsaw on 23 April 1899. Orzeszkowa accused Conrad of deserting Poland by not using his 'talent' to promote the cultural foundations of the nation. Conrad also enjoyed reading Prus, as described in secondhand accounts of his trip to Poland in 1914.
[80] Bross, 'The Missing Theme in Conrad's Political Consciousness,' 67.

and obscurantism – with the traits of the modern scientific individual. The new Pole would bring the nation out of the backwardness of the Russian Empire into the modern world of Europe by shifting the nation's attention to problems of administration, management, economics, education and industry.'[81] Key influences were Darwin, Herbert Spencer, John Stuart Mill, and particularly Henry Thomas Buckle, whose incomplete *History of Civilisation in England* (1856–61) had been translated into Polish in 1862, becoming an important expression of the Positivist method. For Buckle and Positivism, history constituted not an amorphous mass of mysticism, but an exact and observable science.

Bolesław Prus summed up the Positivist ethos when he wrote in *The Weekly Review* in 1887 that there were 'intermediate times between the idyll and the battle, when it is not possible to either live with a smile, or die with honour, only work, work, work.'[82] This promotion of a conscientious work ethic and newfound tolerance of the present meant the Romantic idealising of the past had no place. If illustrious statesman Prince Adam Czartoryski (1770–1861) represented the ideology and long heritage of the Polish struggles for independence followed by Korzeniowski and Buszczyński, then Positivists could also hold him up as symptomatic of the Romantic philosophies that came to fruition in Cieszkowski and Mickiewicz, and which failed in 1863. In 1803, Czartoryski had famously preached: 'If we wish to progress we must have an object we have not yet attained. And in order to be always in progress we must be capable of conceiving an object which will never be attained.'[83] For Cieszkowski, Mickiewicz, and Słowacki, this unattainable object was Poland's glorious past, which could be regained for the future. Positivism regarded this philosophy as futile, a worldview that, in Bobrowski's words, ensured 'one's whole power of resistance has become consumed in dreaming and there is none left for the sober judgement of facts.'[84]

[81] Porter, *When Nationalism Began to Hate*, 46.
[82] Prus quoted in Porter, *When Nationalism Began to Hate*, 50.
[83] Czartoryski quoted in M. Kukiel, *Czartoryski and European Unity: 1770–1861* (Princeton: Princeton University Press, 1955), 3.
[84] Najder ed., *Conrad's Polish Background*, 153.

Bobrowski's letters to Conrad read like a Bible of the Positivist doctrine, capturing the later mentality of 'Typhoon's' Captain Mac-Whirr, who is 'faithful to facts, which alone his conscience reflected' (*T*, 14). Throughout their correspondence, Bobrowski returns to the same maxims. In 1876: 'I consider it my duty by advice and reminders to keep you on the right path: that is to say on the path of reason and of duty.'[85] In 1880: 'Work and perseverance are the only values that never fail,'[86] and 'Now we need work and endurance, endurance and work.'[87] In 1881: 'We must therefore submit to necessity; – which for sober minds is the ultima ratio';[88] and '"Hope is the Mother of fools and calculation the Father of the sober-minded"; – so goes the proverb.'[89] In 1890: 'As a traditional Polish nobleman I value the certain and less glamorous than a more glamorous uncertainty!'[90] He dismissed the Romantic idealisation of the exceptional individual endowed with genius, writing that 'humanity has a lesser need of producing geniuses than of the already-existing modest and conscientious workers who fulfil their duties.'[91] This was central to the Positivist doctrine, and the '"dream"' became a common positivist trope, allowing them to contrast productive "work" with all sorts of lofty ambitions – most important those of the romantic nationalists.'[92]

Conrad's early political views, as expressed in a letter of 1885 to Joseph Spiridion Kliszczewski on the subject of British politics, may have their origin in Polish Positivism.[93] In an oft-cited outburst, best understood as the sensationalised engagement of one determined to display political awareness, but too frequently taken by critics to consti-tute the already fully-formed politics of the later writer, Conrad

---

[85] Najder ed., *Conrad's Polish Background*, 37.
[86] Najder ed., *Conrad's Polish Background*, 63.
[87] Najder ed., *Conrad's Polish Background*, 65.
[88] Najder ed., *Conrad's Polish Background*, 69–70.
[89] Najder ed., *Conrad's Polish Background*, 73.
[90] Najder ed., *Conrad's Polish Background*, 133.
[91] Najder ed., *Conrad's Polish Background*, 154.
[92] Porter, *When Nationalism Began to Hate*, 49.
[93] Conrad's correspondent was in fact Welsh, the son of Polish watchmaker and goldsmith Władysław Spiridion Kliszczewski (1819–91). For details on the Polish background of the Kliszczewskis, see J.H. Stape, 'The Kliszczewski Document,' and Władysław Spiridion Kliszczewski, 'A Short Account of My Early Life,' *The Conradian* 34.1 (2009): 1–37.

despaired of the spectre of rising socialism: 'Where's the man to stop the rush of social-democratic ideas...Socialism must inevitably end in Caesarism' (*CL* 1, 16). Although the Positivism that Bobrowski instilled in Conrad regarded itself as progressive, as one historian has noted, 'Despite all the talk of inclusion, [Positivists] still equated the intelligentsia with "society" and set "the people" aside as an object to be worked upon, to be elevated.'[94] A formative factor in Conrad's fear of the unruly mob can perhaps be seen in the Positivists' use of the metaphor of the 'social organism' in their portrayal of society. In 1882, Prus wrote that '"in a social organism we see a division of labour between various organs, mutually supporting each other." The class structure of Polish society was thus cast as a benign system of mutual support – precisely the imagery the nobility had once used in referring to serfdom. The Positivists remained embedded in this sort of reasoning, even as they tried to talk about making the nation more inclusive and less hierarchical.'[95] For Bobrowski, every individual should think of himself as 'a modest tiny ant which by its insignificant toil in fulfilling its modest duty secures the life and existence of the whole nest.'[96] Bobrowski's earlier assertion that he was a 'traditional Polish nobleman' is perhaps revealing in this regard. One of Positivism's most significant spokesmen, Aleksander Świętochowski wrote that 'Poles, in spite of great imagination, could not create more generally appealing utopias because of two reasons: First, they were a society of nobility, which was very resistant to democratic ideas, the soul of utopianism. Secondly with the loss of independent statehood they dreamed only about such a transformation of the world that could bring them back a Fatherland and a sovereign state.'[97]

In his letters to Conrad, Bobrowski outlined his Positivist position, explaining that the advancement of the nation now rested in recognising the present: 'we are deprived of our own political and national rights, we [...] have to preserve our individuality and our own standpoint, till the time comes when Nemesis, as a result of our own efforts, spins out some

---

[94] Porter, 57.
[95] Porter, 55–56.
[96] Najder ed., *Conrad's Polish Background*, 154.
[97] Świętochowski quoted in Ludwikowski, *Continuity and Change in Poland*, 109–10.

situation which will give us the right to have a real national existence
[. . .]. However, one could write many volumes on this subject without
solving the question, which will eventually be solved by time and
events.'[98] Bobrowski's understanding of history opposed Buszczyński's
La Décadence de l'Europe, with the present comprising a moment in the
Hegelian flux that could not be altered:

You will never control the forces of nature, for whether blind or governed by
Providence, in each case they have their own pre-ordained paths; and you will
also never change the roads along which humanity goes, for there exists in social
development an historical evolutionary compulsion which is slow but sure, and
which is governed by the laws of cause and effect derived from the past and
affecting the future.[99]

This aspect of Bobrowski's thought was problematic for Conrad, as it
contrasted dramatically with his Romantic heritage. As Najder has
noted, there 'were in Bobrowski's teachings two salient elements
which Conrad never accepted but kept turning over in his mind and
his work. The first was his general attitude of reconciliation with
existing reality; the second was his historical optimism.'[100]

Conrad was influenced by two acutely divergent views of history.
Aleksander Świętochowski wrote in 1872 that the 'urn of the past is
filled with the ashes of death and not the juice of life.' The past itself
offered no starting point for the re-building of the nation. Świętochowski believed that 'The more we study history the more we understand the present, the more we recognise the needs of the moment, the
more we obtain a measure for action and a guide for progress. The past,
therefore, will give us no ideals, models, or principles – it only places us
in a given position.'[101] Positivism respected the past but understood
that history was a progressive narrative in which Poland must find its
present place, using that as a basis for movement forward. Bobrowski's

---

[98] Najder ed., *Conrad's Polish Background*, 80.

[99] Najder ed., *Conrad's Polish Background*, 154. Bobrowski was not immune from
the Polish desire to linger in the past. In 1892, he wrote to Conrad saying 'such an
"échappée" of sad thoughts usually assails me during our national festivities, sanctified
as they are by our customs [. . .]. It is nothing in fact but the result of thinking of the
past, which one usually finds more beautiful than the present!' Najder ed., *Conrad's
Polish Background*, 159.

[100] Najder, *Conrad in Perspective*, 66.

[101] Świętochowski quoted in Porter, *When Nationalism Began to Hate*, 61.

most sympathetic letter to Conrad, in 1891, laid out the cultural conflict in Poland, giving insight into Conrad's uneasy inheritance of Romanticism and Positivism: 'Pessimism ruins the individual and his life and stultifies his actions; on the other hand excessive optimism may, in its worst form, render a man stupidly self-satisfied and absurd.... Between these two extremes there is the 'golden mean' which contains, I suppose, the basic truth of life.' Bobrowski concluded by explaining: 'The devotion to duty interpreted more widely or narrowly, according to circumstances and time – this constitutes my practical creed.'[102] Bobrowski's creed was adopted by Conrad, but only as a tempering influence on the beliefs that had already moulded his outlook. Conrad's youth, at the crossroads of Romanticism and Positivism, ensured that his literary style represented both romantic and realistic modes of historical thought.

ROMANTICISM AND POSITIVISM IN *THE NIGGER OF THE 'NARCISSUS'*

In his discussion of Conrad's relationship with Positivism and Romanticism, Addison Bross concludes that Conrad simply excised the Positivist doctrine from Polish history. However, contrary to Bross's assertion that Conrad displayed complete 'silence before the great Polish debate of his era,'[103] the dispute informs Conrad's narrative experimentation and his reflections on history. As one of the generation that later succeeded the Romantics, Conrad supports Norman Davies's view that 'after 1863, the Positivists gained the upper hand, though by no means a monopoly.'[104]

An early manifestation of Bobrowski's Positivism and Korzeniowski's Romanticism appears in *The Nigger of the 'Narcissus'* (1897). The novel endorses 'the importance of the solidarity of people working as a team in a patriotic cause,' but it also 'clearly manifests the tensions between Romanticism and realism, between the Aesthetic outlook and the

---

[102] Najder ed., *Conrad's Polish Background*, 152–53 and 155.
[103] Addison Bross, '*Almayer's Folly* and the Polish Debate about Materialism,' *Conrad's Century*, 44.
[104] Norman Davies, *God's Playground: A History of Poland*, vol. 2 (Oxford: Clarendon Press, 1981), 51.

practical outlook [. . .] between a faith in a hierarchic yet "organic" community and a contrasting knowledge that such an ideal is the material for obsequies rather than for campaigns.'[105] The spirit of the crew of the 'Narcissus,' a crew of 'disenchanted philosophers' (*NN*, 138), represents Conrad's ambiguous adoption of Positivist values and their co-existence with the fading ideals and traditions of the 1863 insurrection. Conrad's Preface opened in Positivistic language, asserting that the quality of art must be evident in its workmanship: 'A work that aspires, however humbly, to the condition of art should carry its justification in every line' (*NN*, vii). Bobrowski had instructed the young Conrad that Romantic genius should reveal itself by scientific work: 'nobody has the right to call himself the former until he has proved it by deeds.'[106] Conrad therefore polarises the philosopher and the scientist: 'Impressed by the aspect of the world the thinker plunges into ideas, the scientist into facts' (*NN*, vii). The 'changing wisdom of successive generations discards ideas, questions facts, demolishes theories' (*NN*, viii). For the artist, however, it is different, and his task is to accommodate 'innumerable temperaments whose subtle and resistless power endows passing events with their true meaning and creates the moral, the emotional atmosphere of the place and time' (*NN*, ix).

Conrad's observation of history sees him fulfil this ambition to capture the sensations of place and time. In one respect, writing becomes a Positivist endeavour, where 'to accomplish that creative task, to go as far on that road as his strength will carry him, to go undeterred by faltering, weariness or reproach, is the only valid justification for the worker in prose' (*NN*, ix). *The Nigger of the 'Narcissus'* strongly advocates the necessity of labour. Donkin is condemned for 'shirking work': 'They all knew him! He was the man [. . .] that dodges the work on dark nights' (*NN*, 10). James Wait is abused for 'the monstrous suspicion that this astounding black-man was shamming sick, had been malingering heartlessly in the face of our toil' (*NN*, 72). The mate, Mr Baker, states the crew's true purpose: 'No rest till the work is done. Work till you drop. That's what you're here for' (*NN*, 93). The crew

---

[105] Cedric Watts ed., Joseph Conrad, *The Nigger of the 'Narcissus'* (London: Penguin, 1989), xiii and xxiv.
[106] Najder ed., *Conrad's Polish Background*, 154.

'boasted of our pluck, of our capacity for work, of our energy' (*NN*, 100). However, despite the crew's ability to fulfil its positivist duty and to go on 'scraping, polishing, painting the ship from morning to night,' it is also suggested that a spiritual 'hunger lived on board of her' (*NN*, 142–43). The Positivist ethos is insufficient, and its realism is juxtaposed with a necessary Romanticism.

The Nigger of the 'Narcissus' displays an overt consciousness of the historical process. The artist's task is to grapple with history and to capture a moment that is passing, or has passed, from potential future into past: 'To snatch in a moment of courage, from the remorseless rush of time, a passing phase of life is only the beginning of the task. The task approached in tenderness and faith is to hold up unquestioningly, without choice and without fear, the rescued fragment before all eyes and in the light of a sincere mood' (*NN*, x). Positivism and the work of the artist have their ultimate goal in the Romantic endeavour of rescuing a phase of life that has passed.[107] The artist works to 'reveal the substance' and 'inspiring secret' (*NN*, x) of the past, and the 'exacting appeal of the work' (*NN*, 16) remains connected to this objective. The Positivistic purpose of work is aligned with a desire to rescue Romanticism. The Polish Romantic response to Hegel intrudes into Conrad's fiction in this resistance to dynamic time. The experience of documenting and fictionalising the past, as Conrad practices in his writing, becomes a method of protecting history: 'After all it is my work. The only lasting thing in the world. People die – affections die – all passes – but a man's work remains with him to the last' (*CL* 1, 293). Conrad admits that both doctrines of his youth must inevitably co-exist in his work, but the end product will be the artist's unique voice: 'but they all: Realism, Romanticism, Naturalism [. . .] all these gods must, after a short period of fellowship, abandon him – even on the very threshold of the temple – to the stammerings of his conscience and to the outspoken consciousness of the difficulties of his work' (*NN*, x–xi). Conrad's experimental style, with a technique Ian Watt has labelled 'delayed-decoding,' originates in an effort to prolong the sensations of the past, emanating from Conrad's Hegelian awareness that 'all finite things are temporal, because sooner or later they are subject to

---

[107] Ian Watt has placed the preface in the context of English Romanticism in *Conrad and the Nineteenth Century* (London: Chatto & Windus, 1980), 76–88.

change.'[108] In Conrad's case, time moves towards an uncertain future, as he noted in a letter to Edward Garnett in 1896: 'If we are "ever becoming – never being" then I would be a fool if I tried to become this thing rather than that; for I know well that I never will be anything' (*CL* 1, 268).

Conrad's novel concerns a passing phase of life.[109] If it sets the seal on the age of sail, it also marks the end of a certain type of seaman in the character of Singleton. Although he contributes his share of the work on the ship, Singleton stands apart because he represents a previous era. Singleton 'resembled a learned and savage patriarch, the incarnation of barbarian wisdom serene in the blasphemous turmoil of the world' (*NN*, 6). Like the Positivist's earlier questioning of Polish Messianists such as Mickiewicz, the source of such mystical wisdom is undermined by Conrad's revelation that Singleton is absorbed in Edward Bulwer-Lytton's popular novel *Pelham* (1828): 'Mystery! Is it the fascination of the incomprehensible? - is it the charm of the impossible?' (*NN*, 6). Ian Watt has emphasised that 'Conrad's deepest sympathies [. . .] go out to the past,' but while he 'sets Singleton against the succeeding generation,' Conrad 'does not pretend that Singleton is a viable model in the contemporary world.'[110] The old seaman adds mysticism to the novel by predicting order will not be restored until Jimmy Wait dies in sight of land (*NN*, 130). Singleton's conception of the task of guiding the ship is differentiated from the younger crew, and his seamanship appears to originate from some preternatural source. Young Charley is in awe of Singleton, 'glancing out of the corners of his restless eyes at the old seaman, who took no notice of the puzzled youngster muttering at his work' (*NN*, 7–8). Singleton mistrusts the new crew, and, while asserting the soundness of the ship, questions those who now take control of its ultimate destiny: 'Ships are all right. It's the men in them!' (*NN*, 24).

---

[108] Hegel, *Philosophy of Nature*, 36.
[109] For a discussion of English history and nationalism in the story, see Allan H. Simmons, '*The Nigger of the "Narcissus"*: History, Narrative, and Nationalism,' in *Joseph Conrad: Voice, Sequence, History, Genre*, edited by Jakob Lothe, Jeremy Hawthorn, & James Phelan (Columbus: Ohio State University Press, 2008), 141–59.
[110] Watt, *Conrad in the Nineteenth Century*, 123–24.

In a remarkable passage, Singleton endures as the lone survivor of an old way of thought, one viewed with scepticism in the new world. In a sense, he embodies the dying Romanticism of post-1863 Poland:

Singleton stood at the door with his face to the light and his back to the darkness. And alone in the dim emptiness of the sleeping forecastle he appeared bigger, colossal, very old; old as Father Time himself [...]. Yet he was only a child of time, a lonely relic of a devoured and forgotten generation. He stood, still strong, as ever unthinking; a ready man with a vast and empty past and with no future, with his childlike impulses and his man's passions already dead within his tattooed breast. The men who could understand his silence were gone – those men who knew how to exist beyond the pale of life and within sight of eternity. [...] Their successors are the grown up children of a discontented earth ... But the others were strong and mute; they were effaced, bowed and enduring, like stone caryatides that hold up in the night the lighted halls of a resplendent and glorious edifice. They are gone now – and it does not matter [...]. [A] truth, a faith, a generation of men goes – and is forgotten, and it does not matter! Except, perhaps, to the few of those who believed the truth, confessed the faith – or loved the men. (*NN*, 24–25)

Conrad's language pays tribute to the ageing seaman and registers a complex amalgamation of attitudes to both Romanticism and a passing period of life. Singleton is perceived with a mixture of awe, respect, and confusion. Singleton belongs to an 'indispensable' generation (*NN*, 25), and his delineation evokes Conrad's later representation of the Polish Romantics. In his 'Author's Note' to *A Personal Record*, Conrad recollected his childhood impressions of his father's contemporaries and the meetings of the underground Polish 'National Committee,' where 'the people appearing and disappearing in that immense space were beyond the usual stature of mankind as I got to know it in later life' (*PR*, x). Yet, despite Singleton's mythic stature, he is subject to the forces of history. Singleton is a 'child of time,' a member of a 'forgotten generation,' and a man 'with a vast empty past and with no future.' He is the last emissary of a people whose ideas and philosophy no longer register, with his creed – '[t]he thoughts of all his lifetime could have been expressed in six words' (*NN*, 26) – already being misrepresented.

Singleton, however, is just one part of the crew who make up the world of the ship, a world with 'her own future' (*NN*, 29–30). The narrator periodically identifies himself with the rest of the crew 'intent on our work' (*NN*, 46), referring to 'Our little world' (*NN*, 103). The ship, which carries myriad hopes and ideas, nevertheless, despite the prominence of Positivist values, receives its inspiration from an inextinguishable source. At the height of the storm, as the crew struggle to maintain direction and control, the Romantic figure of Singleton guides the ship, with the old sailor's sense of duty merging both Romantic and Positivist conceptions of fidelity to the ship/nation:

> Apart, far aft, and alone by the helm, old Singleton had deliberately tucked his white beard under the top button of his glistening coat. Swaying upon the din and tumult of the seas, with the whole battered length of the ship launched forward in a rolling rush before his steady old eyes, he stood rigidly still, forgotten by all, and with an attentive face. [...] He steered with care.   (*NN*, 89)

Just as the text is concerned with a Romantic goal of capturing a moment of time, so the spirit of Romanticism guides the Positivistic labour of the crew. *The Nigger of the 'Narcissus'* strongly evokes the imagery of Adam Mickiewicz's poem 'The Tempest' from the *Crimean Sonnets* (1826), in which the poet called attention to the responses of a ship's crew to elemental danger, ultimately singling out 'A traveller [who] stood silent and apart, / Imbued with thought.'[111] The 'Narcissus' 'carried Singleton's completed wisdom' (*NN*, 99). Singleton seems extracted from Polish history and legend, and he appears 'beyond the light [...] in the smoke, monumental, indistinct, with his head touching the beam; like a statue of heroic size in the gloom of a crypt' (*NN*, 129). As Cedric Watts notes, a 'visit to Poland may nevertheless do more to illuminate Conrad than may the reading of numerous commentaries.'[112] The crypt of the Polish kings and poets in the Royal Cathedral on Wawel Hill in Cracow guards the historic legacy of Poland and the remains of those in the Polish historical imagination who, like Singleton, 'knew how to exist beyond the pale of life and within sight of eternity.' For the edifice of the 'Narcissus' to stand against the elements, the past with all its traditions, whether realistic or futile, must be carried. The present hardships of the ship require Singleton's knowledge:

---

[111] Adam Mickiewicz, *Selected Poems*, edited by Clark Mills (New York: Noonday Press, 1956), 81.
[112] Cedric Watts, *A Preface to Conrad*, 2nd ed. (Harlow: Longman, 1993), 198.

All looked at Singleton, gazing upwards from the deck, staring out of the dark corners, or turning their heads with curious glances. They were expectant and appeased as if that old man, who looked at no-one, had possessed the secret of their uneasy indignations and desires, a sharper vision, a clearer knowledge. [...] They heard his voice rumble in his broad chest as though the words had been rolling towards them out of a rugged past. [...] [W]ho could tell through what violence and terrors he had lived! (*NN*, 129–30)

Throughout the ordeal, Singleton 'radiated unspeakable wisdom, hard unconcern, the chilling air of resignation' (*NN*, 130), and his shouldering of the Romantic burden ensures the past is carried into the present and holds meaning for the future.

The concluding pages of *The Nigger of the 'Narcissus'* bring together concerns of Conrad's writing over subsequent years. The experience of the voyage, for all its focus on the task and the work, becomes romanticised in the pages of the author. The very land becomes a keeper of memory, 'the stones of the Tower gleaming, seemed to stir in the play of the light, as if remembering suddenly all the great joys and sorrows of the past' (*NN*, 172). The 'remembering and mute stones' (*NN*, 172) absorb the voices and faces that have passed that way. Conrad's narrator too, vacillating throughout the text in his commitment to the crew, believes the experience of this voyage is protected in his memory, enshrined there, and given meaning. There is also a questioning of the Cieszkowskian vision of a charted future in the dying moments of Jimmy Wait. Wait turns to 'the regions of memory that know nothing of time,' but he 'was very quiet and easy amongst his vivid reminiscences which he mistook joyfully for images of an undoubted future' (*NN*, 149). Jimmy's death scene is intensified by the narrative's focus on the 'remorseless rush of time' introduced earlier in the Preface. To Donkin, the 'night seemed to go by in a flash; it seemed to him he could hear the irremediable rush of precious minutes' (*NN*, 154). *Lord Jim* also later contemplates how life is navigated 'in cross lights, watching every precious minute and every irremediable step' (*LJ*, 35). Wait's death further affects the crew of the 'Narcissus,' forcing them to consider time and history: 'his death, like the death of an old belief, shook the foundations of our society' (*NN*, 155). There is uneasiness in the text that memory's power is destined to fail in the encounter with history, and the crew of the 'Narcissus' are 'marked by the desolation of time' (*NN*, 73–74).

If one follows Paul Ricoeur's interpretation of narrative, Conrad's bridging of the gap between past and present in both his fictional narrative structures and his autobiographical reminiscences only increases awareness of time. Drawing on the work of St Augustine, and following Hegel's view that remembrance without the vehicle of language is useless, Ricoeur states that recollection itself makes time an ever-present reality: 'time becomes human to the extent that it is articulated through a narrative mode, and narrative attains its full meaning when it becomes a condition of temporal existence.'[113] Conrad's framed narratives and his juxtaposition of contrasting periods in his narrators' lives – usually distinguishing between an active past with an inactive present – imparts to his fiction a dramatic awareness of the passage of time made even more lucid by the process of narration itself. Recalling his sea years in *The Nigger of the 'Narcissus,'* Conrad acknowledged that time was taking him away from those very experiences: 'Twenty years of life went to the writing of these few last lines. "Tempi passati!" The old time – the old time of youth and unperplexed life!' (*CL* 1, 421). In fictionalising his past, Conrad gave it a reality that heightened the contrast between the then and now.

In 'A Familiar Preface' to *A Personal Record*, Conrad first signed himself J.C.K, indicating his fidelity to his Polish past. His drawing of the scenes of his childhood saw his autobiography produce the effect that Polish Romantics wanted the writing of history to engender. Zygmunt Kaczkowski (1825–96), a Polish novelist, noted that in dealing with history 'you will confront [...] the life-like representation of the world gone by long ago, its assemblies, gatherings, actions and struggles, and seeing peoples' faces, homes and hearts so closely and vividly you will feel as if the spirit of those days has been reincarnated in yourself.'[114] Conrad recalled the culture of Poland in which debates about time and history dominated, finding himself 'in hours of solitude and retrospect meeting arguments and charges made thirty-five years ago by voices now forever still' (*PR*, 121). Conrad's meandering backward glance o'er the travelled roads of his 'two lives' (*PR*, 112) escorts the reader along the fringes of the formative points of nineteenth-century

---

[113] Paul Ricoeur, *Time and Narrative*, translated by Kathleen McLaughlin and David Pellauer, vol. 1, (London and Chicago: University of Chicago Press, 1984), 52.
[114] Quoted in Eile, *Literature and Nationalism*, 106.

Polish history; from the dark years of the 1863 insurrection to the comically represented splendour of the Napoleonic period. *A Personal Record* emerges as an autobiography overwhelmingly concerned with the problematic issue of historical authenticity. Asserting that 'Books may be written in all sorts of places' (*PR*, 3), throughout the text Conrad draws attention to the difficulty of acquiring literary and historical coherence through images of discarded letters, manuscripts, and vacant maps. Conrad recalls his father burning his manuscripts, only to remember that they mysteriously turned up again in the library in Cracow in 1914; the 'wandering pages' of *Almayer's Folly* survive various mishaps (*PR*, 19); Nicholas B. destroys most of his papers and letters; his house is later sacked, destroying Nicholas B.'s remaining correspondence, books, and medals. The character of X 'displayed great cleverness in the art of concealing material documents (he was even suspected of having burnt a lot of historically interesting family papers)' (*PR*, 51). Later, Conrad's desk during the composition of *Nostromo* becomes a Stendhalian battlefield of manuscripts, filled with valiant, wounded, and dying volunteers: 'There were pages of MS. on the table, and under the table, a batch of typed copy on a chair, single leaves had fluttered away into distant corners; there were living pages, pages scored and wounded, dead pages that would be burned at the end of the day – the litter of a cruel battlefield, of a long, long and desperate fray' (*PR*, 100).

A Personal Record brings together the consequences of Conrad's childhood experience of Polish historicism. For the artist, 'Inspiration comes from the earth, which has a past, a history, a future' (*PR*, 95), but the act of writing, of dealing with this history, this past, of contemplating the future, leads to an intricate involvement with history. Later, in 1907, while working on *Under Western Eyes*, Conrad wrote to R.B. Cunninghame Graham, expressing the contradictory emotions of carrying the burden of the past: 'Living with memories is a cruel business. I – who have a double life one of them peopled only by shadows growing more precious as the years pass – know what that is. [. . .] Tempi passati!' (*CL* 3, 491–92).

Nineteenth-century Polish literature informed Conrad's writing, as shown by Andrzej Busza, Zdzisław Najder and Susan Jones, amongst others, and Romantic philosophy was an essential foundation of Polish literary culture. Conrad's youth was shaped by philosophies of history. That is not to say that Conrad adhered to the idea of a future that would restore the past. On the contrary, Conrad's exposure to these ideas through his family history ensured he accepted such philosophies' awareness of time, yet adopted a sceptical view of the future and a resigned longing for the past. When he left Poland and later embarked on a literary career, Conrad was 'well acquainted with a rich and lively literary tradition'[115] greatly influenced by the philosophy and historiography of nineteenth-century Poland.

[115] Najder ed., *Conrad's Polish Background*, 16.

2

Narrative and History:
Tales of Unrest to *Lord Jim*

When Conrad settled in England in the 1890s, he entered a cultural climate as concerned with history as that of nineteenth-century Poland. Late-Victorian Britain evaluated the experience of empire and progress, with works such as J.A. Hobson's *Imperialism* in 1902 and Max Nordau's polemical attack on burgeoning Modernism *Degeneration* (1895) analysing contemporary politics, economics and art. While preoccupied politically with the rise of the Labour movement, and militarily with its African colonies, especially at the time of the Second Boer War (1899–1902), Conrad's new setting was a society where 'it was not the physical but the biological sciences which had the deepest and the most pervasive effect upon the way man viewed his personal and historical destiny.'[1] In 1893, neo-Hegelian Idealist David G. Ritchie published *Darwin and Hegel*, stating that the ideas of Darwin and Herbert Spencer dominated the discourse of contemporary society: 'Evolution is in every one's mouth now, and the writings of Mr. Spencer have done a great deal (along with the discoveries of Darwin) to make the conception familiar.'[2] Ritchie drew comparisons between Hegel's philosophy of history and emerging historical debate. Christopher GoGwilt has discussed the appearance of Hegelian notions of historical and social development in England in the 1890s, citing Benjamin Kidd's *Social Evolution* (1894), 'which grafts Hegelian idealism onto Spencerian social Darwinism to produce a formulation that anticipates

---

[1] Ian Watt, 'Ideological Perspectives: Kurtz and the Fate of Victorian Progress,' *New Casebooks: Joseph Conrad*, edited by Elaine Jordan (Basingstoke: Macmillan, 1996), 32.
[2] David G. Ritchie, *Darwin and Hegel, with Other Philosophical Writings* (London: Swan Sonnenschein, 1893), 42.

Oswald Spengler's *The Decline of the West* and Toynbee's surveys of
world history: "to obtain a just conception of our Western civilization,
it is necessary to regard it from the beginning as a single continuous
growth, endowed with a definitive principle of life, subject to law, and
passing, like any other organism, through orderly stages of development."[3] Such discussions were also contemporaneous with resurgence
in interest in time and history in philosophy. As one thinker noted in
the journal *Mind* in 1898, 'it is clear that the idea of progress in its
current acceptation is essentially knit up with time.'[4] The pages of *Mind*
in the late-1890s carried dialogue between British neo-Hegelian Idealists such as F.H. Bradley and Bernard Bosanquet over the perplexities of
time and history as subjects of philosophic study. Also writing was the
influential thinker J.M.E. McTaggart, whose later article 'The Unreality
of Time' (1908) still represents the source for modern studies of the
philosophy of time.[5] Neo-Hegelians treated subjects that would form
the major philosophical investigations of Conrad's writing, and according to Peter Nicholson, the Hegelian tradition gave a 'crucial historical
dimension to the British Idealists' political philosophy.'[6]

Conrad's work can also be placed in a longer nineteenth-century
British tradition of historical philosophy, represented by Thomas Car-
lyle, and continued in Conrad's time by F.H. Bradley, on the respective
values of a romantic approach to history or a sceptical view of the past.
The problems of history and representation voiced in Carlyle's essay
'On History' (1830) and Bradley's later 'The Presuppositions of Critical
History' (1874) addressed topics reflecting philosophical debates in
Poland between Romanticism and Positivism. As noted, the thought
of nineteenth-century British thinkers, such as Darwin, Spencer and
Buckle, was already familiar to Conrad through Bobrowski and Polish
Positivism, as both borrowed from English Liberalism. In his early
fiction, Conrad fused the concerns of his native culture with English

[3] Christopher GoGwilt, *The Invention of the West: Joseph Conrad and the Double-Mapping
of Europe and Empire* (Stanford, CA: Stanford University Press, 1995), 54.
   [4] J.M. Baillie, 'Truth and History,' *Mind* 7 (1898): 521.
   [5] For McTaggart's article, see *Mind* 17 (1908): 457–74. It is reprinted in Robin Le
Poidevin and Murray MacBeath eds., *Oxford Readings in Philosophy: The Philosophy of
Time* (Oxford: Oxford University Press, 1993), 23–34.
   [6] Peter P. Nicholson, *The Political Philosophy of the British Idealists: Selected Studies*
(Cambridge: Cambridge University Press, 1990), 1–2.

treatments of time and history. In his appropriation of writers such as William Hazlitt and Carlyle, and in negotiating issues that occupied neo-Hegelian Idealists, Conrad interacted with English writing reminiscent of the Polish response to German Idealism. In the case of Carlyle, Conrad recognised a towering figure in English letters who, along with Coleridge, had helped familiarise English literature and philosophy with the German tradition of Goethe, Kant and Hegel. Just as *The Nigger of the 'Narcissus'* was Conrad's artistic acknowledgement of the necessary coexistence of Romanticism and Positivism in the evaluation of history, intense retrospective reflection also engendered his other important early works. 'Karain,' 'Youth,' 'Heart of Darkness,' and *Lord Jim* examine the romantic past, yet these texts are complicated by Conrad's narrative experimentation. Conrad's early work can be read in conjunction with the evolution of the philosophy of time, problems of representation in historiography, and, as in Poland, in the context of Hegelian Idealism.

'YOUTH,' TIME AND LITERARY TRADITION

Let me, oh Lord, whilst I rest here on this seashore, on these rocks and cliffs and bathed in the golden rays of the sun – narrate the story of creation, the tale hid in the memory of my past lives.

(Juliusz Słowacki, *Genesis from the Spirit*)[7]

Of all the figures in Polish literature, Conrad held Słowacki in the highest regard. The Polish Romantic's narrator in *Genesis from the Spirit* turns to the past to extract meaning from his experience. With the publication of *Tales of Unrest* (1898), Conrad focused largely on the narrative problems of extricating the tale hid in the memory of past lives. Central to his narrative complexity is Conrad's concern with representing the remorseless rush of time, as outlined in the Preface to *The Nigger of the 'Narcissus.'* Before the appearance of Marlow in 'Youth' in 1898, Conrad's most accomplished stories treat characters contemplating the past. In 'An Outpost of Progress,' published in

---

[7] Słowacki, *Genesis from the Spirit*, 1.

Cosmopolis in 1897, Conrad's two hapless imperial functionaries are thrown into the depths of Africa only to lament their previous existences, and ultimately to succumb to madness and death in their new surroundings. The encounter with an environment being destroyed by a ruthless capitalistic imperialism is presented as a darkly unsettling comic farce. In 'The Lagoon,' published in *Cornhill Magazine* in January 1897, and 'Karain: A Memory,' which appeared in *Blackwood's* in November 1897, Conrad's characters recount their troubling personal histories, with the narratives exploring how the past impinges on the present.

'Karain' is a seminal story in Conrad's development as a writer, as the author for the first time successfully employed a frame narrator. This allowed Conrad to present the effect of time on both his narrator and on the central character, Karain, who recalls his own history within the narrator's past. Andrzej Busza has detected the influence of Mickiewicz's ballad *Czaty*, [*The Ambush*] on the story, analysing folk motifs and plot similarities, revealing Polish Romanticism's presence in Conrad's early writing.[8] Karain's people are unaware that time tortures their leader: 'in his august care they had forgotten all the past, and had lost all concern for the future' (*TU*, 8). Karain's thoughts of his homeland see him transformed into a Polish Romantic exile: 'Now and then his big dreamy eyes would roll restlessly; he frowned or smiled, or he would become pensive, and, staring in silence, would nod slightly for a time at some regretted vision of the past' (*TU*, 14). These regretted visions, in which the frame narrator is also in the process of engaging by recalling his encounter with Karain, are intensified by Conrad's presentation of the human perception of time. As Karain prepares to recount his harrowing past, 'the silence became so profound that we all could hear distinctly the two chronometers in my cabin ticking along with unflagging speed against one another' (*TU*, 23). Along with the voice of the narrator, Karain's language also registers acute consciousness of time. When told that his past will one day cease to haunt him, Karain indicates that his physical movements serve as a reminder of the rush of the present: '"Am I a woman, to forget long years before an eyelid has had the time to beat twice?" he exclaimed, with bitter resentment' (*TU*,

---

[8] Busza, 'Conrad's Polish Literary Background,' 209–15.

43–44). This sensitivity to the dynamism of time is developed further in 'Youth' and 'Heart of Darkness,' along with an elaboration of the underlying philosophy of 'Karain': the incommunicability of experience.

Before transmitting Karain's narrative from that distant night, the narrator maintains 'It is impossible to convey the effect of his story. It is undying, it is but a memory, and its vividness cannot be made clear to another mind, any more than the vivid emotions of a dream. One must have seen his infinite splendour, one must have known him before – looked at him then' (*TU*, 26). An avowal of the impossibility of conveying experience also controls 'Heart of Darkness,' where Marlow affirms 'it is impossible to convey the life-sensation of any given epoch of one's existence – that which makes its truth, its meaning – its subtle and penetrating essence. It is impossible' (*Y*, 82). Time takes the individual away from the past, its reality gradually eroded by the needs of the present, which shape memory. On 21 December 1898, Conrad explained to Graham that 'Time overtakes us. Time! Voilà l'ennemi' (*CL* 2, 134). Nevertheless, Conrad's awareness of the fleeting years brought a corresponding acknowledgement of the benefits of retrospection: 'I had in years gone by a certain reputation for courage. Now, no doubt, all this is changed the spirit being brushed out of me by the tyranny of mysterious sensations, yet still a spark, a dim spark exists somewhere – a vestige of the old fire under the tepid ruins' (*CL* 2, 97). Conrad suggests that memory can hold up the tepid ruins of the present. In praise of Cunninghame Graham's *The Ipané* (1899), which recreated the world of Graham's youthful travels in South America, Conrad wrote that there 'are things in that volume that are like magic and through space, through the distance of regretted years convey to one the actual feeling, the sights, the sounds, the thoughts; one steps on the earth; breathes the air and has the sensations of your past' (*CL* 2, 179).

The regretted years are central to Conrad's portrayal of a sense of loss in his early short fiction. Conrad expressed this sentiment as he worked on 'Youth,' and to W.E. Henley – editor of the *New Review*, where *The Nigger of the 'Narcissus'* was first serialised in 1897 – Conrad pointed to a contemporary inspiration for 'Youth'; Rudyard Kipling's tale of reincarnation, 'The Finest Story in the World' (1893). Kipling's Charlie Mears, like Słowacki's narrator in *Genesis from the Spirit*, recalls his previous incarnations, as 'The Fates that are so careful to shut the doors of each successive life behind us had, in this case, been neglectful.'[9] Conrad wrote to Henley: 'It has been a fine story to me; so fine that I have suddenly regretted the years gone by, regretted not being young when the future seems as vast as all eternity and the story could go on without end; so fine – you are to understand – that when it comes to setting it down the gods of life say nay and one can only mutter "no doubt – but the door is shut."'[10] Conrad indicated that 'Youth' was 'my "Finest Story in the World"' (*CL* 2, 108–9), his own walkway between past and present.

Conrad began 'Youth' in late spring of 1898, and the story was published in *Blackwood's Magazine* in September that year. The tale of the comically ill-fated voyage of the *Palestine*, Conrad later drew attention to 'Youth' for marking the 'first appearance in the world of the man Marlow, with whom my relations have grown very intimate in the course of years' (*Y*, v). Marlow allows Conrad to achieve the effect he sought in 'Youth,' with the story becoming a 'feat of memory' (*Y*, vii). The success of this feat of memory centres on the middle-aged narrator who conveys 'the notion of something lived through and remembered' (*CL* 2, 167). Ian Watt has praised the tale as a 'simple thing beautifully done.'[11] The relegation of 'Youth' to understudy to 'Heart of Darkness' is justified, but in presenting his middle-aged narrator and his recollection of experience, 'Youth' 'was supposed to give the note' (*CL* 2, 271) that 'Heart of Darkness' would develop. Najder has suggested the tone of 'Youth' can be found in an essay on Cooper and Marryat that Conrad submitted to *Outlook* magazine. Published on 4 June 1898 – the day after 'Youth' was completed – the essay, entitled 'Tales of the Sea,' found Conrad, as Najder observes, enthusing that these writers 'awakened one's regret for the bygone romanticism and zest for adventure of youth.'[12] However, the deeper impulse provoking 'Youth' and 'Heart of Darkness' can be found earlier that year in Conrad's first extant attempt at the essay. In an appreciation of Alphonse Daudet, published in *Outlook* in April 1898, Conrad unveiled the philosophy of his fortieth

---

[9] Rudyard Kipling, 'The Finest Story in the World,' *Many Inventions* (1893; London: Macmillan, 1949), 106.

[10] Here Conrad quotes the Indian doctor in Kipling's story.

[11] Watt, *Conrad in the Nineteenth Century*, 133, 134.

[12] Najder, *Conrad: A Chronicle*, 229.

year, one that moulded his most famous protagonist: 'One must admit regretfully that today is but a scramble, that tomorrow may never come; it is only the precious yesterday that cannot be taken away from us' (*NLL*, 21). This glance to the precious yesterday directs Marlow's narrative in 'Youth.' Marlow asks his listeners, 'wasn't that the best time?' (*Y*, 42) Marlow's resurrection of the precious yesterday is a result of the scramble of the present and the uncertainties of the future.

In an essay on Henry James in 1905, Conrad wrote that the 'only possible form of permanence in this world of relative values' was 'the permanence of memory' (*NLL*, 16). The genre of the literary essay was one that attracted Conrad, and he used his essays to consider history, travel, politics, seamanship and literature. As he struck the note of 'Youth' in his essay on Daudet, Conrad echoed whom many consider to be the greatest English essayist, William Hazlitt (1778–1830). J.H. Stape has noted that although Conrad 'was familiar with Lamb and Carlyle, little influence from the English tradition as it developed through the nineteenth century is immediately discernible' in his essay writing.[13] However, Conrad was perhaps drawn to figures in English literary history that fit the pattern of his Polish influences, particularly regarding time, history and memory. Conrad alluded to Hazlitt's essays in his correspondence with Henry James (*CL* 2, 414) echoes of 'The Indian Jugglers' appear in *The Secret Agent*, and Conrad directly quoted from Hazlitt's father in *Lord Jim*.[14]

In 'On the Past and Future' (1821) and 'Why Distant Objects Please' (1821), Hazlitt produced fluidly perceptive English Romantic writing on time and memory, insisting that 'the past is as real and substantial a

---

[13] J.H. Stape, introduction, Joseph Conrad, *Notes on Life and Letters* (Cambridge: Cambridge University Press, 2004), lii.

[14] In *The Secret Agent*, Inspector Heat 'felt at the moment like a tight rope artist might feel if suddenly, in the middle of the performance, the manager of the Music Hall were to rush out of the proper managerial seclusion and begin to shake the rope. Indignation, the sense of moral insecurity engendered by such a treacherous proceeding, joined to the immediate apprehension of a broken neck, would, in the colloquial phrase, put him in a state' (*SA*, 92). In 'The Indian Jugglers,' Hazlitt remembers 'Richer, the famous rope-dancer,' who was 'matchless in his art,' and compares his skill to the laboured painting of Joshua Reynolds: 'If the rope-dancer had performed his task in this manner . . . he would have broke his neck long ago . . . Is it then so easy, (comparatively) to dance on a tight-rope?' William Hazlitt, 'The Indian Jugglers,' *Table Talk, or Original Essays* (London: Dent, 1908), 79, 80.

part of our being, that it is as much a bona-fide, undeniable consideration in the estimate of human life as the future can possibly be.'[15] In
words evoking Marlow's faith in the 'good old time' (*Y*, 42), Hazlitt
warned not to 'quit our hold on the past when perhaps there may be
little left to bind us to existence.'[16] In 'On the Feeling of Immortality in
Youth,' first published in *Winterslow* (1850), its title inviting comparisons with 'Youth' and *Lord Jim*, Hazlitt set out the path that must be
trod from youth to maturity. The young Marlow in 'Youth', like Jim
later, can, in Hazlitt's words, see 'no line drawn, and we see no limit to
our hopes and wishes. [...] [W]e have as yet found no obstacle, no
disposition to flag, and it seems that we can go on so forever.'[17] The
transition from youth to maturity involves acceptance that the once
boundless future slips inexorably away, and it becomes the main theme
of 'Youth,' which nostalgically recalls Marlow's past.

Hazlitt provided a kindred voice in the evaluation of the past, with
the essayist believing that individual experience gave meaning to the
contemplation of time: 'the objects we have known in better days are the
main props that sustain the weight of our affections and give us strength
to await our future lot. The future is like a dead wall or a thick mist
hiding all objects from view: the past is alive and stirring with objects,
bright or solemn, and of unfading interest.'[18] At the close of 'Youth,' the
ageing Marlow, through the 'permanence of memory,' almost succeeds
in entering his bright past: 'I see it now – the wide sweep of the bay, the
glittering sands, the wealth of green infinite and varied, the sea blue like
the sea of a dream, the crowd of attentive faces, the blaze of vivid colour'
(*Y*, 41). In 'Youth,' Marlow creates an ideal past 'conceived of by the
mind's eye.'[19] The past offers security as it 'certainly existed once, has
received the stamp of truth, and left an image of itself behind.'[20]
Conrad's story exploits the relationship between an intense image of
the past and the action of the conceiver in the present, stressing that

[15] William Hazlitt, 'On the Past and Future,' *Table Talk, or Original Essays*, 22. See
also 'On the Feeling of Immortality in Youth,' *Sketches and Essays / Winterslow* (London:
George Bell & Sons, 1909), 299–306.
[16] Hazlitt, 'On the Past and Future,' 23.
[17] Hazlitt, 'Immortality on Youth,' 299.
[18] Hazlitt, 'On the Past and Future,' 25.
[19] Hazlitt, 'On the Past and Future,' 22.
[20] Hazlitt, 'On the Past and Future,' 22–23.

nostalgia, while providing momentary release, polarises romantic past and mundane present.

Conrad's narrative technique in 'Youth' periodically returns to the present to acknowledge that the past remains an elaborate mental construct. In this way, Conrad's story, despite its obvious Romantic melancholy in the tradition of Hazlitt's essays, exposes its proto-modernism. The role of the past in the individual's consideration of time acquired prominence throughout the nineteenth century, with retrospective contemplation becoming less a Romantic reverie than a burden to be carried. By the close of the century, Friedrich Nietzsche contended that awareness of passing through time distinguished humans from the rest of the natural world. According to Nietzsche, animals live un-historically, but in human beings pain, melancholy and boredom are consequences of our consciousness of time. Indeed, this awareness constitutes human identity: 'He cannot learn to forget but always re-mains attached to the past; however far and fast he runs, the chains run with him.'[21] Conrad also pronounced that 'what makes mankind tragic is not that they are the victims of nature, it is that they are conscious of it' (*CL* 2, 30). Conrad's scrutiny of experience through memory does not allow him to escape, like Hazlitt, from the ravages of time, but sees him become cognisant of individual history. In Conrad's case, we can agree with Bryan S. Turner when he suggests that 'man is ontologically nostalgic because memory is always a consciousness of ageing and death. Our awareness of time is also an awareness of passing through time.'[22]

In an historical context, Conrad had already been steeped in this judgement, as Polish patriotism espoused the need to retain the past as a means of enduring the present. 'It is a peculiar characteristic of nine-teenth-century Polish political thought that its dominant trends are at the same time progressive and traditionalist.'[23] However, a variation of this notion also emerged in psychology and philosophy. The French philosopher Henri Bergson's *Matière et Mémoire* [*Matter and Memory*]

---

[21] Friedrich Nietzsche, *On the Advantages and Disadvantages of History for Life* (Indianapolis: Hackett, 1980), 8–9.

[22] Bryan S. Turner, 'Aging and Identity: Some Reflections on the Somatization of the Self,' *Images of Aging: Cultural Representations of Later Life*, edited by Mike Featherstone and Andrew Wernick (London: Routledge, 1995), 249.

[23] Najder, 'Conrad and Rousseau,' 88.

of 1896 argued further that 'memories constitute the human soul and
thereby transfigure the quotidian self,' and Bergson's influential concept
of *dureé* analysed how the human perception of time involved an
amalgamation of both past and present states.[24] F.H. Bradley wrote in
a similar vein in 1908 when he asserted that 'no one can deny that in a
sense we depend on past experience. For, apart from any other consideration, it is from past experience that in the main our minds are filled.
And generally to suppose that without the past we should have an
intelligible present seems obviously absurd.'[25] Marlow can also be
located within this turn-of-the-century culture; his 'feat of memory'
transcends nostalgia and is transformed into an investigation of identity.
However, it is worth reiterating that Marlow's comprehension of time is
effectively a psychological variation on the questions of identity, history
and representation that were ubiquitous in partitioned Poland.

Conrad's meticulous concern with temporal dynamism in 'Youth'
and the early fiction is contemporaneous with an extended treatment of
time in philosophical circles in the 1890s. In *Mind* in April 1897, a
dialogue between philosophers Bernard Bosanquet, S.H. Hodgson and
G.E. Moore questioned: 'In what Sense, if any, do Past and Future
Time Exist.'[26] The exchange addresses the subject of the closing passages of 'Youth,' undertaking to isolate and explain the human perception of time. For Conrad, time is the ultimate intangible, something
that 'while it is expected is already gone – has passed unseen, in a sigh,
in a flash – together with the youth, with the strength, with the
romance of illusions' (*Y*, 42). 'Youth' ponders whether time approaches
from the future, becomes present for an instant, and then recedes into
the past, and such subtleties dominated the philosophical analyses that
inspired J.M.E. McTaggart's seminal article 'The Unreality of Time' in
1908.[27] In *Mind,* Bosanquet alluded to Bradley's *Appearance and Reality*

---

[24] Rick Rylance, 'Twisting: Memory from Eliot to Eliot,' *Memory and Memorials,
1789–1914: Literary and Cultural Perspectives,* edited by Matthew Campbell, Jacqueline
M. Labbe and Sally Shuttleworth (London: Routledge, 2000), 99.

[25] F.H. Bradley, 'On Memory and Judgement,' *Mind* 17 (1908): 156.

[26] *Mind* 6 (1897): 228–40.

[27] 'The Unreality of Time' presents two modes of understanding time, the static time
series and the dynamic time series. The static mode attributes to an event a specific temporal
location, such as the publication of *Almayer's Folly* in 1895. The dynamic series of time
accepts that every event is in flux, and that, as the publication of Conrad's first novel was
once in the future, (say, in 1880) was once present, (in 1895), and is now in the past, then in

(1893) and stressed that 'Though the conception of a flux or succession may seem to imply a present which perishes in appearing, it is evident that in fact our present is not of this nature, but includes duration, and is variable in its extension. Thus we are not brought face to face with a mere series of vanishing points.'[28] In response, Shadworth H. Hodgson wrote that time 'cannot be perceived, imagined, or thought of, save as a continuum [...]. Time is an essential element in experience, and therefore in our conception of reality.'[29] For Hodgson, responsiveness to time implies consciousness of its perceived dynamism. In words that reproduce the rendering of time in 'Youth,' Hodgson explained: 'All contents of experience, then, since they have time as an element in them, are constantly passing [...]. The content of an empirical present moment, thought of before it actually enters consciousness, is thought of as future; one thought of after it has disappeared is thought of as past.'[30] In 'Youth, time consists of a series of vanishing points, an overpowering phenomenon that brings the future into a present devoid of tangible duration, and then immediately recedes into the depths of history.

Time and perception feature prominently in Conrad's early fiction. In 'Karain,' the 'silence was profound; but it seemed full of noiseless phantoms, of things sorrowful, shadowy and mute, in whose invisible presence the firm, pulsating beat of the two ship's chronometers ticking off steadily the seconds of Greenwich Time seemed to me a protection and a relief' (*TU*, 40). Greenwich Time aids the illusion of time as a flowing phenomenon, in this instance puncturing the oppressive silence

this series the event simultaneously occupies three temporal positions. McTaggart admits the need for a dynamic understanding of time if time is to be considered real. While accepting that human perception indeed sees time in flux, McTaggart in turn argues that if an event does in fact approach from the future, become present and then subsequently become past, it must ultimately have three temporal positions. But, as Tim Crane has pointed out in his analysis of McTaggart's thought, 'being past, being present and being future are jointly incompatible: nothing can be past, present, and future. And nothing with incompatible features can exist – for example, nothing can be red and not red. But if an event has one location in the dynamic time series, it has all the other incompatible ones too. Therefore being past, being present, and being future cannot exist: so there is no dynamic time series.' See A.C Grayling ed., *Philosophy 1: A Guide Through the Subject* (Oxford: Oxford University Press, 2001), 195-96.

[28] Bosanquet in *Mind* 6 (1897): 229.
[29] Hodgson in *Mind* 6 (1897): 231.
[30] Hodgson in *Mind* 6 (1897): 232.

of the present. In *The Secret Agent* (1907), Conrad expanded this idea by allowing the modern embodiment of time – the clock – to enter imposingly into the relationships between his characters. As Mr Verloc returns home, 'All was so still without and within that the lonely ticking of the clock on the landing stole into the room as if for the sake of company' (*SA*, 137). For Mrs Verloc, the present remains empty of duration: 'She let the lonely clock on the landing count off fifteen ticks into the abyss of eternity' (*SA*, 138). Chief Inspector Heat, however, attempts to rise 'above the vulgar conception of time' (*SA*, 71) in imagining the last moments of Stevie's life. Newspaper reports of Stevie's death present his destruction as 'Instantaneous' (*SA*, 71), yet Heat 'evolved a horrible notion that ages of atrocious pain and mental torture could be contained within two successive winks of an eye' (*SA*, 71). Treating the 1894 attempt to bomb the Greenwich Observatory, *The Secret Agent* documents the Modern fixation with time in literature and philosophy, juxtaposing the burlesque world of attempted anarchist destruction and the ineluctable devastation wrought by time, which silently pervades Conrad's imagined worlds.[31]

In *Mind* in 1897, G.E. Moore concluded by writing: '[N]either Past, Present, nor Future exists [. . .]. On the other hand I think we may say that there is more Reality in the Present than in the Past or Future, because, though it is greatly inferior to them in extent of content, it has that co-ordinate element of immediacy which they entirely lack.'[32] For Conrad, the fleeting immediacy of the present instigates a subjective need to unearth the past. In *A Personal Record*, recalling Poland and remembering his mother, Conrad wrote: 'It must have been 1864, but reckoning by another mode of calculating time, it was certainly in the year in which my mother obtained permission to travel south and visit her family, from the exile into which she had followed my father' (*PR*, 23). This subjective, other mode becomes a way of engaging with history and challenging the apparent temporal flow, taking precedence over the formulaic, chronological charting of time. In 'Heart of Darkness'

[31] See Ian Watt ed., *Conrad, The Secret Agent: A Casebook* (Basingstoke: Macmillan, 1973). For an analysis of *The Secret Agent* in the context of contemporary discussions relating to physics, see Michael W. Whitworth, 'Things Fall Apart: *The Secret Agent* and Literary Entropy,' in *Einstein's Wake: Relativity, Metaphor, and Modernist Literature* (Oxford: Oxford University Press, 2001), 58–82.

[32] *Mind* 6 (1897): 240.

Conrad again considered these issues, focusing on history and its subjective representation. While Marlow's audience were resigned to the nostalgia of 'Youth' and the disquieting movement of time, 'Heart of Darkness,' which documents the *fin de siècle* European fascination with Africa through Marlow's exposure to the dark world of torture in the Congo, outlined the difficulties of constructing an authoritative history.

HISTORY AND REPRESENTATION IN 'YOUTH' AND 'HEART OF DARKNESS'

It has been claimed that 'Conrad was steeped in the literary culture of his adopted country and formed himself, consciously or unconsciously, in the "great tradition" of nineteenth-century British fiction.'[33] Many critics have pointed to the parallels between 'Heart of Darkness' and Thomas Carlyle's work.[34] Avrom Fleishman has written on Conrad's immersion in the English organicist tradition, looking at Conrad's indebtedness to Carlyle.[35] For Fleishman, Conrad's adoption of an English tradition influenced by German Idealism follows naturally from his childhood in Poland. He has also examined Conrad's emergence as an author in the 1890s, a time when F.H. Bradley and Bernard Bosanquet were writing, suggesting that 'these two philosophers [. . .] bear a remarkable number of similarities to the novelist on ethical and social issues.'[36] A consideration of history helps to further illuminate this relationship.

In 1874, Bradley published his first philosophical essay, 'The Presuppositions of Critical History.'[37] He discussed the impossibility of

---

[33] Avrom Fleishman, *Conrad's Politics: Community and Anarchy in the Fiction of Joseph Conrad* (Baltimore: Johns Hopkins University Press, 1967), 55.

[34] See V.J. Emmett, Jr., 'Carlyle, Conrad, and the Politics of Charisma: Another Perspective on "Heart of Darkness,"' *Conradiana* 7.2 (1975): 145–55; Alison L. Hopwood, 'Carlyle and Conrad: Past and Present and "Heart of Darkness,"' *Review of English Studies* 23 (1972): 162–72.

[35] Fleishman, *Conrad's Politics*, 49–77.

[36] Fleishman, *Conrad's Politics*, 67.

[37] The essay is reprinted in F.H. Bradley, *Collected Essays*, vol. 1 (Oxford: Clarendon Press, 1935), 1–70.

facts in history, examining the imposition of the standpoint of the historian in the account of the past:

> [H]istory stands not only for that which has been, but also for that which is; not only for the past in fact, but also for the present in record; and it implies the union of these two elements: it implies, on the one hand, that what once lived in its own right lives now only as the object of knowledge, and on the other hand that the knowledge which now is possesses no title to existence save in right of that object, and, though itself present, yet draws its entire reality from the perished past.[38]

'Heart of Darkness' focuses on the subjective evaluation of past events, with a coherent present identity only attainable, if at all, through an elucidation of history. The tenebrous quest for the enigmatic Kurtz reflects the historical and semantic contexts of European exploration in Africa, which introduced a discourse of epistemological uncertainty to the documenting of geographical and historical fact. Explorers such as Richard Burton (1821–90), John Hanning Speke (1827–64), and missionary David Livingstone (1813–73) sought to survey and chart the Dark Continent, but with the work of journalist and explorer Henry Morton Stanley (1841–1904), contracted by the *New York Herald* to find Livingstone in Africa in 1871 as a sensational journalistic stunt, Africa became synonymous with protean historical legend. Stanley himself became the subject of various black legends associated with his violent character and his involvement in the barbarity of King Leopold's Congo (1885–1908),[39] and his search for Livingstone was obscured by the contemporary mythology surrounding the man: 'The newspapers described him as worthy of the Christian world's best regard; privately men whispered strange things of him. One was that he had married an African princess and was comfortably domiciled in Africa; another that he was something of a misanthrope, and would take care to maintain a discreet distance from any European who might be tempted to visit him.'[40]

---

[38] Bradley, 'Presuppositions of Critical History,' *Collected Essays*, 8.

[39] See Adam Hochschild, *King Leopold's Ghost: A Story of Greed, Terror, and Heroism in Colonial Africa* (London: Pan, 2006).

[40] Henry Morton Stanley, *In Darkest Africa*, vol. 2 (London, 1890), 208–9. See Frank McLynn, *Stanley: Dark Genius of African Exploration* (London: Pimlico, 2004).

F.H. Bradley's contemporaneous thought in 'The Presuppositions of Critical History,' which investigates the effacing of historical truth, and his later work *Appearance and Reality* (1893), represents a philosophical corridor between the Victorian and Modern imaginations, particularly considering T.S. Eliot's doctoral thesis on Bradley, and Eliot's subsequent interest in Conrad.[41] 'The Presuppositions of Critical History' 'is in fact something of a pioneer work,' being 'the first serious piece of writing in English on truth and fact in history, the first to argue that historical facts are "constructions."'[42] Bradley stated that 'Our interest in the past is our feeling of oneness with it, is our interest in our own progression.'[43] History is 'an event which perishes as it arises. It dies and it can never be recalled. It cannot repeat itself, and we are powerless to repeat it [...] and then from our knowledge of the present too we deplore our ignorance in the past.'[44] As W.H. Walsh has emphasised, although Bradley's article does not employ any specific language from Hegel, 'Bradley's text can scarcely disguise the Hegelian affinities of the whole set of ideas.'[45] This is best captured in Bradley's Hegelian assurance that history is progressive. While Bradley and Bosanquet were directly interested in Hegel's logic for their own studies, the shadow of the German philosopher's historical thought was also visible elsewhere in England. In September 1894, *The Philosophical Review* published an article entitled 'The Problem of Hegel' by John Watson. Watson wrote: 'Hegel seems to me to be the epitome of that remarkable period of intellectual activity which burst upon the world at the beginning of this century, and to understand him is to comprehend one of the most important movements of modern thought.'[46] According to Fleishman, although Conrad was 'probably not directly exposed to the systematic theories of the neo-Hegelians, his explicit statements

[41] In *Victory* (1915), Conrad wrote: 'Appearances – what more, what better can you ask for? In fact you can't have better. You can't have anything else' (*V*, 204).

[42] W.H. Walsh, 'Bradley and Critical History,' *The Philosophy of F.H. Bradley*, edited by Anthony Manser and Guy Stock (Oxford: Clarendon Press, 1984), 34.

[43] Bradley, 'Presuppositions of Critical History,' 36.

[44] Bradley, 'Presuppositions of Critical History,' 41–42.

[45] Walsh,'Bradley and Critical History,' 47.

[46] John Watson, 'The Problem of Hegel,' *The Philosophical Review* 3.5 (1894): 548.

on politics and the dramatic structure of his novels both attest to the presence of his intellectual milieu.'[47]

In addition to neo-Hegelian philosophy, Conrad's fiction responded to a longer tradition of British historical writing represented by Thomas Carlyle. However, although critics have dwelt on Conrad's promotion of the work ethic of Victorian Britain, Conrad had already inherited a much stronger sense of this philosophy from Bobrowski and the Polish response to Hegelian Idealism. Conrad's identification with Carlyle is not an appropriation of a new English voice so much as one that corresponded to his already formed Polish mentality. The emphasis on work that surfaced in *The Nigger of the 'Narcissus'* again features in 'Youth': 'But they all worked. That crew of Liverpool hard cases had in them the right stuff' (*Y*, 25). This capacity for the task becomes a force in history as it has 'a completeness in it, something solid like a principle, and masterful like an instinct – a disclosure of something secret – of that hidden something, that gift of good or evil that makes racial difference, that shapes the fate of nations' (*Y*, 28–29). In his lectures on aesthetics, Hegel had noted the contribution of work to the meaning of individual identity: 'man is realised for himself by his *practical* activity [...]. This purpose he achieves by the modification of external things upon which he impresses the seal of his inner being.'[48] In 'Heart of Darkness,' Marlow advocates the necessity of work in the establishment of a stable identity: 'I don't like work – no man does – but I like what is in the work, – the chance to find yourself. Your own reality – for yourself, not for others – what no man can ever know. They can only see the mere show, and never can tell what it really means' (*Y*, 85). Again, in *Nostromo*, Conrad writes that 'In our activity alone do we find the sustaining illusion of an independent existence as against the whole scheme of things of which we form a helpless part' (*N*, 497). As Zdzisław Najder observes while considering Conrad's relationship with the author of *Sartor Resartus*, Carlyle 'was not the father to but only a stepson of a certain political tradition, and therefore a comparison with him will drive us into a side-alley of the history of ideas.'[49] Conrad's focus on

---

[47] Fleishman, *Conrad's Politics*, 67.

[48] G.W.F. Hegel, *On Art, Religion, and the History of Philosophy: Introductory Lectures* (Indianapolis: Hackett, 1997), 58.

[49] Najder, 'Conrad and Rousseau,' 78.

work possessing something 'masterful' and 'secret' is rooted primarily in Hegelianism and only secondly in Carlyle's English philosophy.[50]

Carlyle's work, however, does appear within the text of 'Youth.' Marlow tells of his literary interests at the time of his voyage in the *Judea*, noting that in reading both the soldier and the philosopher, he gained, and still retains, more respect for the man of action than the man of thought: 'I read for the first time *Sartor Resartus* and Burnaby's *Ride to Khiva*. I didn't understand much of the first then; but I remember I preferred the soldier to the philosopher at the time; a preference which life has only confirmed. One was a man, and the other was either more – or less' (*Y*, 7).[51] Despite this affinity with the man of action, Marlow, like many before and after him, has since become the amateur philosopher. He continues: 'However, they are both dead... and youth, strength, genius, thoughts, achievements, simple hearts – all dies.... No matter' (*Y*, 7). This illuminates Conrad's development in 'Youth' of the problems of representation and truth that cloud 'Heart of Darkness.' As Ian Watt summarises, 'Marlow is in effect his own author, and so there is no reliable and comprehensive perspective on him or his experience.'[52]

Conrad's epistemological scepticism articulates in part the understanding of history found in Carlyle's essay 'On History' of 1830, which first appeared in *Frazer's Magazine*. The essay reads like an early response to Hegel's philosophy of history, and Carlyle anticipates the thought of August Cieszkowski's *Prolegomena zur Historiosophie*. Carlyle stated: 'Let us search more and more into the Past; let all men explore it, as the true fountain of knowledge; by whose light alone, consciously or unconsciously employed, can the Present and the Future

---

[50] According to Bertrand Russell, Conrad 'adhered to an older tradition, that discipline should come from within. He despised indiscipline, and hated discipline that was merely external.' See Bertrand Russell, *Portraits From Memory* (London: Allen & Unwin, 1956), 84.

[51] Carlyle's *Sartor Resartus* consists of an overblown satire on Hegelianism. For Carlyle's German professor Teufelsdrock, 'Our whole terrestrial being is based on Time, and built of Time; it is wholly a Movement, a Time-impulse; Time is the author of it, the material of it... O Time-Spirit, how hast thou environed and imprisoned us, and sunk us so deep in thy troublous dim Time-Element' (99). See Thomas Carlyle, *Sartor Resartus* (1838; Oxford: Oxford University Press, 1987).

[52] Watt, *Conrad in the Nineteenth Century*, 209.

be interpreted or guessed at.'[53] Carlyle points out what Bradley and Conrad later enlarge on; namely that as much as the past and the future can be understood from the perspective of the present, the present can also be shaped by exploration of the past. For Carlyle, the historian's task in the present is controlled by the forces of retrospection and anticipation: 'It is a looking both before and after; as, indeed, the coming Time already waits, unseen, yet definitely shaped, predetermined and inevitable, in the Time come; and only by the combination of both is the meaning of either completed.'[54]

Marlow acknowledges that history must be understood in the tradition of Cieszkowski and Carlyle: 'The mind of man is capable of anything – because everything is in it, all the past as well as all the future' (*Y*, 96). 'Youth' and 'Heart of Darkness' view time as a tripartite division of interrelated and dependent concepts. Carlyle, Cieszkowski, and Conrad grant that in the contemplation of time, the past must enlighten the present and plot the future. Noting the natural human urge towards retrospective narration, Carlyle wrote:

> A talent for History may be said to be born with us, as our chief inheritance. In a certain sense all men are historians. [...] Thus, as we do nothing but enact History, we say little but recite it; nay rather, in that widest sense, our whole spiritual life is built thereon. For, strictly considered, what is all Knowledge too but recorded Experience, and a product of History.[55]

For the Marlow of 'Youth,' the memory of his voyage of initiation takes on the semblance of a glorious historical epic as he combines his own experiences with his chief inheritance, his awareness of history. Marlow 'thought of men of old who, centuries ago, went that road in ships that sailed no better, to the land of palms, and spices, and yellow sands, and of brown nations ruled by kings more cruel than Nero the Roman, and more splendid than Solomon the Jew' (*Y*, 18). The boundaries between fiction and history are blurred in Marlow's narratives, as his story vies for its place amongst the epic tales of world history. Conrad later conceded that fiction and recollection were forms of historiography:

---

[53] Thomas Carlyle, 'On History,' *Critical and Miscellaneous Essays*, vol. 1 (London: Chapman & Hall, 1887), 500.
[54] Carlyle, 'On History,' 495.
[55] Carlyle, 'On History,' 495–96.

Fiction is history, human history, or it is nothing. But it is also more than that; it stands on firmer ground, being based on the reality of forms and the observation of social phenomena, whereas history is based on documents, and the reading of print and handwriting – on second-hand impression. Thus fiction is nearer truth. But let that pass. A historian may be an artist too, and a novelist is a historian, the preserver, the keeper, the expounder, of human experience. (*NLL*, 19)

Conrad's scepticism regarding historical truth – 'let that pass' – reveals that his retrospective narrative style combines Carlyle's human need for recollection with Bradley's later scepticism about definitive judgement on the past.

Marlow embodies the urge to historical narrative, while exposing the difficulty of asserting any truth about history. For characters as ambiguous as Marlow, 'Historical and fictional narratives will reveal themselves to be not distortions of, denials of, or escapes from reality, but extensions and configurations of its primary features.'[56] In 'Heart of Darkness,' the need to order the past, as in Carlyle's description of the need to recite history, forms part of Marlow's identity. Marlow promotes a retrospective narrative urge as endowing him with a European character. On his journey to Kurtz, Marlow is culturally displaced and correspondingly cut off from his past. He feels he is entering a land that does not have an historical consciousness: 'Going up that river was like travelling back to the earliest beginnings of the world' (*Y*, 92). Marlow's appreciation of history and his Cieszkowskian reliance on the past are central to his European identity: 'I don't think a single one of them had any clear idea of time, as we at the end of countless ages have. They still belonged to the beginnings of time – had no inherited experience to teach them as it were' (*Y*, 103). Marlow's inherited experience drives his narrative, with his tale born of Conrad's correlation of the reconstructed past with the present moment of narration. History is subject to constant change by the flux of the present, and Marlow's story is 'the attempt to dominate the flow of events by gathering them together in the forward-backward grasp of the narrative act.'[57]

---

[56] David Carr, *Time, Narrative, and History* (Indianapolis: Indianapolis University Press, 1986), 16.
[57] Carr, *Time, Narrative, and History*, 62.

HISTORY AND ORAL NARRATIVE
TRADITION IN 'HEART OF DARKNESS'

On 5 August 1897, Conrad wrote to Cunninghame Graham, whose pointed attack on British imperialism and the brutality of European involvement in Africa 'Bloody Niggers' was published in *The Social Democrat* that year: 'And suppose Truth is just around the corner like the elusive loafer it is? I can't tell. No one can tell. It is impossible to know. It is impossible to know anything tho' it is possible to believe a thing or two' (*CL* 1, 370). 'Heart of Darkness' investigates whether through the embracing of history one can ever unveil 'truth stripped of its cloak of time' (*Y,* 97). In Conrad's novella, which updated a European tradition of polemical historiography and travel writing begun by Bartolomé de Las Casas' *A Short Account of the Destruction of the Indies* (1542), time shapes and forms the truths required in the present by the surveyor of the past. In October 1898, as Conrad worked on 'Heart of Darkness,' the philosophical stance of his letter to Graham was treated in *Mind,* which featured an article by J.B. Baillie, the future translator of Hegel's *Phenomenology of Mind,* entitled 'Truth and History.' The article carried forward issues raised in F.H. Bradley's essay on critical history.[58] In language reminiscent of a Conradian narrator with academic training, Baillie, asserting that time and change were inseparable, wrote that 'every object which we can consider has a temporal aspect [...]. [But] there must thus be an inner kernel or content of identical (*i.e.,* unchangeable) import which remains and endures through all change.'[59] 'Heart of Darkness' questions whether a timeless truth exists, exploring the implication of present judgement in evaluation of the past.

---

[58] These arguments prefigure much twentieth-century debate on the nature of history and historical writing, particularly the work of E.H. Carr and Hayden White. For an accomplished summary of these debates, see Keith Jenkins, *On 'What is History?' From Carr and Elton to Rorty and White* (London: Routledge, 1995). In literary studies, the most influential work on the nature of historical writing has been Hayden White's study of literary devices and narrative structures by nineteenth-century historians and philosophers, *Metahistory: The Historical Imagination in Nineteenth-Century Europe* (London: Johns Hopkins University Press, 1973).

[59] Baillie in *Mind* 7 (1898): 507.

It is indicated by Marlow's loquacity that the tale aboard the *Nellie*, as presented by the frame-narrator, is just one possible version of events. This is reinforced by the knowledge that Marlow is working in the oral narrative tradition. Baillie's essay reads like an analysis of Marlow's narrative:

The dilemma is briefly this: The discussion of the *history* of a judgment, let us say, is admitted to be a perfectly legitimate and independent inquiry; the discussion of its *truth*, its *validity* for knowledge, is likewise a legitimate and independent inquiry. [...] [But] the judgement under discussion, because having a history in time, must and does change. [...] But if the first conclusion is true, then the judgement can *never* be universally true or valid, for it is *always* in time, in process, and that means change. [...] [F]or process is knit up with change and time, and that means history.[60]

Marlow's interpretations of his past are provoked by and subject to the effects of time. Baillie insists that the 'truth which a judgement expresses is not contained inside the shell of factual existence in the mind which can be thrown aside and leave the truth, if we are ingenious enough to separate the two.'[61] Conrad's story hints at the same conclusion; a separation of truth from the method of arriving at truth is not feasible.

British Idealist philosophy accepted the interdependence of ideological and philosophical contrasts. Bradley's *Ethical Studies* (1876), particularly its chapter 'My Station and Its Duties,' argued in a tradition of Hegelian dialectic that an individual could only exist within the confines of society, with society allowing the confirmation of individuality.[62] Such problems recall Hegel's influential Master-Slave dialectic in the *Phenomenology of Mind* (1807), which outlined the futile struggle for mastery between two self-conscious beings whose identities are essentially founded on oppositional recognition. According to Hegel's formulation, 'Self-consciousness exists in and for itself, in that, and by the fact that it exists for another self-consciousness; that is to say, it *is* only by being recognised.'[63] In 'Falk,' a tale of cannibalism that

[60] Baillie in *Mind* 7 (1898): 509–10.
[61] Baillie in *Mind* 7 (1898): 512.
[62] For a sympathetic discussion of Bradley's moral and political philosophy, see Nicholson, *Political Philosophy of the British Idealists*, 6–53.
[63] G.W.F. Hegel, *The Phenomenology of Mind*, translated, with an introduction and notes by J.B. Baillie, 2nd ed. (London: Allen & Unwin, 1961), 229.

appeared in *Typhoon and Other Stories* (1901), and which with 'The Return' from *Tales of Unrest* (1898) remained Conrad's only other fiction not to be accepted for magazine publication, the narrator asserts that 'Selfishness presupposes consciousness, choice, the presence of other men' (*T*, 198). In fact, Conrad's texts usually employ Hegelian language to register awareness of the inextricable complexities of individual and communal identity. In *Under Western Eyes*, Razumov wonders: 'Have I then the soul of a slave? No! I am independent – and therefore perdition is my lot' (*UWE*, 362). In *Nostromo*, Captain Fidanza thinks 'with the resolution of a master and the cunning of a cowed slave' (*N*, 528). In *Lord Jim*, 'all these things that made him [Jim] master had made him a captive, too' (*LJ*, 247), and 'he was imprisoned within the very freedom of his power' (*LJ*, 283). 'Heart of Darkness' adopts this philosophical duality in its approach to historiography, and Conrad 'calls into question whether literature, or any kind of writing for that matter, can represent history.'[64] This is apparent from the frame narrator's verdict on Marlow's narrative, which adopts Baillie's philosophy: 'to him the meaning of an episode was not inside like a kernel but outside, enveloping the tale which brought it out only as a glow brings out a haze' (*Y*, 48). The complications of historical truth are increased in 'Heart of Darkness' by Conrad's representation of Marlow as historian of his own experience working in the oral narrative tradition, enveloping and embellishing his story.

For Conrad, the act of recollection corresponds with the work of an historian, as narrative is the ordering of experience in the attempt to construct an intelligible record. However, Marlow has a 'propensity to spin yarns' (*Y*, 48). Zdzisław Najder has discussed the role of the traditional Polish folk tale, the *gawęda*, on the development of Conrad's early narrative style: 'Most of these tales were "reminiscences" of old soldiers, friars, or travellers [...]. In some cases a "tale" inserted in a larger work was used as a vehicle to convey the moral or political significance of the whole.'[65] Count Henryk Rzewuski's (1791–1866) *Pamiątki Soplicy* [*The Memoirs of Sophlica*] (1839), 'a series of sketches

---

[64] Hunt Hawkins, 'Conrad's *Heart of Darkness*: Politics and History,' *Conradiana* 24.3 (1992): 208.
[65] Najder ed., *Conrad's Polish Background*, 16.

from the life of the eighteenth century, old-fashioned Polish gentry,'[66] is a characteristic example of such a style. The retrospective mood of these narratives emerged from the Polish literary tradition, with the scene of narration subject to elemental and human interferences, highlighting the construct that was the story. In *A Personal Record*, Conrad's auto-biographical method likewise connects to an oral narrative tradition, seeking to assemble impressions whose 'accumulated verisimilitude of selected episodes puts to shame the pride of documentary history' (*PR*, 15). Conrad strives for this effect in 'Heart of Darkness,' and, as Michael Greaney has written, 'Conrad prefers on the whole to let it appear that his writings originate in informal conversation or oral tradition.'[67] By returning to the scene of narration, Conrad reinforces the presence of the frame-narrator, the audience, and that Marlow's tale unfolds at the turn of the tide in London:

It had become so pitch dark that we listeners could hardly see one another. For a long time already he, sitting apart, had been no more than a voice. There was not a word from anybody. The others might have been asleep, but I was awake. I listened, I listened on the watch for the sentence, for the word, that would give me the clue to the faint uneasiness inspired by this narrative that seemed to shape itself without human lips in the heavy night air of the river. (*Y*, 83)

Because Marlow is working in the oral narrative tradition, his history emerges from his own voice, while also consisting of myriad independent past voices, all conveyed through Marlow's recollection of the Harlequin, the Station Manager, the Doctor, Kurtz, and the Intended. The ambiguity of Marlow's tale originates in his reliance on memory and his incorporation of conflicting accounts into his story. 'Heart of Darkness,' although a text, thus represents a classic oral narrative.

Oswyn Murray observes that the oral narrative history consists of a 'chain of testimonies' whose 'reliability is primarily affected, not by the length of the chain, but by the mode of transmission [...]. And the same mode of transmission affects the character of a story.'[68] Marlow's

[66] Walicki, *Philosophy and Romantic Nationalism*, 230.

[67] Greaney, *Conrad, Language, and Narrative*, 3.

[68] Oswyn Murray, 'Herodotus and Oral History,' *Achaemenid History: Proceedings of the Groningen Achaemenid History Workship II. The Greek Sources*, edited by Heleen Sancisi-Weerdenburg and Amúlie. Kuhrt (Leiden: Nederlands Instituut voor het Nabije Oosten, 1987), 97.

mode of transmission on the deck of the *Nellie* is coloured by various concerns; his lingering nostalgia for his youth that carries over from 'Youth,' his reluctance to fully share the experience with his listeners, and his complicated position with regard to Kurtz. In his study of covert plots in Conrad's work, Cedric Watts has analysed the conspiracy against Kurtz through the sabotage of Marlow's steamer.[69] Marlow relays his conversation with the manager, who affirms: 'Well, let us say three months before we can make a start. Yes. That ought to do the affair.' Marlow wryly comments: 'Afterwards [. . .] it was borne in upon me startlingly with what extreme nicety he had estimated the time requisite for the "affair"' (*Y*, 75). For Watts, the 'reticently elliptical presentation of this plot enables [Conrad] to maintain the general atmosphere of futile, pointless activity.'[70] Marlow's elliptical presentation fulfils the requirements of the oral narrator/historian, as every 'testimony and every tradition has a purpose and fulfils a function. It is because of this that they exist at all. For if a testimony had no purpose, and did not fulfil any function, it would be meaningless for anyone to pass it on, and no-one would pass it on.'[71] The voices Marlow recalls all have significance, but readers must evaluate their import.

There are signposts within the text that Marlow is working in the oral narrative tradition. As Murray points out, 'Literacy [. . .] encourages certain mental forms, the most common of which, the table and the list, belong especially to bureaucratic practices.'[72] Marlow's discovery of *Towson's Inquiry* highlights the contrast between a methodological approach to knowledge and the fluidity of the oral narrative:

Its title was *An Inquiry into some Points of Seamanship*, by a man Towser, Towson – some such name – Master in His Majesty's Navy. The matter looked dreary reading enough, with illustrative diagrams and repulsive tables of figures, and the copy was sixty years old. [. . .] Not a very enthralling book; but at the first glance you could see there was a singleness of intention, an

[69] See Cedric Watts, *The Deceptive Text: An Introduction to Covert Plots* (Brighton: Harvester Press, 1984).

[70] Watts, *A Preface to Conrad*, 120.

[71] Jan Vansina, *Oral Tradition: A Study in Historical Methodology*, translated by H.M. Wright (London: Routledge & Kegan Paul, 1973), 77. See also Jan Vansina, *Oral Tradition as History* (London: James Currey, 1985); Jack Goody, *The Domestication of the Savage Mind* (Cambridge: Cambridge University Press, 1977).

[72] Murray, 'Herodotus and Oral History,' 109.

honest concern for the right way of going to work, which made these humble pages, thought out so many years ago, luminous with another than a professional light. (*Y*, 99)

The thorough, systematic textual *Inquiry* stands in stark contrast to Marlow's meandering oral tale. Nevertheless, if the reliability of Marlow's narrative is questioned, then so is the idea of an authoritative textual history. 'Heart of Darkness' questions the possibility of any such thing as 'a readable report' (*Y*, 138). Kurtz's report for the International Society for the Suppression of Savage Customs is 'Seventeen pages of close writing [. . .]. But it was a beautiful piece of writing' (*Y*, 117–18). However, time interferes with Marlow's judgement of the work: 'The opening paragraph, however, in the light of later information, strikes me now as ominous' (*Y*, 118). Kurtz's degeneration in the heart of Africa invalidates Marlow's original interpretation of his elegant treatise, 'the unbounded power of eloquence – of words – of burning noble words' (*Y*, 118). Time and shifting judgement ensure the work comes to be seen as that of a psychotic. Marlow encounters Kurtz's postscript: 'Exterminate all the brutes!' Marlow further distorts the truth of the document by later tearing off the postscript to protect Kurtz's memory and to counter the emerging black legend of his exploits. History is a series of recurring postscripts influencing our interpretation of the past, and the close of the story encourages this interpretation, as Marlow sits in the darkness 'in the pose of a meditating Buddha' (*Y*, 162). He who began in the pose of a 'Buddha preaching' (*Y*, 50) now contemplates whether there can be any truth to our knowledge of history.

LORD JIM AND HISTORIOGRAPHY

Lord Jim underlines the transformation of oral narrative into textual form, with the shift from third person narrator to Marlow's oral and written narratives complementing Conrad's thematic focus on Jim's development. The surviving notebook containing the earliest known fragment of *Lord Jim* represents a family heirloom retained by Conrad and contains poems in the handwriting of Teofila Bobrowska, Conrad's maternal grandmother. Conrad's inheritance of Polish Romanticism and Positivism colours the text, and central to its structure is the antagonism between the abstract and the practical, between Jim's Romantic plight and the cold logic of Positivist facts: 'They wanted facts. Facts! They demanded facts from him, as if facts could explain anything!' (*LJ*, 29). Marlow also rails against the 'solicitation of ideas. Hang ideas! They are tramps, vagabonds, knocking at the back-door of your mind' (*LJ* 43). *Lord Jim* remains indeterminate, scorning both facts and the image of the Hegelian 'thinker evolving a system of philosophy from the hazy glimpse of truth' (*LJ*, 24). Acknowledging the 'doubt that is the inseparable part of our knowledge' (*LJ*, 221), Conrad analyses whether one can acquire as an individual what Stein sees perfected in nature: 'the balance of colossal forces' (*LJ*, 208).

Lord Jim also wears its German Romantic credentials on its sleeve with the epigraph from Novalis and Stein's quotation of Goethe's *Torquato Tasso* (1790). Stein, as a veteran of the barricades of the 1848 revolution, delicately balances his Romantic, republican heritage with his modern scientific detachment as a naturalist, which Conrad modelled on British naturalist Alfred Russell Wallace and his celebrated work *The Malay Archipelago* (1869). Stein's speech on the 'destructive element' analyses the complexities of engaging with both the romance and the reality of the past. According to Cedric Watts, Stein's speech can be reduced to the contradictions of Conrad's polarised philosophical inheritance: 'Be a realist, not an idealist; yet be an idealist, not a realist.'[73] Polish Romanticism intensifies Conrad's study of the passing of youth. The course of the *Patna* is expressed in the language of acute historical and temporal awareness: 'Such were the days, still, hot, heavy, disappearing one by one into the past, as if falling into an abyss for ever open in the wake of the ship.' While the past can be observed, history continues 'on her steadfast way' (*LJ*, 16). Further, as Zdzisław Najder has pointed out, 'the main character of Mickiewicz's greatest work *Pan Tadeusz*, Jacek Soplica, alias Father Robak, is shown as trying to atone, by many years of heroic service to Poland, for a moment of weakness in his youth when his private feelings made him forget his national obligations: a perfect forerunner of Conrad's Jim.'[74]

---

[73] Cedric Watts, notes, Joseph Conrad, *Lord Jim*, edited by Robert Hampson (London: Penguin, 1989), 360.
[74] Najder ed., *Conrad's Polish Background*, 15.

Conrad's appropriation of Romantic influences sees him turn, as in 'Youth,' to the English Romanticism exemplified by William Hazlitt. According to Marlow, Jim 'had a conscience, and it was a romantic conscience' (*LJ*, 276), and *Lord Jim* treats the subject of Hazlitt's essay 'On the Feeling of Immortality in Youth.' The essayist wrote of the evaporation of a youthful feeling of immortality, stressing the need to accept the past as the possibilities of the future diminish: 'The future was barred to my progress, and I turned for consolation and encouragement to the past. It is thus that while we find our personal and substantial identity vanishing from us, we strive to gain a reflected and vicarious one in our thoughts.'[75] Whereas Marlow symbolises an acceptance of this view, Jim's failure to admit that his youthful opportunity for heroism has vanished propels him forward in a frantic bid to undo his past cowardice. Conrad openly revealed his indebtedness to Hazlitt in *Lord Jim*. Jim's Englishness is constructed on the knowledge that he is the son of an English Parson. The letter from Jim's father that comes into Marlow's possession consists of phrases borrowed from a letter written by the Reverend William Hazlitt to his son in March 1790.[76] As Marlow notes, 'There are four pages of it, easy morality and family news' (*LJ*, 341).

Lord Jim's questioning of whether life can ever offer a 'clean slate' (*LJ*, 185) receives a gloomy negation in Conrad's letters at the time of the novel's composition: 'Life starts again, regrets, memories and a hopelessness darker than night' (*CL* 2, 151). Marlow's tendency to lapse into memory and 'make the past live for a short and precious moment' (*CL* 2, 171) has a controlling influence on the narrative of *Lord Jim*. Adapting oral narrative techniques, the novel strives to be 'fundamentally oral in form: it is patterned as a succession of stories independent of each other and often without obvious connections; the resonances and repetitions give the impression of being folk-tale motifs, traditionally accepted devices to explain motivation or actions.'[77] Conrad's narrative method investigates the discrepancy between the facts of history and

---

[75] Hazlitt, 'Immortality in Youth,' 304.
[76] Patricia Dale, 'Conrad: A Borrowing from Hazlitt's Father,' *Notes and Queries* ns 10 (1963): 146.
[77] Murray, 'Herodotus and Oral History,' 112.

their representation.[78] The various stories that *Lord Jim* presents are the subjective memories of figures from Marlow's past. Each newly introduced individual feels impelled, like Marlow, to relate his own story. Marlow, ironically, seems unaware of this, and this is best revealed in his dismissal of the second helmsman of the *Patna*, '*the* sensation of the second day's proceedings' of the inquiry into Jim's desertion from the ship:

[S]uddenly, with shaky excitement he poured upon our spellbound attention a lot of queer-sounding names, names of dead-and-gone skippers, names of forgotten country ships, names of familiar and distorted sound, as if the hand of dumb time had been at work on them for ages. They stopped him at last. [. . .] [T]his extraordinary and damning witness that seemed possessed of some mysterious theory of defence. (*LJ*, 99)[79]

Marlow is oblivious to the fact that this is an exact description of his own narrative. In his use of various dead-and-gone people to add new perspectives to his story, Marlow spins a seemingly interminable oral tale. Captain Brierly, Mr. Jones, Chester, Robinson, the French Lieutenant, Stein, and Gentleman Brown all have a tendency to recount their pasts as Marlow does, thus shaping the structure of *Lord Jim*.[80]

In writing the novel, Conrad had been swayed by subjective memories. Just as 'Heart of Darkness' had been 'mainly a vehicle for conveying a batch of personal impressions' (*CL* 2, 460) of the Congo, in a letter to Hugh Clifford, Conrad admitted that a great deal of *Lord Jim* relied on the memory of past encounters: 'I want to put into that sketch a good many people I've met – or at least seen for a moment – and several things overheard about the world. It is going to be a hash of episodes, little thumbnail sketches of fellows one has rubbed shoulders with and so on' (*CL* 2, 226–27). Conrad revealed that *Lord Jim* engaged

---

[78] For a fine analysis of the ambiguity of language in *Lord Jim*, see Alexis Tadié, 'Perceptions of Language in *Lord Jim*,' *The Conradian* 31.1 (2006): 16–36.

[79] Although most of its short, unsigned review of *Lord Jim* was favourable, on 14 November 1900 *Sketch* accused Marlow of being, in effect, similar to the second helmsman mentioned above, saying the 'story – the little story it contains – is told by an outsider, a tiresome, garrulous, philosophising bore.' See Sherry ed., *Conrad: The Critical Heritage*, 118.

[80] See J.H. Miller, '*Lord Jim*: Repetition as Subversion of Organic Form,' *Fiction and Repetition: Seven English Novels* (Cambridge, MA: Harvard University Press, 1982), 22–41.

him in the role of historian collecting and arranging various individual accounts.[81]

Jakob Lothe has explored how *Lord Jim* 'appropriates and cumulatively combines aspects of other subgenres of fiction, including the sketch, the tale, the fragment, the episode, the legend, the letter, the romance, and the parable.'[82] *Lord Jim* also connects with the genres of historiography and travel writing going back to the father of Western history, Herodotus (c.484 BC—c. 425 BC), who presented colourful accounts of the ancient Greek world and the Persian Wars in the fifth century BC.[83] Like Herodotus and early historians, Marlow has gathered various oral testimonies on his wide travels and presented them to his audience, first through his own oral narrative, and later through his written account of Jim's fate. According to Philip A. Stadter, in the *Histories* Herodotus 'provides a bewildering number of individual accounts. [. . .] In a technique both powerful and daunting, everything in the *Histories* seems connected to everything else.'[84] Whereas for Herodotus the coming of the Persian Wars is his unifying centre, for Marlow, everything relates to Jim. For the oral historian, the narrative to a group of listeners is the initial stage in constructing a written account. Herodotus's method involved 'investigation and judgement. Investigation depends on two sources, personal observation and oral report. [...] He himself probably originally presented many of the segments of his work as stories recounted to small audiences during his travels. [. . .]. Only later would the stories have been organised and written down as the book we now possess.'[85] Marlow uses the testimonies

---

[81] The celebrated incident with the steamship *Jeddah* in 1880 – the facts of which correspond to the *Patna* episode in the novel – form the definite source-material for *Lord Jim*. Conrad may have met Augustine Podmore Williams (1852–1916), first mate on the *Jeddah*, in Singapore in 1883. The abandonment of the Jeddah 'created a scandal that would not die out.' See Sherry, *Conrad and his World* (London: Thames and Hudson, 1972), 44.

[82] Jakob Lothe, 'Conrad's *Lord Jim*: Narrative and Genre,' *Joseph Conrad: Voice, Sequence, History, Genre*, edited by Jakob Lothe, Jeremy Hawthorn, & James Phelan (Columbus: Ohio State University Press, 2008), 236.

[83] See John Burrow, *A History of Histories: Epics, Chronicles, Romances and Inquiries from Herodotus and Thucydides to the Twentieth Century* (London: Allen Lane, 2007).

[84] Philip A. Stadter, 'Historical Thought in Ancient Greece,' *A Companion to Western Historical Thought*, edited by Lloyd Kramer and Sarah Maza (Oxford: Blackwell, 2002), 40.

[85] Stadter, 'Historical Thought in Ancient Greece,' 41–42.

he has gathered to hold both an audience and a readership, thereby negotiating the boundary of oral and written narrative traditions.

Zdzisław Najder has remarked that in the 'immense critical literature on Conrad there is not a single general study dealing with the presence of Greek and Latin traditions in his work.'[86] The strongest evidence for associating *Lord Jim* with the Greek originator of Western historiography appears within the text of Herodotus's *Histories*. Book One relates a tale of the Lydian king Croesus that unequivocally resonates with *Lord Jim*.[87] Digressing from the main narrative of the build up to the Persian War, Herodotus focuses on Lydian society. Croesus dreams that a blow from an iron weapon will kill his son, Atys. As a precaution, Croesus orders that henceforth Atys should not be allowed into battle. Later, at Atys's wedding, a Phrygian stranger named Adrastus, who has been exiled from his community for accidentally killing his brother, comes to Lydia. The unfolding tale betrays numerous parallels to Jim's relationship with Doramin and Dain Waris in Patusan.

Adrastus establishes a position of importance within his new environment until the Mysians ask Croesus for the assistance to rid their community of a dangerous wild boar. Croesus decides he will send a party of soldiers but, remembering his dream, refuses to allow Atys to engage in combat. Atys points out that Croesus's dream mentioned only that a blow from an iron weapon would kill him, and that a wild boar cannot wield such a weapon. Croesus relents:

The king then sent for Adrastus the Phrygian, and said to him: 'Weighed down by great misfortune, Adrastus, you came to me in great distress. I gave you ritual purification, welcomed you to my house, and have spared no expense to entertain you. Now, I expect a fair return for my generosity: take charge of my son on this boar hunt; protect him from highwaymen and cut-throats on

---

[86] Zdzisław Najder, 'Joseph Conrad and the Classical World: A Sketch of an Outline,' *The Ugo Mursia Memorial Lectures: Second Series*, edited by Mario Curreli (Pisa: Edizioni ETS, 2005), 19.

[87] In *The Polish Shades and Ghosts of Joseph Conrad*, Gustav Morf notes that the third Persian campaign was amongst subjects taught in history at St. Anne's Gimnazjum in Cracow, which Conrad is believed to have attended (75). The student file of Conrad's contemporary in France, Arthur Rimbaud (1854–91), was filled for 1864/65 with 'allusions to Alexander, Darius, and "their cronies" and to "that filthy language," Greek.' See Graham Robb, *Rimbaud* (London: Picador, 2000), 21.

the road. In any case it is your duty to go where you can distinguish yourself: your family honour demands it, and you are a stalwart fellow besides.'

'Sire,' Adrastus answered, 'under ordinary circumstances I should have taken no part in this adventure. A man *under a cloud* has no business to associate with those who are luckier than himself. Indeed I have no heart for it, and there are many reasons to prevent my going. But your wishes make all the difference. It is my duty to gratify you in return for your kindness: so I am ready to do as you ask. So far as it lies in my power to protect your son, you may count on his returning safe and sound.'[88] (Emphasis added)

On the hunt, Adrastus fires an arrow at the boar. Its iron point misses the beast and strikes Atys, killing him, making Croesus's dream come true:

A messenger hurried off to Sardis, and Croesus was told of the encounter with the boar and the death of his son. The shock of the news was dreadful; and the horror of it was increased by the fact that the weapon had been thrown by the very man whom the king had cleansed from the guilt of blood. In the violence of his grief Croesus prayed to Zeus, calling on him as God of Purification to witness what he had suffered at the hands of his guest; he invoked him again under his title of Protector of the Hearth, because he had unwittingly entertained his son's murderer in his own house; and yet again as God of Guest-Friendship, because the man he had sent to guard his son had turned out to be his bitterest enemy.

Before long the Lydians arrived with the body, followed by the killer. He took his stand in front of the corpse, and stretching out his hands in an attitude of submission begged the king to cut his throat there and then upon the dead body of his son.

'My former trouble,' he said, 'was bad enough. But now that I have ruined the man who absolved me of my guilt, I cannot bear to live.'

In spite of his grief Croesus was moved to pity by these words.

'Friend,' he said, 'as you condemn yourself to death, there is nothing more I can require of you. Justice is satisfied. This calamity is not your fault; you never meant to strike the blow, though strike it you did. Some god is to blame – some god who long ago warned me of what was to happen.'

Croesus buried his son with all proper ceremony; and as soon as everything was quiet after the funeral, Adrastus – the son of Gordias, the grandson of Midas: the man who had killed his brother and destroyed the host who gave

---

[88] Herodotus, *The Histories*, edited by John M. Marincola (London: Penguin, 1996), 17.

him purification – convinced that he was the unluckiest of all the men he had ever known, stabbed himself and fell dead upon the tomb.[89]

The echoes of Jim's flight from his own world into Doramin's protection on Patusan are striking. Adrastus's appeal for death to Croesus recalls Jim's voluntary demise at the hands of Doramin. When Croesus, unlike Doramin, pardons Adrastus, the ritualistic suicide nevertheless occurs. Determined that the 'dark powers should not rob him twice of his peace' (*LJ*, 409), Adrastus, like Jim later, dies aware that he 'had retreated from one world [...] and now the other, the work of his own hands, had fallen in ruins upon his head' (*LJ*, 408).

Marlow resolutely states his claim as inheritor of the Herodotean tradition, not only through his narrative ornamentation and his apparent contempt for facts, but by committing Jim's story to writing so that he will not be 'doomed to forgetfulness in the end' (*LJ*, 275).[90] Herodotus opened his *Histories* with a similar justification; presenting history 'so that human achievements may not become forgotten in time, and great and marvellous deeds...may not be without their glory.'[91] The extravagant writings of Herodotus also evoke divisive perspectives on historical knowledge, a conflict central to Conrad's historical investigations. Famously labelled the 'father of lies' as well as the 'father of history' by Roman statesman and philosopher Cicero (106 BC–46 BC) for his seemingly unreliable historiography, Herodotus was 'one of the earliest victims of what might be called the positivist character' of modern historical scepticism; 'ignorance and fantasy, as well as malicious invention, has been attributed to Herodotus and Plutarch; and these charges against narrative history had been repeated at intervals by those who preferred certainty to conjecture.'[92] While the

---

[89] Herodotus, *Histories*, 18.

[90] Ernest Bevan writes that Marlow 'is a historian of sorts, whose narrative attempts to create a unified history which will make Jim's present comprehensible in terms of the young seaman's past.' Ernest Bevan, Jr., 'Marlow and Jim: The Reconstructed Past,' *Conradiana* 15.3 (1983): 193–94.

[91] Herodotus, *Histories*, 3.

[92] Isaiah Berlin, 'The Sciences and the Humanities,' *The Proper Study of Mankind: An Anthology of Essays*, edited by Henry Hardy and Roger Hausheer (London: Pimlico, 1998), 331. Conrad's essays 'Geography and Some Explorers' (originally titled 'The Romance of Travel') and 'Travel' in *Last Essays* (1926) lamented the omniscience of the scientific world of the twentieth century, a time when 'there is nothing new left now, and but very little of what may be called obscure' (88).

correspondences between *Lord Jim* and the *Histories* may illuminate Conrad's analysis of epistemological concepts, Herodotus also 'shared the common Greek belief that any act of insolence or overweening pride (*hybris*) inevitably leads to some destruction (*nemesis*),'[93] and the inescapable power of fate in Greek tragedy structures Marlow's account: 'there is to my mind a sort of profound and terrifying logic in it, as if it were our imagination alone that could set loose upon us the might of an overwhelming destiny' (*LJ*, 342). In Marlow's eyes, historical determinism ensures Jim's demise, as 'Something of the sort had to happen' (*LJ*, 342–43), and the novel shows how Jim's hubristic Romantic obstinacy leads to his untimely destruction.

In his affinities with Herodotus, Marlow represents what Hegel defined as an 'Original Historian,' one who recalls the events of his own lifetime and historical epoch. According to Hegel, in his introductory lectures to the philosophy of history, the writing of history can be divided into Original history, Reflective history, and Philosophic history:

[The Original Historian] describes more or less what he has seen, or at least lived through. Short spans of time, the individual patterns of men and events – these are the singular, unreflected features out of which he composes his portrait of the time, in order to bring that picture to posterity with as much clarity as it had in his own direct observation or in accounts of other direct witnesses. He is not concerned with offering reflections on these events, for he lives within the spirit of the times and cannot as yet transcend them.[94]

Marlow relies 'on the reports and accounts of others, since it is not possible for one person to have seen everything. But they use these sources as ingredients only [. . .]. These historians bind together what is vanishing down the stream of time, and place it all in the Temple of Memory to give it immortality.'[95] In envisaging the young Jim, like Adrastus, 'under a cloud' (*LJ*, 277, 339, 416), Marlow hopes to 'bring that picture to posterity' by grounding his story in documentary form. Marlow's story will lack profound reflection on Jim: 'there shall be no message, unless such as each of us can interpret for himself from the

---

[93] John M. Marincola, introduction, *Histories*, xxi. See also Dorothy Van Ghent, *The English Novel: Form and Function* (Holt, Reinhart & Winston, 1953) for a discussion of elements of classical tragedy in *Lord Jim*.

[94] Hegel, *Philosophy of History*, 4.

[95] Hegel, *Philosophy of History*, 3–4.

language of facts, that are so often more enigmatic than the craftiest arrangement of words' (*LJ*, 340). J.H. Stape has written that 'Conrad's insistent refusal to ground the text by continuously undermining narrative authority purposefully encourages a nostalgic, almost wistful longing for a once present centre.'[96] In his 'Author's Note' to the novel, written in 1917, Conrad described the story as a 'free and wandering tale' (viii), ironically addressing the criticisms of some early reviews that had called into question the unfeasible length of Marlow's after dinner recital.[97] However, the novel's evolution from oral to written narrative is part of its thematic focus on development, with the narrative mode of the novel mirroring Jim's regression towards youth by undergoing a simultaneous shift towards the traditional adventure story. Although perhaps not as deliberate an example of a stylistic use of cliché and anecdote as the 'Eumaeus' episode of Joyce's *Ulysses*, where Stephen Daedalus and Leopold Bloom sit after midnight, exhausted, listening to an old sailor, *Lord Jim* is aware of its 'becoming' a romance, or a Romantic history.[98] The longer the story goes on the more Marlow is inclined to become sentimental and Romantic, and he admits that 'all this may seem to you sheer sentimentalism' (*LJ*, 222).

The third-person narrator in *Lord Jim* returns to introduce Marlow's written history, locating 'Marlow's tale on the borderland between speech and writing.'[99] Living in an unnamed city, the packet the privileged reader receives from Marlow two years after his oral narrative consists of the conclusion of Jim's story. It arrives 'addressed in Marlow's upright and angular handwriting' (*LJ*, 292). The aborted letter from Jim and the letter from his father which accompany Marlow's

---

[96] J.H. Stape, 'Lord Jim,' *The Cambridge Companion to Joseph Conrad*, edited by J.H. Stape (Cambridge: Cambridge University Press, 1996), 67.

[97] For example, a review in *The Academy* (10 November 1900, 443) claimed that Marlow's narrative must have lasted eleven hours.

[98] For an interesting account of connections between Joyce and Conrad – especially in *Ulysses* – see Jane Ford, 'James Joyce and the Conrad Connection: The Anxiety of Influence,' *Conradiana* 17.1 (1985): 3–18. Ford proposes that the old sailor in the 'Eumaeus' episode may in fact represent Conrad, especially as his audience wait 'in the hope that the rover might possibly by some reminiscences but he failed to do so, simply letting spurt a jet of spew into the sawdust, and shook his head with a sort of lazy scorn.' James Joyce, *Ulysses*, edited by Jeri Johnson (Oxford: Oxford University Press, 1993), 585.

[99] Greaney, *Conrad, Language, and Narrative*, 79.

package stress that Marlow's final words on Jim are a written document, with their textuality not subject to the fluidity of his oral tale. Conrad notes the materials Marlow has used in the production of his account: 'A good many pages closely blackened and pinned together; a loose square sheet of greyish paper with a few words traced in handwriting he had never seen before, and an explanatory letter from Marlow. From this last fell another letter, yellowed by time and frayed on the folds' (*LJ*, 338). Marlow's indebtedness to oral history emerges in his lamentation for Jim's voice: 'I wonder how he would have related it himself. He has confided so much in me that at times it seems as though he must come in presently and tell the story in his own words' (*LJ*, 343). Marlow, however, fulfils his role as original historian, as such 'original historians, then, transform the events, actions, and situations present to them into works of representation.'[100] Marlow's written narrative places Jim firmly within the romantic tradition, his story unfolding as an 'astounding adventure' (*LJ*, 342).

Marlow constructs his story in conjunction with his investigations, and his main source, Gentleman Brown, exposes the difficulties of engaging with a witness and representing a received testimony. Marlow reports: 'Till I discovered the fellow my information was incomplete [...]. Fortunately he was willing and able to talk between the choking fits of asthma, and his racked body writhed with malicious exultation at the bare thought of Jim. [...] He gloated over his action' (*LJ*, 344). Brown creates a 'harrowing and desperate story' (*LJ*, 356), illustrating the pitfalls of the oral tradition: 'We know now that even participants and observers regularly adjust their memories to habitual or fitting narratives; events become mythologised with astounding rapidity.'[101] In conclusion, Marlow reports the testimony of a native of Patusan, Tamb' Itam, ensuring that henceforth 'events move fast without a check, flowing from the very hearts of man like a stream from a dark source, and we see Jim amongst them, mostly through Tamb' Itam's eyes' (*LJ*, 389). Tamb' Itam is 'evidently overawed by a sense of deep inexpressible wonder, by the touch of an inscrutable mystery' (*LJ*, 351), and Marlow correspondingly colours Jim's death with the language of romantic adventure; the 'sky over Patusan was blood-red, immense,

---

[100] Hegel, *Philosophy of History*, 4.
[101] Stadtler, 'Historical Thought in Ancient Greece,' 42.

streaming like an open vein. An enormous sun nestled crimson amongst the tree-tops, and the forest below had a black and forbidding face' (*LJ*, 413). By enshrining him within the romantic adventure tradition, Marlow sees Jim locked eternally located within a romantic past. Marlow acknowledges Jim's death as a 'pitiless wedding with a shadowy ideal of conduct' (*LJ*, 416). However, Marlow indicates that his history has preserved Jim: 'And that's the end. He passes away under a cloud, inscrutable at heart, forgotten, unforgiven, and excessively romantic. Not in the wildest days of his boyish visions could he have seen the alluring shape of such an extraordinary success!' (*LJ*, 416). Jim's extraordinary success lies in his final entombment in Marlow's written account, which, in its opaque history, demonstrates the confluence of 'traditional storytelling and modernist reflexivity' in Conrad's writing.[102]

[102] Greaney, *Conrad, Language, and Narrative*, 6.

3

History and Nation: *Nostromo,*
The Secret Agent, and *Under Western Eyes*

Nostromo (1904), *The Secret Agent* (1907), and *Under Western Eyes*
(1911) firmly engage with European historical philosophy. These political novels analyse the role of the nation in history, as Conrad explores
both historical and modern understandings of nationality. Conrad's
writing addresses both contrasting positions that have come to dominate debate on the origins of nationalism in the late twentieth and early
twenty-first centuries. Eric Hobsbawm has written that 'the basic characteristic of the modern nation and everything connected with it is its
modernity. This is now well understood.'[1] *Nostromo*, with its sceptical
focus on the origins of the new nation of Sulaco, 'whose flourishing and
stable condition is a matter of common knowledge now' (*N*, 303),
concurs with Hobsbawm's view of the modernity of nations. The
impact of the San Tomé silver-mine on the construction of the Occidental Republic of Sulaco illustrates Ernest Gellner's belief that 'nationalism is an essential component of modernisation, or the transition from
agrarian to industrial society – the latter requiring a state that can
produce and be maintained by one common, literate and accessible
culture.'[2] *Nostromo*, however, also details an existent, multifarious
Costaguanan culture that has developed throughout the country's
Spanish colonial and post-colonial history. Incorporating 'the worn-
out antiquity of Sulaco' (*N*, 97), Costaguana authentically represents
the hybrid and evolving identity of a South American nation.

[1] Eric Hobsbawm, *Nations and Nationalism since 1780* (Cambridge: Cambridge
University Press, 1990), 14.
[2] Brendan O'Leary, 'On the Nature of Nationalism: An Appraisal of Ernest Gellner's
Writings on Nationalism,' *British Journal of Political Science* 27 (1997): 198.

In support of the historical validity of nations, Adrian Hastings has written that 'Nation-formation and nationalism have in themselves almost nothing to do with modernity. Only when modernisation was already in the air did they almost accidently become part of it.'[3] In his writing on the Polish nation, most notably in 'Prince Roman' and essays such as 'Poland Revisited' and 'Autocracy and War,' Conrad adheres to a vision of a diverse but immutable Polish national identity that has its origins in the depths of the past, something Conrad consistently discusses in a metaphysical sense; what he calls the 'invincible soul of a nation' (*NLL*, 99). Further, in *Under Western Eyes*, Conrad envisages a natural division of peoples into distinct nations so that he can analyse 'the very soul of things Russian' (*CL* 4, 8). Throughout his writing, Conrad engages with both views of the nation, those of both the believer and the sceptic, and Conrad's treatment of nationalism confirms that 'scepticism and credulity can coexist productively. Nationalism's adherents seem to be capable of believing in national myths and celebrating supposed national traditions, even while suspecting them to be false in one case and of recent vintage in the other.'[4]

Although nationalism continues to form an open field of discussion, it is necessary to return to the main currents of European thought to properly ground Conrad's view of the nation. Deeply embedded in *Nostromo* and *Under Western Eyes* lies Conrad's response to two closely associated and influential figures in European philosophical history, Johann Gottfried von Herder (1744–1803) and Jean-Jacques Rousseau (1712–88) respectively. Although Rousseau's connection to *Under Western Eyes* has been noted by many critics,[5] the role of Herder's thought in *Nostromo* and in Conrad's idea of the nation has not previously been explored. Considering Herder's position in European history as both the promotor of Slavic cultural rejuvenation and as the

---

[3] Adrian Hastings, *The Construction of Nationhood: Ethnicity, Religion and Nationalism* (Cambridge: Cambridge University Press, 1997), 205.

[4] Yoon Sun Lee, *Nationalism and Irony: Burke, Scott, Carlyle* (Oxford: Oxford University Press, 2004), 8.

[5] See particularly Fleishman, *Conrad's Politics*, and Najder, 'Conrad and Rousseau.' According to Bertrand Russell, Conrad's 'point of view, one might perhaps say, was the antithesis of Rousseau's.' *Portraits from Memory*, 82. For an extended treatment of Herder's role in European philosophy, see the work of Isaiah Berlin, especially *Vico and Herder: Two Studies in the History of Ideas* (London: Hogarth Press, 1992).

foremost exponent of cultural nationalism, room exists for an analysis of Herder's importance in Conrad's presentation of nation and history. Further, the absence of a clearly defined boundary between a purely cultural nationalism that follows Herder's philosophy and a political nationalism in the tradition of Rousseau also calls for Conrad's relationship with the latter to be re-evaluated.[6]

Conrad labelled Rousseau an 'artless moralist' (*PR*, 95) in *A Personal Record* for the unwieldy size of his *Confessions*, but as Edward Said has pointed out, 'if Conrad's hatred of Rousseau was at all like his well-known hatred of Dostoevsky, it may have been that Conrad perceived in the loquacious Swiss a temperament uncomfortably similar to his own.'[7] Rousseau's works on political nationalism, most notably *The Social Contract* (1762) and his *Discourse on Political Economy* (1758), presuppose the existence of a people upon which the framework of a political order must be placed: 'It would be better, before examining the act by which a people gives itself to a king, to examine that by which it has become a people.'[8] As F.M. Barnard has stressed, while 'Herder and Rousseau saw the transition from national becoming to political becoming in divergent terms, there was full agreement between them that some matrix of national becoming must precede political becoming for the latter to be able to build upon the former.'[9] *The Social Contract* indicates a division of peoples into separate identity groups and analyses 'the rules of society best suited to nations,' each of which Rousseau sees possessing its own unique character.[10]

---

[6] See F.M. Barnard, 'National Culture and Political Legitimacy: Herder and Rousseau,' *Journal of the History of Ideas* 44.2 (1983): 231.

[7] Edward Said, *Joseph Conrad and the Fiction of Autobiography* (Cambridge, MA: Harvard University Press, 1966), 53.

[8] Jean-Jacques Rousseau, *The Social Contract and Discourses*, translated with an introduction by G.D.H. Cole (London: Dent, 1963), 11. The most problematic aspect of Rousseau's thought for Conrad was Rousseau's insistence on the subjection of the individual to the state, expressed in *The Social Contract* as follows: 'The better the constitution of a state is, the more do public affairs encroach on private in the minds of the citizens. Private affairs are even of much less importance, because the aggregate of the common happiness furnishes a greater proportion of that of each individual, so that there is less for him to seek in particular cares' (78).

[9] F.M. Barnard, *Herder on Nationality, Humanity, and History* (London: McGill-Queen's University Press, 2003), 40.

[10] Rousseau, *Social Contract*, 32.

In his political writings, particularly 'Autocracy and War,' Conrad follows Rousseau and Herder in his insistence upon the rights of every nation to its own political identity and peaceful coexistence. Rousseau's ideas associating the nation with the people have, of course, been accepted as a determining factor in the articulation of the goals of the French Revolution. For Conrad, the philosophy that inspired the Revolution contained an 'elevated' idea in its identification of the people with the nation. However, aware of the transformation of the Revolution into the Terror of 1793, and the eventual emergence of Napoleon, Conrad wrote in 'Autocracy and War' that, ultimately, 'the glorified French Revolution itself, except for its destructive force, was in essence a mediocre phenomenon. The parentage of that great social and political upheaval was intellectual, the idea was elevated: but it is the fate of any idea to lose its royal form and power, to lose its "virtue" the moment it descends from its solitary throne to work its will among the people' (*NLL*, 73). Conrad's language, linking the emergence of liberal, progressive ideas with monarchy, the 'royal form and power,' is characteristically ironic, and it reflects the periodically conservative slant of Conrad's politics and his sceptical view of human nature.[11] Although Conrad appears to condemn Rousseau's 'general will' in his allusion to the political immaturity of the people, the upheaval in France between 1789–1815 remains problematic because of the 'degradation of the ideas of freedom and justice at the root of the French Revolution' (*NLL*, 73). In *Nostromo*, Conrad wrote of 'something inherent in the necessities of successful action which carried with it the moral degradation of the idea' (*N*, 521). Rousseau's philosophy is notoriously ambiguous, but Conrad, it seems, opposes the rampant will of the majority, and not the general will, which is supposed to check the wrongful desires of the majority will. What Conrad objects to is not the association of the people with the nation, but later, extreme, populist

---

[11] On this subject, Conrad distinguished his views from those of H.G. Wells in the following manner: 'The difference between us, Wells, is fundamental. You don't care for humanity but think they are to be improved. I love humanity but know they are not!' Quoted in Rupert Hart Davis, *Hugh Walpole: A Biography* (London: Macmillan, 1952), 168.

interpretations of Rousseau and Herder's philosophies of nationalism, what Julia Kristeva has called 'the ambiguity of the great Herder.'[12]

In 'Autocracy and War,' Conrad voiced his fear of popular, chauvinistic nationalism unrestrained by some higher authority: 'No leader of a democracy without other ancestry but the sudden shout of a multitude [...] will have any interest in calling brother the leader of another democracy – a chief as fatherless and heirless as himself' (*NLL*, 87). For Conrad, the 'sin of the old European Monarchies was not the absolutism inherent in every form of government; it was the inability to alter the forms of their legality grown narrow and oppressive with the march of time' (*NLL*, 84). In Conrad's view, Germany since Bismarck was the apotheosis of modern, violent interpretations of nationalism, and in Conrad's essay Germany emerges as 'a powerful and voracious organism full of unscrupulous self-confidence, whose appetite for aggrandisement will only be limited by the power of helping itself to the severed members of its friends and neighbours' (*NLL*, 86). At the time of writing *Nostromo* and 'Autocracy and War,' Conrad would also doubtless have been aware that the Romantic understanding of the Polish nation, with its emphasis on diversity and plurality, that had driven and inspired thinkers such as Cieszkowski, Buszczyński, and Korzeniowski, was being usurped and promoted as a reactionary, exclusionary concept with the rise of Roman Dmowski's anti-semitic National Democratic Party in Poland in the late-1890s.[13] Conrad is representative of what the early theorist of nationalism Carlton Hayes, writing in 1931, labelled 'humanitarian nationalism,' exemplified by those such as Rousseau and Herder, who 'believed in the natural division of the human race into

---

[12] Julia Kristeva, *Nations without Nationalism*, translated by Leon S. Roudiez (New York: Columbia University Press, 1993), 32.

[13] Throughout his life, Dmowski (1864–1939) sought to work within Russian power structures for Poland's cause, and he was the persistent ideological opponent of Marshal Józef Piłsudski (1867–1935), Poland's first post-war Chief of State (1918–22), and later dictator between 1926 and 1935. While both Piłsudski and Dmowski's view of Polish nationality invariably reproduced nineteenth-century Romantic political rhetoric, they had divergent understandings of Polish identity. For Piłsudski, an inspirational figure for Conrad in the re-establishing of Poland's independence, ethnic purity was not paramount, whereas it became the foundation of Dmowski's xenophobic politics. In 1917, Dmowski sent to Capel House a copy of his *Problems of Central and Eastern Europe* (1917), a work attacking German imperialism as Poland's principal enemy, for which he received a brief reply from Conrad (*CL* 6, 127).

distinct nationalities, all of which should be allowed to govern their own destinies and to follow their own path to freedom.'[14]

Herder's vision of Europe consisted of independent yet mutually respectful nations, similar to that promoted later by Stefan Buszczyński in his *La Décadence de l'Europe* and Conrad in 'Autocracy and War.' Conrad distinguishes between two types of nationalism. Europe is dominated by the 'doctrine of nationalities' (*NLL*, 86). This can be interpreted positively, as each nation enjoys independence while accepting the entitlement of other nations to the same right. However, Conrad also notes the tendency of individual nations to impose on the balance of European power. Seeing a degree of European harmony as the only way towards a peaceful unfolding of history, Conrad observes that the 'evolution of the idea of nationality as we see it concreted at the present time' has been effective in 'creating close knit communities possessing the ability, the will and the power to pursue a common ideal' alongside a 'wider solidarity.' However, 'the solidarity of Europeanism which must be the next step towards the advent of Concord and Justice [...] [and] the only possible goal of our progress' was being held back by the 'fatal worship of force and the errors of national selfishness' (*NLL*, 81).

The concept of the nation forms a recurring theme in Conrad's writing in the early years of the century. Alongside the detailed representation of nineteenth-century South American politics and history in *Nostromo*, between 1904 and 1911 Conrad publicly grappled with his Polish identity in 'Autocracy and War' (1905), *A Personal Record*, 'Prince Roman,' in which the author portrayed early nineteenth-century Poland and the rising of 1830, and, of course, *Under Western Eyes*, where Conrad addressed the subject of Russia. In these works, Conrad revealed his Polish origins to the new national environment of his English readership. An illuminating example of the weight Conrad attached to nationality exists in his response to Robert Lynd's review of *A Set of Six*, published in the *Daily News* in August 1908. The question of identity resurfaced for Conrad when Lynd wrote: 'Mr. Conrad, without either country or language, may be thought to have

---

[14] Paul Lawrence, *Nationalism: History and Theory* (London: Longman, 2005), 88. See Carlton J. H. Hayes, *The Historical Evolution of Modern Nationalism* (1931; New York: Macmillan, 1949), 13–42.

found a new patriotism for himself in the sea. His vision of men, however, is the vision of a cosmopolitan, of a homeless person.'[15] Lynd addressed sensitive subjects to a Pole raised in the traditions of early nineteenth-century Polish philosophy, particularly Conrad, who had recently been accused of deserting Poland by Eliza Orzeszkowa in her essay 'The Emigration of Talent' in 1899. Lynd adopted a Herderian approach to dispossessing Conrad, announcing that a 'writer who ceases to see the world coloured by his own language – for language gives colour to thoughts and things in a way that few people understand – is apt to lose the concentration and intensity of vision without which the greatest literature cannot be made. It was a sort of nationalism of language and outlook that kept wanderers like Turgénieff and Browning from ever becoming cosmopolitan and second rate.'[16] In presenting Conrad as a literary vagabond, Lynd, who later came to respect Conrad's work, deprived the author of his nationality, culture, language, and, significantly, assumed Conrad's patriotism – a venerated concept in Polish history – to be mere loyalty to the ocean.[17]

It is worth reiterating that a distinction between an inclusive patriotism and an aggressive nationalism, such as that outlined by theorist Elie Kedourie, is relevant to Conrad.[18] In the context of Polish history, as Brian Porter has explained, to write about such issues is to 'enter a terminological minefield,' for while patriotism is regarded as a noble and benign idea, nationalism 'is unambiguously an expression of opprobrium, so to speak (in Polish) of a nationalist tradition that extends across the entire nineteenth century and includes such diverse figures as [Stanisław] Staszic, Mickiewicz, and Dmowski is either absurd or incendiary.'[19] This distinction applies to 'Autocracy and War,' which encourages 'conceptions of legality, of larger patriotism, of national duties and aspirations,' while at the same time condemning emerging doctrines of popular nationalism that cultivate 'the fatal worship of force and the errors of national selfishness' (*NLL*, 81).

---

[15] Sherry ed., *Critical Heritage*, 211.

[16] Sherry ed., *Critical Heritage*, 210–11.

[17] On the evolution of Lynd's attitude to Conrad, see Richard Niland, '"Who's that Fellow Lynn?": Conrad and Robert Lynd,' *The Conradian* 33.1 (2008), 130–44.

[18] See Elie Kedourie, *Nationalism* (1960; Oxford: Blackwell, 1993), 68.

[19] Porter, *When Nationalism Began to Hate*, 13.

Nostromo gains its ironic power from its exposé of those who distort the language of patriotism for the advancement of material interests, be they Monterists seeking the subjection of Sulaco and control of the San Tomé silver-mine, or those such as Martin Decoud pursuing the creation of the Occidental Republic of Sulaco. As Decoud notes: 'What is a conviction? A particular view of our personal advantage either practical or emotional. No one is a patriot for nothing. The word serves us well' (*N*, 189). Still, for Conrad, patriotism is interpreted as a noble concept, one easily exploited by those seeking political power. In 'Prince Roman,' Conrad observed 'some exchange of ideas about patriotism – a somewhat discredited sentiment, because the delicacy of our humanitarians regards it as a relic of barbarism' (*TH*, 29). If, as Kedourie notes, patriotism, unlike nationalism, allows for the absence of commitment to a particular political order, then Conrad likewise appears to interpret it as such, with the essence of true patriotism holding a degree of Platonic perfection. Conrad understands patriotism as an inherited duty to the spiritual nation, particularly one enslaved by the aggressive power of another nationalism. Nationalism, on the other hand, raises connotations of that great concern of Conrad's writing, the danger of the individual being subsumed within a larger social or political identity.

Reacting to Robert Lynd's review, Conrad wrote to Edward Garnett lamenting that he had been labelled 'a man without country and language. It is like abusing a tongue-tied man. For what can one say. The statement is simple and brutal; and any answer would involve too many feelings of one's inner life, stir too much secret bitterness and complex loyalty' (*CL* 4, 108). The complex loyalty Conrad felt in relation to his Polish background becomes one of the reasons why Conrad deals with both traditional and modern understandings of nationalism. The years before the First World War found Conrad living in a culture where 'theorists were beginning to step outside the paradigm of nationalism, to think conceptually about the issues involved and to question received assumptions pertaining to the antiquity of nations and the desirability of the nationalist principle.'[20] In his influential 1882 lecture *Qu'est-ce qu'une nation?* French theologian Ernest

---

[20] Lawrence, *Nationalism: History and Theory*, 50.

Renan recalled Herder and explored ideas that historians such as Ernest Gellner and Benedict Anderson later developed. For Renan, nations 'are not something eternal. They have begun, they will end. [...] At the present time the existence of nations happens to be good, even necessary. Their existence is a guarantee of liberty.'[21] Renan's essay, like 'Autocracy and War,' was influenced by the French defeat in the Franco-Prussian War and the direction of a Europe dominated by an increasingly powerful Germany. For Conrad, the 'war of 1870 [...] was the first characterised by a special intensity of hate, by a new note in the tune of an old song for which we may thank the Teutonic thoroughness' (*NLL*, 87). In the same pages where he warned of the rise of German nationalism, Conrad also articulated his belief in a benign Polish nationality constituting an inherited past and shared culture. Equally, Renan wrote that neither race, language, religion, community of interests, nor geography were enough to constitute a nation. He declared that 'a nation is a soul, a spiritual principle,' and its determining bond was the 'possession in common of a rich legacy of remembrances. [...] To have common glories in the past, a common will in the present.'

Although Renan acknowledged that recognition of the national idea was a particularly modern phenomenon, the identity of the nation nevertheless stretched into the historical past: 'A nation is a grand solidarity constituted by the sentiment of sacrifices which one has made and of those that one is disposed to make again. It presupposes a past, it renews itself especially in the present by a tangible deed: the approval, the desire, clearly expressed, to continue the communal life.'[22] While Conrad negotiates with such contemporary adoptions of Herder's thought, his language of nationality, particularly in *Nostromo* – with Giorgio Viola's worship of legendary Italian patriot Giuseppe Garibaldi (1807–82), his condemnation of Count Cavour (1810–61), and the novel's allusion to the political art of Francisco de Goya

---

[21] Ernest Renan, 'Qu'est-ce qu'une nation?' *Nationalism*, edited by John Hutchinson and Anthony D. Smith, 17–18.

[22] Renan, 'Qu'est-ce qu'une nation?' 17–18.

(1746–1828) – also connects to a broader popular tradition of European nationalism.[23]

The Italian patriot and thinker Giuseppe Mazzini (1805–72) embraced Herder's philosophy in his articulation of his 'Young Italy' movement in the 1840s, and Conrad's sympathetic depiction of Viola in *Nostromo*, the inheritor of Mazzini and Garibaldi's liberal nationalism, is consistent with Conrad's broad historical support for national independence movements, particularly those opposing the empires that controlled Poland. Viola is 'the Idealist of the old, humanitarian revolutions' (*N*, xix). For Mazzini, 'Natural divisions, the spontaneous tendencies of the peoples will replace the arbitrary divisions sanctioned by bad governments. The countries of the people will rise, defined by the voice of the free, upon the ruins of the countries of Kings and privileged castes.'[24] In Conrad's *Suspense* (1925), which reworked aspects of Stendhal's *La Chartreuse de Parme* (1839) in its historical and geographical settings, Conrad portrayed the beginnings of nationalist sentiment in the territories of Italy controlled by the Austrian Empire that Mazzini and Garibaldi would later oppose. The Austrian chancellor Metternich, the most influential politician in the relatively settled Europe after the Congress of Vienna of 1815, famously dismissed Italy as a mere

---

[23] Gustav Morf suggests that Conrad's use of 3 May – the only date mentioned in *Nostromo* – is a reminder of the Polish constitution of 1791. Conrad, however, knew Goya's work (*CL* 4, 299), and he owned a copy of William Rothenstein's *Goya* (1900). In writing of Don José Avellanos's torture by the regime of Guzman Bento, Conrad evokes Goya's *Executions of the 3ʳᵈ of May* (1814), which depicts French military reprisals on Spanish civilians during the Peninsular War (1807–14): 'A lucky one or two of that spectral company of prisoners would perhaps be led tottering behind a bush to be shot by a file of soldiers. [...] The irregular report of the firing squad would be heard, followed sometimes by a single finishing shot' (*N*, 138). Also, the gatekeeper's memory of Don Enrique Gould's execution is rendered in Goyan tones: '[He] had, on that fatal morning, followed the firing-squad; and, peeping from behind one of the cypresses growing along the wall of the Franciscan Convent, had seen, with his eyes starting out of his head, Don Enrique throw up his hands and fall with his face in the dust' (*N*, 382).

[24] G. Mazzini, *The Duties of Man* (London: Dent, 1907), 52. Regarding Conrad's relationship with central figures in nineteenth-century European nationalism, one could trace a web of influences from Conrad's creation of Viola through Garibaldi, Mickiewicz, Mazzini, and Herder, particularly given Mickiewicz's friendship with Mazzini and the importance of Herder's philosophy in the development of Mazzini's 'Young Italy' movement. See Harry Hearder, *Italy in the Age of Risorgimento* (London: Longman, 1983). Further, one of Conrad's sources for *Nostromo* was the *Mémoires de Garibaldi*, translated by Alexandre Dumas *père*. See Cedric Watts, *Joseph Conrad: Nostromo* (London: Penguin, 1990), 28.

'geographical expression.' Yet, it was the fate of such geographical expressions – Greece, Belgium, Germany, and Italy – to achieve reasonably stable political identities during the nineteenth century. Conrad's position as a Pole immersed in the philosophy of his native country, a philosophy developed during Metternich's rule of part of historic Poland, contributes to *Nostromo's* engagement with discourses of nationalism in nineteenth-century Europe.

HERDER, CIESZKOWSKI, AND THE POLISH ROMANTIC NATION

Lord Acton, Cambridge professor of history, in his essay 'Nationality' (1862), associated modern concepts of nationalism, particularly an insistence on political identity, with the third partition of Poland in 1795: 'Thenceforth there was a nation demanding to be united in a State, – a soul, as it were, wandering in search of a body in which to begin life over again.'[25] In 'The Crime of Partition' (1919), written before the Versailles peace conference confirmed the reappearance of Poland on the political map of Europe, Conrad echoed Acton, explaining that the disappearance of the Polish state in 1795 gave birth to the peripatetic and yearning national soul: 'the spirit of the nation refused to rest therein. It haunted the territories of the Old Republic in the manner of a ghost haunting its ancestral mansion [...]. Poland deprived of its independence, of its historical continuity, and with its religion and language persecuted and repressed, became a mere geographical expression.' (*NLL*, 96). Conrad reveals not only his indebtedness to a European discourse of nationality, but also, as discussed earlier, to the language of Polish patriotism, which adopted cultural philosophies of nationalism after the 1795 partition.[26]

[25] Lord Acton, *Essays on Freedom and Power*, edited with an introduction by Gertrude Himmelfarb (London: Thames, 1956), 146.

[26] For the extent of Conrad's indebtedness to Józef Retinger's *La Pologne et l'équilibre européen* (1916) in the composition of 'The Crime of Partition,' see Stape ed., *Notes on Life and Letters*, 420–25.

In Poland of the Romantic period and in Conrad's discussions of the nation, the 'distinction between a geopolitical Poland and an ideal Poland – "national spirit" – [which] was the foundation of early nineteenth-century nationalism,' is paramount.[27] Conrad suggests that political independence will ensure the re-emergence of Poland's ruptured historical continuity, with the spirit of the nation providing justification for Poland's right to political restoration. In its promotion of a cultural nationalism in place of political dispossession, Polish Romantic philosophy was influenced by Herder in developing the idea of the spiritual nation in the absence of the Polish state. In *Ideas for a Philosophy of the History of Mankind* (1784–91), Herder expressed the hope that Slavs would 'awake refreshed from your long listless slumber and, having shaken off the chains of slavery, will enjoy again the possession of your fair lands.'[28] In Central and Eastern Europe, it 'was music to the ears of an aspiring nationalist to be told that existing states were only phantoms while ethnic cultures were the expression of true reality, merely awaiting development.'[29]

The manifestation of Herder's ideas in Poland can be seen in the work of philosopher Maurycy Mochnacki, who gave his most Herderian view of the nation in *On Polish Literature in the Nineteenth Century* (1830), writing: 'the nation is not a collection of people living on a territory defined by certain borders. Rather, the essence of a nation is the collection of all concepts and feelings regarding religion, political institutions, legislation, [and] customs. [The national essence] even has a tight bond with geographical location, climate and other factors of empirical existence.'[30] August Cieszkowski refers to Herder throughout

---

[27] Porter, *When Nationalism Began to Hate*, 21.

[28] Barnard, *Herder on Nationality, Humanity and History*, 13–14.

[29] F.M. Barnard, 'National Culture and Political Legitimacy: Herder and Rousseau,' 245–46. Conrad's view of Polish nationhood perhaps represents a subdued version of the ideas of Friedrich Engels (1820–95), whose 'support for the restoration of historical Poland was thus combined with an outspoken refusal to acknowledge the right of self-determination by Ukranians, Lithuanians, and Belorussians. In his view "historical nations" (like Poland) had a right to separate and independent existence while ethnic "nonhistorical" nationalities did not have such a right, because separatism contradicted the centralist tendency of progress.' Andrzej Walicki, *The Enlightenment and the Birth of Modern Nationhood: Polish Political Thought from Noble Republicanism to Tadeusz Kołciuszko* (Notre Dame: University of Notre Dame Press, 1989), 121.

[30] Quoted in Porter, *When Nationalism Began to Hate*, 21.

the *Prolegomena zur Historiosophie*, and, as André Liebach has noted, Cieszkowski 'appealed to the authority of Schiller and Herder' in his outlining of his new philosophy.[31] In the chapter of the *Prolegomena* entitled 'The Teleology of Universal History,' Cieszkowski, directly echoing Schiller, wrote of '*culture, humanity, the aesthetic education of mankind*,' praising Herder for his focus on 'the empirical matter of universal history.'[32] The initial basis of Cieszkowski's philosophy was an acceptance of the cultural nation in the tradition of both Herder and philosopher Johann Gottlieb Fichte's later *Addresses to the German Nation* (1808), with the culture and empirical matter of the nation becoming the foundation of what Mickiewicz would portray as Poland's messianic, spiritual existence.

Conrad's conception of the Polish nation also promotes the national character and a mystical national spirit. In 'A Note on the Polish Problem,' written during the Great War, Conrad insisted that 'Poland exists as a spiritual entity to-day as definitely as it ever existed in her past' (*NLL*, 108). He later claimed in 'The Crime of Partition' that the re-emerging Polish state would be bonded by the national spirit: 'Polish loyalty will be rooted in something much more solid and enduring [. . .]. It will be rooted in the national temperament which is about the only thing on earth that can be trusted' (*NLL*, 129). Conrad's representation of Poland consistently advocates the nation as an ideal construct bound by the spirit of its cultural heritage, existing above, although always conscious of, the confines of any political reality.

In his only story set in nineteenth-century Poland, 'Prince Roman,' Conrad offered a tableau of the nation grounded in Polish Romantic philosophy. Conrad's narrator announces that the Polish nation 'demands to be loved as no other country has ever been loved' (*TH*, 51). The eponymous prince communes with the landscape and the spiritual nation: 'And this familiar landscape associated with the days without thought and without sorrow, this land the charm of which he felt without even looking at it soothed his pain, like the presence of an old friend who sits silent and disregarded by one in some dark hour of life.' (*TH*, 38) The nation and the individual merge through the unifying bonds of geography and shared history. Importantly, an

---

[31] Cieszkowski, *Selected Writings*, 13.
[32] Cieszkowski, *Selected Writings*, 66.

embracing, inclusive national spirit inhabits this landscape. Roman encounters 'the Jew Yankel, innkeeper and tenant of all the mills on the estate, [who] was a Polish patriot' (*TH*, 39). Conrad's narrator explains: 'It requires a certain greatness of soul to interpret patriotism worthily – or else a sincerity of feeling denied to the vulgar refinement of modern thought which cannot understand the august simplicity of a sentiment proceeding from the very nature of things and men' (*TH*, 29–30). Conrad's language envisages a harmonious bond between the individual and his cultural background, concurring with Herder's view that 'the cultural bonds which linked members of a nation into a relational whole were not *things* or artefacts imposed from above but living energies (*Kräfte*) emanating from within, shared meanings and sentiments which in time form a people's collective soul.'[33] Along with his Jewish ethnicity and culture, Yankel also sees his identity connected to the history of the Polish nation: 'I was already a married man when the French and all the other nations passed this way with Napoleon. Tse! Tse! That was a great harvest for death, *nu*! Perhaps this time God will help' (*TH*, 39). Conrad's Poland, with its emphasis on shared historical memory, maintains Herder and Polish Romanticism's inclusiveness.

An insistence on national diversity had been promoted by Polish Romantics to increase the numbers of those prepared to engage in patriotic activity for the return of Poland's political identity. In a Polish Romantic context, 'the link between ethnicity and the nation was always uncertain. [...] Joachim Lelewel [1786–1861], one of the most influential patriotic writers of the era (and its leading historian), instructed his countrymen not to 'differentiate the sons of Poland, whether they speak the Ruthenian, Polish, or Lithuanian language.'[34] In addition to ethnic and linguistic concord, Polish Romanticism advocated a broad imagining of the nation in a social context. August Cieszkowski's *Słowa*

---

[33] F.M. Barnard, 'National Culture and Political Legitimacy: Herder and Rousseau,' 242.

[34] Porter, *When Nationalism Began to Hate*, 19–20. While Conrad had misgivings about Wincenty Lutosławski's messianic nationalism, correspondences exist between the two writers. In *The Polish Nation* (1917), Lutosławski challenged linguistic nationalism, something the trilingual Conrad obviously had no interest in maintaining: 'No national state of Europe stands the test of linguistic unity: everywhere we see languages other than the national language spoken, sometimes totally different from the official language of the State' (15).

wieszcze Polaka wyrzeczone roku [*Prophetic Words of a Pole*] (1848) announced the politicisation of the people: 'As history calls successive peoples to the forefront so too it calls different estates of society in turn to the arena of deeds. The *higher* and *middle* estates have already played splendid roles in history and have fulfilled salutary missions for humanity. Today begins the era of activity for the *last estate*.'[35] The shifting parameters of those who guard the Polish national spirit were analysed by Conrad in 'Prince Roman,' as the story announces the breakdown of social and cultural barriers. Conrad's narrator speaks of the ruling *szlachta*, remarking: 'No longer born to command – which is the very essence of aristocracy – it becomes difficult for them [noblemen] to do aught else but hold aloof from the great movements of popular passion' (*TH*, 30). When Prince Roman decides to participate in the 1830 insurrection, his father, Prince John, 'moved and uneasy, speaking from a purely aristocratic point of view, mistrusted the popular origins of the movement, regretted its democratic tendencies, and did not believe in the possibility of success' (*TH*, 40). However, through Roman's involvement in the patriotic struggle, Conrad's Poland includes class and ethnic collaboration, collapsing the internal divisions within the nation. Prince John's patriotism leads him to avoid full condemnation of the uprising: 'There are secular principles of legitimacy and order which have been violated in this reckless enterprise for the sake of most subversive illusions. Though of course the patriotic impulses of the heart...' (*TH*, 40).

In *A Personal Record*, Conrad insisted that the 1863 revolt was an assertion of liberal nationalism, a revolt 'against foreign domination,' and that his father never advocated the 'subversion of any social or political scheme of existence. He was simply a patriot in the sense of a man who believing in the spirituality of a national existence could not bear to see that spirit enslaved' (*PR*, vii–viii). While critics have debated the extent of Apollo Korzeniowski's social radicalism, it is certain that Polish thought before the 1863 insurrection considered the extant social order and employed a discourse of inclusiveness. Conrad continued in this tradition, viewing the vista of Polish history in the context of Polish Romantic philosophy. 'A Note on the Polish Problem' presented the

[35] Cieszkowski, *Selected Writings*, 104.

Polish-Lithuanian Commonwealth as a varied entity, 'an organic, living thing capable of growth and development.' When 'Poland lost its independence this alliance and this union remained firm in spirit and fidelity. All the national movements towards liberation were initiated in the name of the whole mass of people inhabiting the limits of the Old Republic, and all the Provinces took part in them with complete devotion' (*NLL*, 98).[36] This idealistic, Romantic vision of Poland ensures that Conrad's Costaguana accommodates a turbulent modern pluralism while in the throes of political upheaval.

Nostromo's presentation 'of national, ethnic, and racial identities determines the manner in which the novel builds up such an inclusive picture of the people and politics of Costaguana.'[37] Conrad felt he had created the 'whole world of Costaguana' (*PR*, 100); a world holding myriad linguistic and cultural traditions including, amongst many others, the *mestizos* and descendants of African slaves who farm the coastal lands of Sulaco to Mrs. Viola's Chinese servants and the Casa Viola's Basque clientele. In his 'Author's Note' to the novel, Conrad wrote: 'Italians were swarming into the Occidental Province at the time' (*N*, xix), and the narrator explains that the natives were an 'outcast lot of very mixed blood' (*N*, 14). While *Nostromo* is relatively muted on the subject of the 'vanished nations' (*N*, 89) of the native population, accurately capturing early nineteenth-century Latin American attitudes to indigenous culture, the Sulacan elite embodies the modern confusion of Costaguanan identity.[38] Appearances in Conrad's writing are notoriously deceptive, so while Charles Gould is descended from a family 'established in Costaguana for three generations' (*N*, 46), he continues to look 'thoroughly English.' However, Gould 'astonished you to hear

---

[36] In 'Autocracy and War,' Conrad insisted that 'Through all the centuries of its existence Poland has never been a menace to anybody [. . .]. The spirit of aggressiveness was absolutely foreign to the Polish temperament' (*NLL*, 97). In *The Books and the Pilgrimage of the Polish Nation*, Mickiewicz presented an identical view of Polish history: 'There was, again, no instance of Polish kings and Polish warriors conquering neighbouring countries with the sword; but they made other nations sharers of their brotherhood, uniting them in the common bond of faith and liberty' (16).

[37] GoGwilt, *Invention of the West*, 206.

[38] Holroyd, the US financier, is also a compound of nationalities and traditions. Holroyd's 'parentage is German and Scotch and English, with remote strains of Danish and French giving him the temperament of a Puritan and an insatiable imagination of conquest' (*N*, 76).

him talk Spanish (Castillan, as the natives say) or the Indian dialect of the country-people so naturally' (*N*, 48). Gould represents a figure that deals fluently if not reflectively with the 'complex loyalty' of his national identity.

The experience of Costaguana inducts immigrants such as Dr. Monygham into the national culture. Monygham's torture by the regime of Guzman Bento 'seemed to bind him indissolubly to the land of Costaguana like an awful procedure of naturalization' and 'did away with his Europeanism' (*N*, 375). Mrs. Gould 'had seen the land with a deeper glance than a trueborn Costaguanera could have done' (*N*, 86), and her travels amongst the 'burdened Indians' brought her 'nearer to the soul of the land' (*N*, 87). Nostromo, with his 'distinct experience of the country' (*N*, 417), represents Rousseau's 'social man,' one who 'only knows how to live in the opinion of others, so that he seems to receive the consciousness of his own existence merely from the judgement of others concerning him.'[39] As Peter Mallios notes, 'the primary significance of Nostromo's being "of the people" is that he provides the novel with its only major character who concretely interfaces with the people in all their diversity.'[40]

In his review of *Nostromo* in the *Speaker* in November 1904, Edward Garnett argued that Conrad provided 'a whole national drama.'[41] Before analysing the various historical trajectories national identity may take, Conrad renders Costaguanan culture through a portrayal of its diverse national traditions. The opening of *Nostromo* binds landscape, inhabitants, and history through the legend of two gringos who have succumbed to the mysterious power of buried treasure in the rocky headlands of the Sulacan coast. The traditions of Costaguana reflect the unfolding plight of Nostromo while illuminating the violent and tumultuous political history of the country: 'The popular lore of all nations testified that duplicity and cunning, together with bodily strength, were looked upon, even more than courage, as heroic virtues by primitive mankind' (*N*, 385). Monygham believes that Costaguanan politics are 'true to the very spirit of the country' (*N*, 315). While

---

[39] Rousseau, *Social Contract*, 220.
[40] Peter Mallios, 'Undiscovering the Country: Conrad, Fitzgerald, and Meta-National Form,' *Modern Fiction Studies* 47.2 (2001): 369.
[41] Sherry ed., *Critical Heritage*, 175.

Conrad links the spirit of Costaguana with its disparate inhabitants, Frederic Jameson notes the polarity of European and indigenous political affiliation at the Casa Viola: 'No native of Costaguana intruded there. This was the Italian stronghold' (*N*, 32).[42] However, as Christopher GoGwilt has countered, the unfolding of Costaguana's history depends 'on an increasing confusion of this clear-cut distinction between European and "native."'[43]

Conrad's ethnic, linguistic, and cultural fusion of native and European emerges distinctly in his representation of popular festivals. The Costaguanan spirit manifests itself in the dynamic culture of the *cargadores*, immigrants, and 'groups of people from the distant campo' (*N*, 126). Nostromo is absorbed by 'music vibrating and shrieking with a racking rhythm, overhung by the tremendous, sustained, hollow roar of the gombo. The barbarous and imposing noise of the big drum, that can madden a crowd, and that even Europeans cannot hear without a strange emotion, seemed to draw Nostromo on to its source' (*N*, 126). According to Carlton Hayes, the Romantic focus on folk traditions assembled 'the stone and mortar for the impressive modern temple of nationalism,'[44] and in unveiling his complex and chaotic portrait of a nation Conrad draws on this early Romantic heritage to present the cultural reality of Costaguana. Once established, *Nostromo* proceeds to foreground competing interpretations of national identity, and the divisive influence of the San Tomé mine ensures that a 'sense of nationhood as an ideal but impossible social limit – both the only effective mechanism of social cohesion imaginable, and a mechanism impossible to imagine in Costaguana – runs throughout the novel.'[45]

[42] See Frederic Jameson, *The Political Unconscious: Narrative as Socially Symbolic Act* (1981; London: Routledge, 2002), 194–271.

[43] GoGwilt, *Invention of the West*, 199.

[44] Carlton Hayes, *Essays on Nationalism* and *The Historical Evolution of Modern Nationalism* (New York: Macmillan, 1931), 53. Russian Westernizer Vissarion Belinsky (1811–48) famously railed against the romanticising of folk traditions, insisting that 'Nationality is not a home-spun coat, bast slippers, cheap vodka, or sour cabbage.' Quoted in Andrzej Walicki, *A History of Russian Thought from the Enlightenment to Marxism* (Oxford: Clarendon Press, 1988), 140.

[45] Mallios, 'Undiscovering the Country,' 377.

NOSTROMO: CREATING THE OCCIDENTAL REPUBLIC

In his unfinished *Project of Constitution for Corsica* (1765), Rousseau wrote that the foundation of a political nation was the national character. Each 'people has or should have one, and if the national character is lacking one must begin by giving it to the people.'[46] *Nostromo* traces the imposition of a new national character onto the province of Sulaco. Martin Decoud sits within Giorgio Viola's L'Albergo d'Italia Una – another signpost of the importance of nineteenth-century nationalism in the novel – formulating his thoughts on the creation of the Occidental Republic of Sulaco. The 'birth of another South American Republic' (*N*, 223) within the hallowed halls of the tradition of nineteenth-century European nationalism sceptically questions the origins of modern national identity. As GoGwilt has written, 'L'Albergo d'Italia Una becomes the locus for an entirely imaginary projection of European political form.'[47] Decoud's secessionist rhetoric 'makes a coincidence of local geography stand for the geopolitical interests of multinational capitalism.'[48] Decoud, echoing Renan's *Qu-est-ce qu'une nation?* promotes the historical continuity of the Occidental province as the foundation of its new national identity: For Decoud, Sulaco has 'always been distinct and separated,' and the 'Occidental territory is large enough to make any man's country' (*N*, 184). The secession of Sulaco and its relationship to the Gould Concession invites the suspicion that once 'the process [of industrialisation] has started, deliberate pioneers and "leaders of national awakening" attempt to cash in by engineering their own versions [of identity], but their actions are only supplementary to the underlying driving force of industrialisation.'[49] Although Decoud endorses a historical national identity for Sulaco, the San Tomé mine has manifestly constructed the allegedly latent bonds of Sulacan solidarity.

[46] Quoted in Josep R. Llobera, *The God of Modernity: The Development of Nationalism in Western Europe* (Oxford: Berg, 1994), 161.
[47] GoGwilt, *Invention of the West*, 200–1.
[48] GoGwilt, *Invention of the West*, 211.
[49] Lawrence, *Nationalism: History and Theory*, 138.

Nostromo divulges how the modern political and economic realities displace the collective folk history of the nation. The San Tomé mine assumes centre stage in the fortunes of Costaguana, and Conrad's language reflects the new binding power in the community: 'The Gould concession was a serious asset in the country's finance, and, what was more, in the private budgets of many officials as well. It was traditional. It was known. It was said. It was credible' (*N*, 402). Economic necessity has eclipsed the cultural bonds that open the novel, and the needs of industrial capitalism will henceforth control the customs of the people. At the festive inauguration of the dictator Don Vincente Ribeira, Charles Gould declares: 'All this piece of land belongs now to the Railway Company. There will be no more popular feasts held here' (*N*, 123). The mine authorises manifestations of the communal spirit and restricts the individuality of the workers during official festivals. The San Tomé mine 'had altered, too, the outward character of the crowds on feast days on the *plaza*,' who wear 'white ponchos with a green stripe affected as holiday wear by the San Tomé miners' (*N*, 97). It is noted that green is 'the colour of hope, being also the colour of the mine' (*N*, 99). As Nostromo points out to the dying Mrs. Viola, the silver of the mine is now a 'greater treasure than the one which they say is guarded by ghosts and devils in Azuera' (*N*, 255). Material interests have devalued cultural tradition.

Nostromo prefigures theories of nationalism and its relationship to modernity developed in the 1960s by historians such as Ernest Gellner and Karl Deutsch. Modernisation theory argued that 'nationalism was a *function* (in some ways a by-product) of the transition to modernity. In other words, not only was nationalism created by the forces of industrialisation and modernisation, rather than by popular will and sentiment, nations per se had not even existed until after the advent of modernity.'[50] With its focus on the erosion of the culture of Costaguana, *Nostromo* anticipates Deutsch's view that as 'men leave the relative security of villages and folk cultures for the mobility and uncertainty of travel, towns, and markets, and for the competition of wealth-getting, politics, and warfare,' they may experience a

---

[50] Lawrence, *Nationalism: History and Theory*, 11–12.

corresponding sense of cultural isolation and loss.[51] *Nostromo* analyses the ease with which modernity creates a sense of national community. Decoud writes of the mutability of the national idea, revealing his manipulation of the people: 'Their sentiment was necessary to the very life of my plan; the sentimentalism of the people that will never do anything for the sake of their passionate desire, unless it comes to them clothed in the fair robes of an idea' (*N*, 239). Decoud illuminates Ernest Gellner's view of modern nation formation: 'Nationalism is not the awakening of nations to self-consciousness: it invents nations where they do not exist.'[52]

One of the concerns of any emerging nation is the nurturing of national consciousness and the empowerment of history as the arbiter of national identity. This is evident in the appeals to the past of Polish Romanticism, the Irish literary renaissance of the 1890s, and of course in Conrad's own writing on Poland, to take but three examples. Conrad's scepticism about the new Sulacan nation and its leaders of national awakening is consolidated by the novel's focus on written history. The necessity of presenting a well-founded national story was articulated amongst Conrad's contemporaries. In the journal *Atlantic Monthly* in 1890, John Franklin Jameson wrote that 'there is almost always a close connection between the course of a nation's political history and the development of its historiography.'[53] *Nostromo* acquires its modernity through awareness of such issues as writing the nation. Peter Mallios has explained that in Costaguana there 'are as many different national plans, moreover, as there are national authors,'[54] including the varied historical perspectives of Gould, Viola, Avellanos, Decoud, and the Monterists. From Conrad's 'use' of Don José Avellanos's *History of Fifty Years of Misrule* as a source for the novel to Captain Mitchell's insistence upon the historical nature of every event in Sulaco – 'This marks an epoch'

[51] Karl W. Deutsch, 'The Growth of Nations: Some Recurrent Patterns of Political and Social Integration,' *World Politics* 5.2 (1953): 182. See also Karl Deutsch, *Nationalism and Social Communication: An Inquiry into the Foundations of Nationality* (London: Chapman & Hall, 1953).

[52] Ernest Gellner, *Thought and Change* (London: Weidenfeld & Nicholson, 1972), 168.

[53] John Franklin Jameson, 'The Development of Modern European Historiography,' *Atlantic Monthly* 66 (1890): 322.

[54] Mallios, 'Undiscovering the Country,' 376.

(*N*, 68) – *Nostromo* watches history unfold, with an accepted and digestible documentation of the past shaping national identity.

The *History of Fifty Years of Misrule*, which seeks to give Costaguana an 'honourable place in the comity of civilized nations' (*N*, 140), fails to diffuse a coherent political identity for Costaguana, engendering a new history of the emerging Sulacan Republic. Conrad contrasts the popular history of Costaguana, transmitted through its folk traditions, with the interpretations of the nation's history amongst the intelligentsia, thereby continuing investigations of the boundaries between oral and written history. Michael Greaney has noted that the 'transformation of Sulaco into an independent republic is accompanied by a remarkable outpouring of writing – letters, front-line reportage, newspaper propaganda, historical memoirs, constitutional documents – as the written word imposes its authority on a raucous oral culture.'[55] The failure of Avellanos's *History* to reach publication, and Costaguana's inability to attain a stable political form, can be attributed to the force of the San Tomé mine and its intrusion into the economic, political, historical, and even literary life of the nation. In composing his historical opus, Avellanos had 'one ever-present aim to preserve the inviolable character of the mine at every cost' (*N*, 112). The *History of Misrule* attempts to bind the troubled past of Costaguana into a cogent history, but the scattering of its pages through the town square of Sulaco symbolises that Avellanos's history of Costaguana has been superseded by an historical positivism, which demands the creation of Sulaco. It falls to Decoud, ostensibly supporting the cause solely for his love of Antonia Avellanos, to use his standing as journalist to rewrite the history of Sulaco. As Conrad observed in 'Autocracy and War,' the 'ground of every revolution has to be intellectually prepared' (*NLL*, 84). Don José Avellanos now asks that Decoud's newspaper the *Porvenir* 'voice the aspirations of the province' (*N*, 158). In analysing the factors involved in the emergence of modern nationalism, Benedict Anderson notes the importance of 'the novel and the newspaper. For these forms provided the technical means for "re-presenting" the kind of imagined community that is the nation.'[56] In re-presenting Sulaco as a separate state through his journalism, Decoud is conscious, however, that his plan of secession is

[55] Greaney, *Conrad, Language, and Narrative*, 116.
[56] Benedict Anderson, *Imagined Communities* (London: Verso, 1991), 24–25.

'contrary to the doctrine [of Costaguanan unity] laid down in the "History of Fifty Years' Misrule"' (*N*, 185). Decoud's articulation of the new identity of Sulaco is merely one version of Costaguanan history.

Nostromo closes with the makers of the Sulacan revolution aiming to stabilise the flux of history into what can be considered a national past. The narrative's focus on Captain Mitchell's mythologising – 'Almost every event out of the usual daily course "marked an epoch" for him or else was "history"' (*N*, 112–13) – symbolises the 'invention of tradition,' incorporating the festivals and monuments of the constructed nation. The myriad ways in which the engineers of the secession, such as Avellanos, Decoud, and Nostromo, have become heroes of national history exposes how quickly the edifice of modern national identity and history can be erected. The monument to Don José Avellanos, the medallion-memorial to Martin Decoud, and Captain Mitchell's role as spokesman for the glory of the revolution betray how modern nationalism developed 'a nationalist ideology and rhetoric by a process of simplification, repetition and the dissemination of symbols and ceremonials.'[57] As Captain Mitchell leads tourists through Sulaco explaining its history, the Occidental Republic has already transformed its past into a recognisable history. However, the fragility of this new nation indicates that hostile ideologies will once more emerge to articulate their aspirations. In his 'Author's Note' to the novel, written in 1920, Conrad reported that the battle for Costaguana was still being fought, with the constructed Sulacan nation now 'a relic of the past disregarded by men awaiting impatiently the Dawns of other New Eras, the coming of more Revolutions' (*N*, xxii).

CIVILISATION AND BARBARISM: LATIN AMERICAN LITERATURE IN *NOSTROMO*

Nostromo's authentically complex world of Latin American politics and history derives from its ironic echoing of 'the single most influential

---

[57] Lawrence, *Nationalism: History and Theory*, 168–69. See *The Invention of Tradition*, edited by Eric Hobsbawm and Terence Ranger (Cambridge: Cambridge University Press, 1983).

literary work of modern Spanish American culture,'[58] Argentine writer
Domingo Faustino Sarmiento's (1811–88) *Facundo, civilización y barbarie* (1845), a stylised historical account treating the rule of political
strongmen and the ruptures between Federalist and Unitarist factions in
Argentina in the nineteenth century.[59] *Facundo*, a hitherto neglected
but essential context for *Nostromo*, was translated into French and
English in the 1850s and 1860s respectively, and since its original
publication in the journal *El Progreso* in 1845 it has had an immeasur-
able effect on the discourse of nationhood in South America. Mary
Mann's 1868 translation entitled *Life in the Argentine Republic in the
Days of Tyrants, or Civilization and Barbarism* uncannily recalls the
work in progress of Don José Avellanos and the riotous world of
Nostromo. By polarising the detached, materialistic European heritage
of Sulaco and the forces of political violence emanating from Costaguana, Conrad sceptically treated Sarmiento's dichotomy of civilisation
and barbarism, with the fictional historiography of *Nostromo* 'intended
for *all* South America in the seventh decade of the nineteenth-century'
(*CL* 6, 231).[60] This political contrast surfaces throughout Conrad's
work, with varying irony and sincerity; from an 'Outpost of Progress'
and 'Heart of Darkness' with their scrutiny of European Imperialism to
'Autocracy and War' and *Under Western Eyes*, where Conrad represents
Poland as an outpost of civilisation before Russian barbarism.

---

[58] Edwin Williamson, *The Penguin History of Latin America* (London: Penguin,
1992), 290.

[59] For a concise overview of Argentine history, see Félix Luna, *A Short History of the
Argentinians* (Buenos Aires: Booket, 2000). My sincere thanks to Laurence Davies for a
generous and detailed exchange of ideas on the subject of Sarmiento and *Facundo*.

[60] In addition to its analysis of the export economy of a South American nation, and
Decoud's portrayal as an Argentine dandy, numerous individual examples in *Nostromo*
indicate that Conrad drew specifically from Argentine history. Just as Conrad's Monteros represent the forces of violence and lawlessness, in *Facundo* Sarmiento notes the rise
of 'provincial, warlike associations, called *montoneras*, legitimate offspring of the tavern
and the field, hostile to the city' (54). *Nostromo's* Don Vincente Moraga is 'a doctor of
philosophy from the Cordova University' (*N*, 144), indicating not, as some critics have
cited, Cordoba in Spain, but as Sarmiento notes, Argentina's 'celebrated University of
Cordova, founded as long ago as the year 1613, and in whose gloomy cloisters eight
generations of medicine and divinity, both branches of law, illustrious writers, commen-
tators, and scholars have passed their youth' (107).

Facundo 'squarely addresses the question of nation-building,'[61] presenting the turbulent history of post-independence Argentina through a detailed anecdotal portrait of federalist *caudillo* (a charismatic and ruthless provincial leader) Facundo Quiroga (1788–1835), outlining his violent politics in the province of San Juan and La Rioja and his rivalry with brutal dictator Juan Manuel de Rosas (1793–1877). Sarmiento regarded his work as 'a summary of contemporary history, illustrated by the bright colors that reflect the costumes and habits of a nation, the dominating ideas, the tendencies of civilisation.'[62] In presenting his vision of Argentina, Sarmiento supported urban development, industry, French cultural influence, and he associated the traditions of the *gaucho* (the Argentine cowboy) with Rosas, Quiroga, and regressive forces hindering Argentina's progress. Life in the provinces, prone to the rule of local dictators, 'induces all the externals of barbarism.'[63] As gaucho culture became romanticised and part of Argentine identity in the later nineteenth century, especially through José Hernández's famous poem *Martín Fierro* (1872), *Facundo*, a fierce critique of the tradition, was absorbed into the national body of writing about the legendary plainsmen.[64] According to Ilan Stavans, by the late nineteenth century *Facundo* was labelled '*el Quijote de América*.'[65]

Just as *Nostromo* unveils the striking geographical features of Costaguana before sharpening its gaze to isolate historical developments in Sulaco, *Facundo* opens with a panoramic view of Latin America, framing the majestic landscape before locating civilisation and progress in the metropolis of Buenos Aires. However, beyond 'the precincts of the city everything assumes a new aspect,' and for Sarmiento the journey from the civilisation of the European-influenced city to the wilds of the interior polarised the 'people composing these two distinct forms of

---

[61] Williamson, *History of Latin America*, 290.

[62] Quoted in Ilan Stavans, introduction, Domingo F. Sarmiento, *Facundo, or Civilisation and Barbarism*, translated by Mary Peabody Mann (London: Penguin, 1998), x.

[63] Sarmiento, *Facundo*, 21.

[64] See Diana S. Goodrich, *Facundo and the Construction of Argentine Culture* (Austin: University of Texas Press, 1996). Sarmiento recognises the poetic potential of gaucho life but is unable to separate this from political manifestations of the culture. For a modern rendering of the gaucho identity, see Jorge Luis Borges, 'A Biography of Tadeo Isidoro Cruz (1829–74), *Collected Fictions*, translated by Andrew Hurley (London: Allen Lane, 1998), 212–14.

[65] Stavans, introduction, *Facundo*, viii.

society, [who] do not seem to belong to the same tradition.'[66] *Facundo* observes that 'two differing kinds of civilization existed in the Argentine Republic: one being Spanish, European, and cultivated, the other barbarous, American, and almost wholly of native growth.'[67] Sarmiento sought to lead Argentina to a modern identity and to free it from the ruthless sway of militaristic warlords:

> Have Facundo and Rosas ever done the least thing for the public good, or been interested in any useful object? No. From them come nothing but blood and crimes. I have given these details at length, because in the midst of horrors such as I am obliged to describe, it is comforting to pause on the few progressive impulses which revive again and again after being apparently crushed by savage barbarians. Civilization will, however feeble its present resistance, one day resume its place. There is a new world about to unfold itself, and it only awaits some fortunate general to put aside the iron heel which has so long crushed it.[68]

Conrad's intricate history adopts Sarmiento's rhetoric, but it destabilises *Facundo's* moralising by making all political ideologies complicit in the violent fragmentation of Costaguana. *Nostromo's* impassive cosmopolitan characters routinely condemn 'the persistent barbarism of our native continent' (*N*, 231), which subjects Costaguana to a cycle of vicious rulers cast in the mould of Quiroga, 'the barbarian of the interior; and Rosas, the bloodhound.'[69] Charles Gould's energetic but passionless development of the San Tomé mine and his support for the puppet dictator Vincente Ribeira is ostensibly inspired by his belief that economic development will eradicate the destructive forces at work in Costaguana: 'What is wanted here is law, good faith, order, security. Any one can declaim about these things, but I pin my faith to material interests' (*N*, 84). Gould aims to rewrite the narrative of Costaguanan history, hitherto a 'tissue of crimes'[70] bloodied by the dictator 'Guzman Bento of cruel memory' (*N*, 47) and later by the ferocious Monteros, whose combined achievements read like a compendium of events from *Facundo*: 'stories of political outrage; friends, relatives, ruined, imprisoned, killed in the battles of senseless civil wars, barbarously executed

---

[66] Sarmiento, *Facundo*, 19.
[67] Sarmiento, *Facundo*, 54.
[68] Sarmiento, *Facundo*, 168.
[69] Sarmiento, *Facundo*, 162.
[70] Sarmiento, *Facundo*, 168.

in ferocious proscriptions, as though the government of the country had been a struggle of lust between bands of absurd devils let loose upon the land' (*N*, 88).

One of Conrad's numerous sources on South American history for *Nostromo*, George Frederick Masterman's *Seven Eventful Years in Paraguay* (1869), treats the rule of Paraguayan dictator Fancisco López (1826–70), capturing the political contrasts of *Facundo*. Masterman notes the 'disturbed condition of the republics of the Plate; indeed, their normal state may be said to be that of revolution, and for the reason, perhaps, that there they are always talking about liberty, patriotism, and progress, without understanding the first, possessing the second, and indebted for the third to aliens, who advance them in spite of themselves.'[71] Antagonism between an avowedly authentic patriotism and an elitist European-shaped national vision appears throughout *Nostromo* and *Facundo*, becoming the unbridgeable gulf separating political factions. The national loyalty of Sulaco is tainted in the eyes of Monterists because of European influence, while for Decoud the native Costaguanan patriotism of General Montero symbolises 'the cry of dark barbarism, the cloak of lawlessness, of crimes, of rapacity, of simple thieving' (*N*, 187). For Sarmiento, 'the consummate Europeanized intellectual,' civilisation and barbarism 'described a land torn by divided loyalty: the desire to emulate Europe and the urge to pursue the unruly, chaotic behaviour symbolized by the primitivism of the Americas.'[72]

Although Costaguana represented a South American 'state in general; thence the mixture of customs and expressions' (*CL* 3, 175), Conrad exploited Robert Cunninghame Graham's rich involvement with Argentina to uncover Sarmiento's work and its polarised politics.[73]

---

[71] George Frederick Masterman, *Seven Eventful Years in Paraguay: A Narrative of Personal Experience Amongst the Paraguayans* (London, 1869), 85.

[72] Stavans, introduction, xiv.

[73] 'Gaspar Ruiz' in *A Set of Six* captures the romance of the South American wars of independence from Spain (1810–24). Argentine, Chilean, and Peruvian independence leader General José de San Martín (1778–1850) features in the story. Conrad explained to Graham (*CL* 8, 65) that he found the germ of the story in Basil Hall's *Extracts from a Journal, Written on the Coasts of Chili, Peru, and Mexico, in the years 1820, 1821, 1822* (1824). Conrad's fascination with the period reveals his interest in national movements, military history, and exploits of Napoleonic proportions. *Nostromo* also makes reference to the liberator Simón Bolívar and his pessimistic view of Latin American politics,

The London literary scene in the early twentieth century also featured
W.H. Hudson, whose travel accounts, memoirs, and South American
romances, such as *Idle Days in Patagonia* (1893), *Green Mansions*
(1904), *South American Sketches* (1909), and *Far Way and Long Ago*
(1918) recall the cultural and geographical landscapes of *Nostromo*. In
1915, Conrad explained that Costaguana had been shaped by 'Mexico,
Argentina and Paraguay, with a dash of Banda Oriental and traces of
Venezuela' (*CL* 5, 325). Graham had travelled to Argentina in 1870
during one of Argentina's periodic civil wars, which erupted after the
death of General Justo José de Urquiza (1801–70), president between
1854–60 but who later controlled Entre Ríos province after relinquish-
ing presidential power to Sarmiento's friend Bartolomé Mitre
(1821–1906). By 1870, however, the forces of barbarism were directed
against Sarmiento himself, who had become Argentine president in
1868. In 'A Vanishing Race' in *Father Archangel of Scotland and Other
Essays* (1896), *Thirteen Stories* (1900), and *Progress and Other Sketches*
(1904), the last dedicated to Conrad, Graham wrote of Rosas, Urquiza,
Quiroga, the Gaucho tradition, and their importance in the formation
of Argentine identity. For Graham, 'Almost all the founders of the
Argentine Republic were of the Gaucho class,' including 'Rosas, the
tyrant of Buenos Ayres.'[74] Sarmiento had earlier written that Rosas
'applied the knife of the gaucho to the culture of Buenos Ayres, and
destroyed the work of centuries – of civilization, law, and liberty.'[75]
Graham also pointed out that 'Urquiza, the great rival of Rosas, also was
originally a country man, and so of [Facundo] Quiroga (the Tiger of the
Llanos).'[76]

While Graham believed that 'Revolutions in the S. American repub-
lics are of too frequent occurrence,'[77] he idealised gaucho culture in his
South American sketches. In 'La Pulperia,' published in *Thirteen Stories*,
Graham wrote that 'Don José Hernández, the Gaucho poet, relates the

expressed in a letter to General Juan José Flores, 9 November 1830: 'America is
ungovernable: those who worked for her independence have ploughed the sea.' Quoted
in Williamson, *History of Latin America*, 232.

[74] R. B. Cunninghame Graham, *Thirteen Stories* (London: Heinemann, 1900), 178.
[75] Sarmiento, *Facundo*, 55.
[76] *Thirteen Stories*, 179.
[77] Quoted in Cedric Watts and Laurence Davies, *Cunninghame Graham: A Critical
Biography* (Cambridge: Cambridge University Press, 1979), 18.

adventures of one Martin Fierro, who suffered many things.'[78] Graham's sympathetic evocation of *Martín Fierro* mirrors the literary and historical nostalgia that coloured later Argentine representations of the gaucho. *Martín Fierro* celebrated life on the pampas just as it was being threatened by modernity. For Graham, modernisation represented, in Conrad's words, the 'material apparatus of perfected civilisation which obliterates the individuality of old towns under the stereotyped conveniences of modern life' (*N*, 96). The culture that Sarmiento had sought to suppress in the middle of the nineteenth century now held some intrinsic national purity: 'As the Gaucho replaced the Indian, the European colonist will replace him, one more type will have faded from the world, one more step will have been made to universal ugliness.'[79] Argentine novels such as Lucio Vincente López's *La gran aldea* [The Big Village] (1884) observed the loss of the country's traditional heritage, while the gaucho featured prominently in fictional representations of modern and traditional identities. Leopoldo Lugones's *La guerra gaucha* [The Gaucho War] (1905) resurrected the exploits of gauchos during the Argentine War of Independence, and the best-known modern work, *Don Segundo Sombra* (1926), by Ricardo Güiraldes, portrayed the position of the gaucho in contemporary Argentine society.[80]

Nostromo's dialogue with *Facundo* displays the novel's indebtedness to early nineteenth-century Latin American literature and history, but *Nostromo*, importantly, also benefits from being read in its immediate historical context. Published following the Spanish-American War of 1898 over Cuba, which inspired the rebirth of Latin American nationalism and the search for the mythic roots of national identity in the pre-Columbian past, Conrad's vision of Costaguana can be positioned alongside the Spanish American Modernism of Rubén Darío (1867–1916) of Nicaragua and José Martí (1853–95) of Cuba. Martí's essay 'Nuestra América' (1891) promoted the diversity of the Americas, encouraged the exploration of history, criticised Europeanised cultural

---

[78] *Thirteen Stories*, 177–78. See José Hernández, *Martín Fierro* (Buenos Aires: Losada, 2005). The poem was originally published in two parts: *El gaucho Martín Fierro* (1872) and *La vuelta de Martín Fierro* (1879). In *Nostromo*, the feared bandit of the highlands is named Hernandez.

[79] *Thirteen Stories*, 167–68.

[80] See Lucio V. López, *La gran aldea* (1884; Buenos Aires: Kapeleusz, 1965), and Ricardo Güiraldes, *Don Segundo Sombra* (1926; Buenos Aires: Agebe, n.d.).

elitism, and observed the rise of North American power.[81] While *Nostromo* overlooks pre-Columbian culture, focusing instead on post-colonial identity, Conrad wondered whether the recent war would 'awaken the Latin race,' and 'Will it be any good if they did awaken?' (*CL* 2, 60). The Spanish-American War encouraged a re-aligning of Latin American literary and political affiliations. In Rubén Darío's 'To Roosevelt,' from *Cantos de vida y esperanza* (1905) the poet stated: 'You are the United States, / future invader of our naive America / with its Indian blood, and America / that still prays to Christ and still speaks Spanish.' The effects of North American geo-political interests following the Monroe Doctrine (1823) and the Roosevelt Corollary (1904) ensured that: 'The United States is grand and powerful. / Whenever it trembles, a profound shudder / runs down the enormous backbone of the Andes.'[82] The poet's suggestion of a dormant continental capacity evoked the image of awakening nations incorporating diverse historical identities, the 'vanished nations' of the indigenous culture that Conrad mentioned in *Nostromo*: 'the America of Moctezuma and Atahualpa, / the aromatic America of Columbus, / Catholic America, Spanish America.' Darío concluded with the cry: 'Long live Spanish America!'[83] Darío's *El canto errante* (1907) featured the poem 'Tutecotezumí,' outlining the poet's desire to excavate the Indian past: 'My pick is working / deep in the soil of this unknown America,' where 'The strange life of a vanished people emerges / from the mists of time.'[84] In 'Song to the Argentine,' Darío also wrote of the modern Latin American nation and the influx of the culture of new European immigrants: 'The docks

---

[81] The original literary influences for Spanish American Modernism were French Parnassian and Symbolist poetry, and consequently both Darío and Martí were initially labelled, like Martin Decoud, as 'Frenchified outsiders' in cultures searching for indigenous purity. See Octavio Paz, prologue, *Selected Poems of Rubén Darío*, translated by Lysander Kemp (Austin: University of Texas Press, 1988), 8. In *Nostromo*, Decoud's desire to 'become a poet like that other foreigner of Spanish blood, José Maria Heredia' (*N*, 151) illustrates Conrad's awareness of Latin American literature. Cuban-born Heredia (1842–1905) became a leader of the Parnassian movement in French poetry.

[82] *Selected Poems of Rubén Darío*, 69. The Monroe Doctrine of 1823 was articulated by US President James Monroe (1758–1831). It declared that the newly independent states of Latin America should remain free of European influence. In 1904, Theodore Roosevelt's (1858–1919) amendment to the Monroe Doctrine, known as the Roosevelt Corollary, approved US intervention in Central America.

[83] *Selected Poems of Rubén Darío*, 70.

[84] *Selected Poems of Rubén Darío*, 97.

bristled with smokestacks; / new ideas and new muscles / landed at the seaports, / sent here by distant nations.'[85] Just as Conrad presents the varied identities of Costaguana, Darío sees Latin America revitalised by the contributions of other nations.[86]

Conrad supported the dying efforts of the Spanish Empire against the US, following coverage of the war in the press. Likewise, 'between 1897 and 1903 Graham was a particularly close student of South American affairs, and many of his articles and letters to the press make bitter comment on the emergence of the United States as a new imperialist power.'[87] In July 1898, Conrad expressed to Graham his own anti-Imperialist views: 'I do like the attitude of the *Maga* on the Spanish business. If one could set the States & Germany by the ears! That would be *real fine*' (*CL* 2, 81). *Blackwood's* asserted in August 1898 that the United States was 'flooded with the wave of Imperialism,'[88] moving from 'the old order of seclusion into the new career of adventure.' Spain's loss of Cuba to American interests led to the resurgence of the Cuban patriotism articulated in the work of José Martí, which was 'sudden, but in every way sincere. As the Cuban insurgents were to the Spaniards, so they are to their American liberators.'[89] Cuban independence had been previously supported by the US, but the war had replaced one Imperialism, Spanish, with another, US. The 'Americans will have to deal not with a population grateful to its liberators, but with a malcontent people well practised in rebellion who think themselves tricked into a change of masters.'[90] This historical transformation inspired different Latin American voices on the subject of national development. Uruguayan writer José E. Rodó's influential essay *Ariel* (1900), which drew from Ernest Renan in its treatment of nationality and history, contrasts the spirituality of Latin America with the soulless utilitarianism of North American economic power in a conscious reworking of Sarmiento's politics of civilisation and barba-

[85] *Selected Poems of Rubén Darío*, 123.
[86] See also, Carola M. Kaplan, Peter Mallios, and Andrea White eds., *Conrad in the Twenty-First Century: Contemporary Approaches and Perspectives* (London: Routledge, 2005).
[87] Watts and Davies, *Cunninghame Graham: A Critical Biography*, 144–45.
[88] *Blackwood's Magazine* 164 (August 1898): 287.
[89] *Blackwood's*, 288.
[90] *Blackwood's*, 289.

rism. *Ariel,* according to Carlos Fuentes, remains 'an essential book in the protracted Latin American search for identity,' constituting 'the emotional and intellectual response of Latin American thought and Latin American spirituality to growing North American imperial arrogance.'[91]

Ariel presents two visions of modern culture: that of Caliban, associated with US economic power and consumer culture, and that of Ariel, connected to a European-influenced Latin American identity that should oppose the rampant forces of global capitalism. For Rodó, in turning to European culture as the guiding light of history, South American 'spiritual idealism... must emphasize its unswerving faith in the future.'[92] While continuing *Facundo's* appreciation of European cultural influence, *Ariel* resonates powerfully with *Nostromo's* portrayal of Holroyd, the US business magnate who symbolises and brutally articulates emerging US dominance in global affairs: the US 'shall run the world's business whether the world like it or not. The world can't help it – and neither can we, I guess' (*N,* 77). At the end of *Nostromo,* Monygham announces that the material progress of the San Tomé mine, formerly held to represent the forces of enlightened civilisation against native barbarism, now embodies a new, utilitarian brutality. Material interests 'have their law, and their justice. But it is founded on expediency, and is inhuman,' ensuring that the Gould Concession 'shall weigh as heavily upon the people as the barbarism, cruelty, and misrule of a few years back' (*N,* 511). Just as Martí's 'Nuestra América,' Rodó's *Ariel,* and Darío's poetry all recall *Facundo,* they were likewise 'written when the relationship between the hegemonic countries and Latin America was altering the dichotomy civilization/barbarism and the values assigned to it.'[93] In its broad and ironically layered portrait of the transience of historical and political contrasts, *Nostromo* similarly captures a half-century of fluctuating Latin American history.

---

[91] José E. Rodó, *Ariel,* translated by Margaret Sayers Peden, prologue by Carlos Fuentes (Austin: University of Texas Press, 1988), 15, 16.

[92] José E. Rodó, *Ariel,* edited with an introduction and notes by Gordon Brotherston (Cambridge: Cambridge University Press, 1967), 94.

[93] Goodrich, *Facundo and the Construction of Argentine Culture,* 81.

FOREIGNNESS AND NATIONALITY IN
THE SECRET AGENT

In *The Secret Agent*, Conrad turned his attention to 'the very centre of the Empire on which the sun never sets' (*SA*, 162). By using the 1894 bomb plot on the Greenwich Observatory as the basis of his story of anarchist activity in London, Conrad brought his understanding of national identity to bear on his adopted country. *The Secret Agent* examines self-proclaimed anarchists and 'foreign political spies' (*SA*, 171), scrutinising those seeking the destruction of capitalism and the counter-efforts of the establishment to safeguard British political and cultural traditions.[94]

Inspired, Conrad claimed in his 'Author's Note,' by a conversation with Ford Madox Ford about anarchism, the opening passages of the novel draw attention to the long British tradition of political asylum for European dissidents. The anarchist publications the *Torch* and the *Gong* on display in Verloc's shop call to mind the exiled Russian socialist Alexander Herzen's (1812–70) review *The Bell*, published in London in 1857.[95] Anarchism preoccupied late-Victorian and Edwardian society. As Barbara Tuchman has written: 'So enchanting was the vision of a stateless society, without government, without law, without ownership of property [. . .] that six heads of state were assassinated for its sake in

---

[94] For a fine selection of documents and centennial essays on *The Secret Agent*, see *The Conradian* 32.1 (2007).

[95] See Robert Hampson, 'Conrad and the Rossettis: "A Casual Conversation about Anarchists,"' *Ugo Mursia Memorial Lectures: Second Series*, 289–304. Hampson discusses Ford Madox Ford's acquaintance with Olive, Arthur, and Helen Rossetti, who founded the anarchist journal *The Torch* in 1891. The publication later adopted the ideologically chaotic sub-title of 'A Revolutionary Journal of Anarchist-Communism' (292). The Rossettis knew Peter Kropotkin (1842–1921), the figurehead of international anarchism since the death of its founding ideologues, Joseph Proudhon (1809–65) and Mikhail Bakunin (1814–76). Herzen had significantly influenced Bakunin's thought in his early years. According to George Woodcock, Bakunin's 'semi-mystical vision of salvation through destruction derived from the Hegelian 1840s that dominated his development from a revolutionary nationalist to an anarchist internationalist.' For Kropotkin, however, the 'conception of evolution as natural process was inevitably more sympathetic than the Bakuninist conception of revolution as apocalypse.' George Woodcock, *Anarchism: A History of Libertarian Ideas and Movements* (Harmondsworth: Penguin, 1986), 172–73.

the twenty years before 1914.'[96] In *The Secret Agent*, the apparent insanity of an attack on the Greenwich Observatory is conceived because of public immunity to shock from the death of political figures. Mr. Vladimir, the official from a foreign Embassy (understood to be Russian), who orders the attack on a British institution, explains his logic to the *agent provocateur* Mr. Verloc: 'An attempt upon a crowned head or on a president is sensational enough in a way, but not so much as it used to be. It has entered the general conception of the existence of all chiefs of state. It's almost conventional – especially since so many presidents have been assassinated' (*SA*, 29). The threat posed by anarchists to political figures and civilians from bomb plots was, more significantly for Conrad, associated with the question of immigration and the distilling of the purity of national identity. In America, Leon Czolgosz, a Polish-American, had assassinated President McKinley in 1901, and press condemnation 'customarily referred to Anarchists as "wild beasts," "crypto-lunatics," degenerates, criminals, cowards, felons, "odious fanatics prompted by perverted intellect and morbid frenzy."'[97] Meanwhile, Bram Stoker's *Dracula* (1897) had popularised the concept of an Eastern European influx of sickness and death into London. By delineating aimless anarchists in *The Secret Agent*, Conrad subverted the idea of a threat from foreign, marginal figures in British society.

Conrad had earlier written about supposedly alien outsiders in England in 'Amy Foster,' first published in the *Illustrated London News* in December 1901. The story recounted the experiences of an Eastern European castaway, Yanko Gooral, exploring his position as a vilified outsider in the traditional and sheltered English community of Colebrook. According to Conrad, 'Amy Foster' treated the 'essential difference of the races' (*CL* 2, 402), and the story echoes 'Heart of Darkness' in presenting England as 'an undiscovered country' (*T*, 112), with Gooral's treatment and tragic fate upsetting conventional notions of civilisation and barbarism.[98]

---

[96] Barbara W. Tuchman, *The Proud Tower: A Portrait of the World before the War, 1890–1914* (New York: Ballantine, 1996), 63. They were President Carnot of France in 1894, Premier Canovas of Spain in 1897, Empress Elizabeth of Austria in 1898, King Humbert of Italy in 1900, President McKinley of the United States in 1901, and another Premier of Spain, Canalejas, in 1912.

[97] Tuchman, *The Proud Tower*, 108.

[98] See Richard Ruppel, 'Yanko Gooral in the Heart of Darkness: "Amy Foster" as Colonialist Text,' *Conradiana* 28.2 (1996): 126–32.

The Secret Agent continued Conrad's study of the 'insular nature of Great Britain' (*SA*, 212). Along with *Chance*, *The Secret Agent* has been considered Conrad's most English novel,[99] owing to its representation of the city of London and British institutions. Conrad unveils a London to rank alongside the work of Hogarth, Dickens, and Conan Doyle, and the novel's stylistic effects, such as the attributing of animation to buildings and objects, indicate that London and British tradition are robust and impervious to destruction by foreignness or anarchism.[100] Mr. Verloc's journey to see Mr. Vladimir takes him 'westward through a town without shadows in an atmosphere of powdered old gold' (*SA*, 15). Conrad's London displays its heritage but also, in the novel's juxtaposition of signs and actual geographical locations, its modern adaptability. Verloc observes 'a yellow wall, which, for some inscrutable reason, had No. 1 Chesham Square written on it in black letters. Chesham Square was at least sixty yards away' (*SA*, 17). However, Verloc is 'cosmopolitan enough not to be deceived by London's topographical mysteries' (*SA*, 17), undermining the traditional anti-Semitic associations of otherness and cosmopolitanism.[101] In *The Secret Agent*, to be cosmopolitan is to be at home in the capital, and Conrad populates London with characters whose national origins are uncertain and shifting, figures subsumed within, and whose marks of nationality are effaced by, the city.

London constitutes a melting pot of national cultures, races, and political ideals, and deep within its arteries, in Brett Street, Winnie's mother 'considered herself to be of French descent, which might have been true' (*SA*, 11).[102] 'Traces of the French descent which the widow

---

[99] See Jacques Berthoud, 'Conrad the Englishman: The Case of *Chance*,' *Conrad's Century*, 133–48.

[100] For discussions of Conrad's presentation of London, see Gene M. Moore ed., *Conrad's Cities: Essays for Hans van Marle* (Amsterdam: Rodopi, 1992).

[101] See Georgias Varouxakis, ' "Patriotism," "Cosmopolitanism," and "Humanity" in Victorian Political Thought,' *European Journal of Political Theory* 5.1 (2006): 100–18; and Cedric Watts, 'Jews and Degenerates in *The Secret Agent*,' *The Conradian* 32.1 (2008): 70–82.

[102] In his marvellous portrait of nineteenth-century European society and politics, *My Past and Thoughts*, Alexander Herzen wrote of the Soho of the 1850s and its assortment of outcasts with a kaleidoscope of political aims: 'It may well be imagined what incongruous elements are caught up from the Continent and deposited in England by those ebbs and flows of revolution and reaction which exhaust the constitution of Europe like an intermittent fever; and what amazing types of people are cast down by these waves and stray about in the damp swamps of London. What must be the chaos of

boasted of were apparent in Winnie too' (*SA*, 11). The ironic voice of the narrator renders obsolete the definition of characters by national origin. When Verloc reveals himself a 'natural born British subject' (*SA*, 23), he immediately disclaims pure English inheritance: 'But my father was French, and so – ' (*SA*, 23), while Vladimir advises him not to be 'too English' (*SA*, 25). Conrad's ostensibly English characters, the Dickensian Toodles and the Assistant Commissioner, are transformed by their interaction with the city from markedly English to decidedly alien personages. In disguise, on his journey of reconnaissance to Soho, the Assistant Commissioner 'was struck by his foreign appearance' (*SA*, 115). His journey into the city at night sees him encounter a confusion of national identities and traditions, all of which have contributed to the development of English culture and the evolving 'national spectacle' (*SA*, 13). After visiting an Italian restaurant, he feels 'that the patrons of the place had lost [. . .] all their national and private characteristics. And this was strange, since the Italian restaurant is such a peculiarly British institution. But those people were as denationalised as the dishes set before them' (*SA*, 115).

London sees national origins lose their exclusive characteristics. The Assistant Commissioner's appearance at Verloc's shop allows Winnie to remark on his physical and linguistic characteristics: 'There was nothing foreign in his accent, except that he seemed in his slow enunciation to be taking pains with it. And Mrs Verloc, in her varied experience, had come to the conclusion that some foreigners could speak better English than the natives' (*SA*, 150). On returning to the centre of British political power, the Assistant Commissioner becomes 'a queer foreign-looking chap' to Toodles (*SA*, 162), and, ultimately, his Englishness dissolves: 'In the dim light, the salient points of his personality, the long face, the black hair, his lankness, made him look more foreign than ever' (*SA*, 164). Conrad's most distinctive presentation of the vigour and flexibility of English national tradition surfaces in the confrontation

---

ideas and theories in these specimens of every kind of moral formation and reformation, of every protest, every Utopia, every disillusionment, and every hope, who meet in the alleys, eating-houses and beer-shops of Leicester Square and the adjoining back streets? "There," as the *Times* puts it, "lives a wretched population of foreigners . . . a miserable, poverty-stricken, harassed population who set all the powerful monarchs of Europe trembling except the Queen of England.' *My Past and Thoughts*, volume 5, translated by Constance Garnett (London: Chatto & Windus, 1926), 2.

between the nihilistic Professor and the folk songs of British culture. As the redoubtable bomber makes his exit from the Silenus Restaurant, the lonely piano 'without as much as a music stool to help it, struck a few chords courageously, and beginning a selection of national airs, played him out at last to the tune of "The Blue Bells of Scotland"' (*SA*, 65).

The important exception to Conrad's representation of national identity lies in the delineation of Mr. Vladimir. While Vladimir's 'somewhat oriental phraseology' (*SA*, 171) leaves his precise national origin ambiguous, it is clear considering the evidence of 'Autocracy and War' and *Under Western Eyes* that Vladimir is uniquely Russian: 'Descended from generations victimized by the instruments of an arbitrary power, he was racially, nationally, and individually afraid of the police. It was an inherited weakness, altogether independent of his judgement, of his reason, of his experience. He was born to it' (*SA*, 169). Vladimir's 'amazingly guttural intonation' is 'not only utterly un-English, but absolutely un-European' (*SA*, 24), and his orchestration of the bomb outrage – allowing Conrad to highlight a malignant Russian influence – guarantees that all 'foreign scoundrels' are suspected by the establishment of being 'likely to throw something,' causing 'a national calamity' (*SA*, 112).

However, Conrad's association of a threat to English order with the political representatives of Russian authority ensures that structures of power, especially British political alliances following Anglo-Russian rapprochement in the early years of the century, are responsible for engendering potential instability. Russian territory encroaches on the geography of London, with Vladimir's planning of the bomb plot occurring 'Theoretically only, on foreign territory, abroad only by a fiction' (*SA*, 172). Despite the contemporary belief that the dangers of foreignness were to be located in 'cosmopolitan slums' (*SA*, 25), *The Secret Agent* unambiguously allows Verloc, Karl Yundt, Tom Ossipon, and Michaelis, to peacefully exist in London society. Michaelis relies on a 'Lady Patroness' (*SA*, 83), and is 'a humanitarian sentimentalist, a little mad, but upon the whole incapable of hurting a fly intentionally' (*SA*, 87). According to the Professor, the terrorist Karl Yundt 'has been a posturing shadow all his life' (*SA*, 57), while Ossipon's opportunistic womanising is complemented by his more intimate knowledge of London, evoked in his final saunter through the city after deserting Winnie: 'He walked through Squares, Places, Ovals, Commons, through monotonous streets with unknown names where the dust of humanity settles inert and hopeless out of the stream of life. He walked. And suddenly turning into the strip of a front garden with a mangy grass plot, he let himself into a small grimy house with a latchkey he took out of his pocket.' (*SA*, 224) Ossipon returns to a domestic English existence by instinctively negotiating the labyrinthine city. The residential districts of London harbour not a dangerous foreigner but a Londoner, just as Brett Street, from 'a certain point of view,' is simply the scene of a 'domestic drama' (*SA*, 168). Meanwhile, the traditional sites of political authority breed the violence that will literally fragment a representative, albeit 'degenerate' (*SA*, 40), English youth.

Conrad claimed to his publisher Methuen in 1907 that the novel treated a 'sensational' subject and had 'no social or philosophical intention' (*CL* 3, 371). Nevertheless, Conrad 'may have wanted to hint at something he dared not say publicly: that the Russian embassy, the English police, and the Home Office were objects of no less ridicule' than the anarchists.[103] Mr. Vladimir's understanding of anarchist activity is based on a confusion of socialist and anarchist principles, something that astonishes Verloc. Mr. Vladimir displayed 'an amount of ignorance as to the real aims, thoughts, and methods of the revolutionary world which filled the silent Mr. Verloc with inward consternation. He confounded causes with effects more than was excusable' (*SA*, 28). Vladimir contributes to, and is the product of, a culture which has willingly obfuscated its understanding of threats to the social order in conjunction with the outpourings of the popular press. In *The Secret Agent*, journalists treat anarchism with 'emotional gush' and 'emotional indignation' (*SA*, 96). As Barbara Melchiori explains, the tendency to 'confuse socialists and anarchists was largely due to biased press reporting,' which sought to convince contemporary readers 'that they were being plotted against, that their lives were at risk, their values at stake and their property in imminent danger of confiscation or destruction.'[104] Conrad condemns the establishment for its failure to understand destructive forces operating within society, while the dangers of terrorism are portrayed as exaggerated and illusory. Sir Ethelred is given

---

[103] Najder, *Conrad: A Chronicle*, 324.
[104] Barbara Arnett Melchiori, *Terrorism in the Late Victorian Novel* (London: Verso, 1985), 9.

an uncomfortable moment of insight when he muses: 'there's but poor comfort in being able to declare that any given act of violence – damaging property or destroying life – is not the work of anarchism at all, but of something else altogether – some species of authorised scoundrelism' (*SA*, 109).

Conrad's view of the Anarchist threat is radical given the exploitative nature of much contemporary writing on the subject.[105] Conrad undertook a 'sustained effort in ironical treatment of a melodramatic subject' (*CL* 3, 491). Melodramatic stories of anarchist outrages featured in contemporary periodicals, with many reinforcing the soundness of the social order. In 1894, *The Strand Magazine* published a translation of a French story by Eugène Moret entitled 'An Anarchist.'[106] In this sensational, conservative tale, a disaffected worker, Jacques, leaves his family, intent on blowing up the house of his employer. On the night of the planned outrage, his employer hosts a gathering for local children, with Jacques's offspring amongst those present. On learning this from his wife, Jacques sounds the alarm, the children are escorted to safety, and Jacques is killed in a desperate attempt to stop the bomb. He will be forever known as '[T]he Anarchist – but who did not hesitate to rush on to death to save us, and accepted that fate as an expiation.'[107] The melodrama of the subject also arose for Conrad from his sceptical view of the sincerity of self-styled revolutionaries. In a letter to R.B. Cunninghame Graham, Conrad felt that 'All these people are not revolutionaries – they are Shams' (*CL* 3, 491). A review of *The Secret Agent* in *The Glasgow News* in October 1907 observed that 'no one who has any knowledge of even the outer side of anarchism can fail to be delighted with this portrayal of some typical anarchists as they are to be met in life, and not as they are wildly imagined by writers of popular fiction.'[108] By

---

[105] See Ian Watt, 'The Political and Social Background of *The Secret Agent*,' *Essays on Conrad* (Cambridge: Cambridge University Press, 2000), 112–26.

[106] Eugène Moret, 'An Anarchist,' *The Strand Magazine* 8 (Jan–June, 1894), 339–47.

[107] Moret, 'An Anarchist,' 347.

[108] Sherry ed., *Critical Heritage*, 196. Herzen echoes Conrad's discourse of anarchist futility. Writing of political exiles in London, Herzen noted: 'Time passed with terrible leisureliness, but it passed; revolution was nowhere in sight, except in their imaginations [. . .]. They had no habit of work; their thoughts, bent on the political arena, could not concentrate on the practical; they caught at anything, but with exasperation, with annoyance, with impatience, without perseverance, and everything slipped through their fingers.' Herzen, *My Past and Thoughts*, 6.

basing his plot around the 1894 anarchist incident at Greenwich, in which Frenchman Martial Bourdin was accidentally killed by his own bomb, Conrad also reinforced that, despite public susceptibility to fears of imminent anarchist outrages, Bourdin, who is transformed into the hapless Stevie in the novel, was the only victim of anarchist violence in England.[109] In *The Secret Agent*, the 'total absence of any real [anarchist] activity'[110] makes the terrorist threat to London appear a manufactured construct.

Instead of embodying an active menace, Conrad's anarchists endlessly debate the philosophy of history, with the ticket-of-leave apostle Michaelis expounding on 'the economic condition of the world responsible for the past and shaping the future; the source of all history, of all ideas, guiding the mental development of mankind and the very impulses of their passion' (*SA*, 40). Later, the Professor denounces all speculative philosophies of history: ' "Prophecy! What's the good of thinking of what will be!" He raised his glass. "To the destruction of what is," he said calmly' (*SA*, 228). While the Professor boldly claims: 'Madness and despair! Give me that for a lever, and I'll move the world' (*SA*, 230), his destructive power, although devastating in its immediate cost to human life, remains as insignificant to unfolding history as the attempt on the Greenwich Observatory.[111] The ending of *The Secret Agent* isolates the decrepitude of the 'incorruptible' (*SA*, 230) Professor, acknowledging him as 'frail, insignificant, shabby, miserable – and terrible in the simplicity of his idea calling madness and despair to the regeneration of the world. Nobody looked at him. He passed on unsuspected and deadly, like a pest in the street full of men' (*SA*, 231). The Professor's faith in destructive action and Michaelis's confidently pronounced theories of historical development are challenged and muted by Conrad's evocative portrayal of the artistic endeavours of Stevie, who, during anarchist meetings, sits drawing 'circles, circles, circles; innumerable circles, concentric, eccentric; a coruscating whirl

---

[109] See Woodcock, *Anarchism*.

[110] Melchiori, *Terrorism in the Late Victorian Novel*, 75.

[111] The Professor remains particularly ineffectual in his desire for the destruction of society in light of transtextual evidence. In Conrad's story, 'The Informer,' published in *Harper's Magazine* in December 1906, the Professor also appeared, but the reader learns he 'perished a couple of years afterwards in a secret laboratory through the premature explosion of one of his improved detonators' (*SS*, 88).

of circles that by their tangled multitude of repeated curves, uniformity of form, and confusion of intersecting lines suggested a rendering of cosmic chaos, the symbolism of a mad art attempting the inconceivable' (*SA*, 40). This juxtaposition of those professing insights into history and the confusion of the work of Stevie, the 'artist' of the novel (*SA*, 40), places *The Secret Agent* alongside Conrad's earlier explorations of the indeterminacy of historical knowledge in 'Heart of Darkness,' *Lord Jim*, and *Nostromo*.

CONRAD AND RUSSIA: 'AUTOCRACY AND WAR' AND *UNDER WESTERN EYES*

In *The Mirror of the Sea* (1906), Conrad reiterated the metaphysical qualities of nationhood: 'we must turn to the national spirit, which, superior in its force and continuity to evil and good fortune, can alone give us the feeling of an enduring existence and of an invincible air of power against the fates.' (*MS*, 194) This trust in an unassailable national identity, it has been argued, was something that Conrad articulated to endear his writing, particularly in 'Youth' and *The Nigger of the 'Narcissus,'* to his English audience.[112] In *Under Western Eyes*, Conrad returned to the subject in the context of Russia.

On 2 November 1905, Conrad considered Russian history, acknowledging that Alexander II's 1861 liberation of the serfs marked 'the starting point of an orderly rational programme in accord with the national spirit' (*CL* 3, 294). Conrad adopted a similar position in his later essay on Turgenev, written in 1917, when he labelled the author of *Fathers and Sons* a 'whole-souledly national' writer (*NLL*, 41). In January 1908, Conrad wrote to John Galsworthy that his proposed story 'Razumov' sought to 'capture the soul of things Russian' (*CL* 4, 8). Yet, Conrad's insistence on the unique attributes of the Russian character should not be understood as an endorsement of that country's heritage. On the contrary, Conrad was setting up the temple of Russian nationhood that he intended to expose as a vaporous mirage. *Under*

---

[112] See Peter D. McDonald, *British Literary Culture and Publishing Practice, 1880–1914* (Cambridge: Cambridge University Press, 1997).

Western Eyes would reveal 'the very essence of things Russian' (*CL* 4, 14): the crushing power of autocracy and the resultant obscure mysticism of writers such as Dostoevsky. Autocracy had 'gone into the [Russian] blood, tainting every mental activity in its source by a half-mystical, insensate, fascinating assertion of purity and holiness' (*NLL*, 82). The correspondences between *Crime and Punishment* and *Under Western Eyes* ensure that Conrad 'challenges the nineteenth-century Russian novel on its own terms: as a novel of ideas' representing Russian national consciousness. Indeed, Conrad asserts 'that Russia has no history.'[113] *Under Western Eyes* aimed to subvert Russian identity, continuing what Conrad had explored in 'Autocracy and War.' If Russia possessed no tradition other than autocracy, this singular history negated Russia's claims to nationhood following the Western models of Herder and Rousseau.

'Autocracy and War,' written at the time of the Russo-Japanese War in 1905, responded to a tide of Russophile literature sweeping England, particularly amongst the circle around the Garnetts.[114] Conrad presented a portrait of Russian identity to counter the pervasive influence of pro-Russian sentiment in literary and, with the new military alliance (1907) between Britain and Russia, political England. Employing a recurring trope in European literature, Conrad contended that Russia does 'not exist,' because it received its character solely from its political structure: 'The truth is that Russia of our fathers, of our childhood, of our middle-age; the testamentary Russia of Peter the Great – who imagined that all the nations were delivered into the hand of Tsardom – can do nothing. It can do nothing because it does not exist' (*NLL*, 76). Whereas Poland's lack of political structure engendered a spiritual existence, Russia was not spiritual but spectral: 'Spectral it lived and spectral it disappears without leaving a memory of a single generous

---

[113] Carola M. Kaplan, 'Conrad's Narrative Occupation of/by Russia in *Under Western Eyes*,' *Conradiana* 27.2 (1995): 97–98.

[114] For example, see Edward Garnett's glowing 1895 introduction to Ivan Turgenev's *On the Eve*. Conrad, of course, respected Turgenev as a literary artist, but for Garnett, Turgenev's 'genius was of the same force in politics as in art; it was that of seeing aright. He saw his country as it was, with clearer eyes than any man before or since. If Tolstoï is a purer native expression of Russia's force, Turgenev is the personification of Russian aspiration working with the instruments of wide cosmopolitan culture.' Edward Garnett, introduction, Ivan Turgenev, *On the Eve*, translated by Constance Garnett (1895; London: Heinemann, 1928), x.

deed, of a single service rendered – even involuntarily – to the polity of nations' (*NLL*, 77). Conrad was even prepared to agree with Bismarck in his dismissal of Russia: '*La Russie, c'est le néant*' (*NLL*, 79).

Conrad's essay augured the futile unrest for the non-existent soul of the Russian nation, which Conrad would enlarge on in *Under Western Eyes*:

Voices have been heard saying that the time for reforms in Russia is already past. This is the superficial view of the more profound truth that for Russia there has never been such a time within memory of mankind. It is impossible to initiate a rational scheme of reform upon a phase of blind absolutism and in Russia there has never been anything else to which the faintest tradition could, after ages of error, go back as to a parting of ways. (*NLL*, 80–81)

For Conrad, a 'revolution is a short cut in the rational development of national needs in response to the growth of world-wide ideals' (*NLL*, 84). Revolution had failed in Russia because there was not the 'faintest tradition' of a cultural nation. The Russian 'soul, kept benumbed by her temporal and spiritual master with the poison of tyranny and superstition will find itself on awakening possessed of no language' (*NLL*, 85). The lack of a language of cultural unity ensures that Russia does not possess Herderian qualities of nationhood, the 'invincible soul' that Conrad believed to exist in Poland. Conrad portrays 'the hard ground of Russia, inanimate, cold, inert . . . without a fireside, without a heart!' (*UWE*, 33).[115] In place of the fireside and heart of a Romantic culture, whenever 'two Russians come together, the shadow of autocracy is with them, tinging their thoughts, their views, their most intimate feelings, their private life, their public utterances – haunting the secret of their silences' (*UWE*, 107). The ubiquitous power of the autocracy deprives Russia of the established European fundamentals of national tradition and identity.

Ironically, Conrad drew heavily from Russian literature and philosophy to illustrate his antagonistic politics. *Under Western Eyes*, as Paul

---

[115] Conrad also turned to Polish Romantic literature to dispossess Russia. The teacher of languages believes Russia is 'like a monstrous blank page awaiting the record of an inconceivable history' (*UWE*, 33), evoking Mickiewicz's poem 'Digression,' in which the Polish poet wrote: 'This level plain lies open, waste, and white, / A wide-spread page prepared for God to write.' Quoted in Keith Carabine, *The Life and the Art: A Study of Conrad's 'Under Western Eyes'* (Amsterdam: Rodopi, 1996), 88.

Kirschner has noted, engages overtly with nineteenth-century Russian historical thought.[116] In his *Lettres philosophiques* (1827–31), the first of which appeared in Russian translation in the journal *Teleskop* in 1836, Pyotr Chaadayev (1794–1856) inaugurated decades of Russian philosophical debate between Westerners and Slavophiles over Russia's geographical isolation and cultural singularity. Chaadayev, a Westernizer with an incongruous mystical philosophy of religion and Russian identity (or, perhaps not so incongruous considering the work of Mickiewicz on Poland), argued that Russia was not a historical nation in the enlightenment tradition, writing: 'Russians come into the world like illegitimate children, without a heritage.'[117] Similarly, Alexander Herzen, who admired the work of Hegel and August Cieszkowski,[118] insisted in *The Russian People and Socialism: An Open Letter to Jules Michelet* (1851) that Europe had an 'attachment to the legacy of the past that is incomprehensible to us.'[119] Conrad's attempted obliteration of Russia forms an overturning of ideas from *The Russian People and Socialism*, with Herzen's essay an important stylistic and political touchstone for understanding Conrad's estimation of Russia. Herzen's analysis of autocracy and Russian culture responded to Jules Michelet's *Poland And Russia: The Legend of Kosciusko* (1852), which stated, as Conrad would later, that 'Russia doesn't exist.'[120] Michelet's account constitutes a typically histrionic nineteenth-century lament for dismembered Poland, adopting a Romantic rhetoric to support the nation's continued vitality: 'Poland, bloody and in shreds, mute, with neither pulse nor breath, *she lives… she lives more and more.*' Conversely: 'I say,

---

[116] See Paul Kirschner ed., Joseph Conrad, *Under Western Eyes* (London: Penguin, 1997) for an analysis of the parallels between *Under Western Eyes* and the work of Turgenev and Dostoevsky.

[117] Quoted in Kirschner ed., introduction, *Under Western Eyes*, xxxv.

[118] In 1838, Herzen wrote of Cieszkowski's *Prolegomena* that he was 'in agreement with the author on all major points.' Quoted in Walicki, *History of Russian Thought*, 129. See *Selected Writings of August Cieszkowski*, 15–16.

[119] Quoted in Kirschner ed., introduction, *Under Western Eyes*, xxxvii. For a detailed survey of the conflict between Slavophiles and Westerners in Russian national philosophy in the nineteenth century, see Andrzej Walicki, *The Slavophile Controversy: History of a Conservative Utopia in Nineteenth-Century Russian Thought* (Oxford: Clarendon Press, 1975).

[120] Herzen, *Russian People and Socialism*, 165.

I affirm, I swear and I will prove that *la Russie n'est pas.*' Russia had stooped to 'a dreadful moral nothingness; she has gone against the world and receded into barbarism.' Russia's greatest crime had engendered its own historical regression, strengthening the spiritual life of Poland while destroying Russian integrity: 'This monstrous crime of the Russian government. An immense crime, the murder of fifty million men! It has divided Poland only to provide her with a stronger sense of life, but in reality, *il a supprimé la Russie.*'[121]

In response, Herzen, resorting to the historicism he had learned from Cieszkowski, and which Conrad adopted in his considerations of Poland, claimed: 'For the Russian people the past is dark: the present is terrible: but for all that, it lays some claim to the future, it *has no belief* in its present condition.' Herzen drew attention to 'the unknown Russian, the Russia of the people,' which would ultimately awaken, insisting that European writers concerned themselves 'too much with the official Russia, the Russia of the Tsar.'[122] However, where Herzen observed the 'agonizing cry of a people awakening in its prison-house,'[123] Conrad deliberately inverted Herzen's thought to re-invigorate the tradition of the Marquis de Custine's *La Russie en 1839* (1843), which viewed Russia as a hollow, barbaric, and spiritless expanse on the edge of Western civilisation.

THE DISCOURSE OF POLISH PHILOSOPHY IN CONRAD'S RUSSIA

Conrad regarded *Under Western Eyes* as his 'most deeply meditated novel' (*CL* 5, 695), and this statement is justified by the writer's psychological breakdown upon its completion in 1910. Conrad later explained that the novel had caused him to navigate the intersections of Polish and Russian history: 'The obligation of absolute fairness was imposed on me historically and hereditarily [...]. I had never been called before to a greater effort of detachment' (*UWE*, xxx–xxxi). Conrad, however, blurs the historical boundaries between Polish and

[121] Jules Michelet, *Pologne et Russie: légende de Kosciusko* (Paris, 1852), 16, 17.
[122] Herzen, *Russian People and Socialism*, 166.
[123] Herzen, *Russian People and Socialism*, 193.

Russian identity. Ford Madox Ford pointed out that Razumov 'was probably more a Pole than a Russian,'[124] and the relationship between the forces of autocracy and revolution sees *Under Western Eyes* adopt the rhetoric of Polish Romanticism and Positivism.[125] Razumov's political creed outlines incompatible attitudes to the nation: 'History not Theory. / Patriotism not Internationalism. / Evolution not Revolution. / Direction not Destruction. / Unity not Disruption' (*UWE*, 66). Conrad's method, as in 'Autocracy and War,' employed a Polish discourse of national history and development, sceptically analysing its obsolescence in a Russian context. Conrad discloses Russia's 'impenetrability to whatever is true in Western thought. Western thought when it crosses her frontier falls under the spell of her autocracy and becomes a noxious parody of itself' (*NLL*, 82).[126]

In Conrad's understanding of Polish history, Romanticism and Positivism struggled to give political form to an existent Polish nation. *Under Western Eyes* imposes the authentic language of political extremism and conservatism from Polish national history onto the 'abyss' of the Russian autocratic tradition.[127] August Cieszkowski's *Prolegomena zur Historiosophie* promoted the idea of a deed as essential to the unfolding of history. Victor Haldin speaks as if schooled in militant interpretations of this philosophy. In his confession to Razumov of the murder of de P-, Haldin explains that he 'resolved to have no sleep until "the deed" was done' (*UWE*, 17). Haldin voices the ideology of the Romantic struggle: 'It's not my life I want to save, but my power to do. I won't live idle. Oh no! Don't make any mistake, Razumov. Men like me are rare' (*UWE*, 20). After Haldin's arrest, Razumov is understood

---

[124] Sherry ed., *Critical Heritage*, 245.

[125] See Andrzej Busza, 'Rhetoric and Ideology in *Under Western Eyes*,' *Joseph Conrad: A Commemoration*, 105–18; Carabine, *The Life and the Art*; and Edward Crankshaw, 'Conrad and Russia,' *Joseph Conrad: A Commemoration*, 91–104.

[126] For a collection of essays on the intersections between Polish and Russian history and philosophy, see David L. Ransel and Bozena Shallcross eds., *Polish Encounters, Russian Identity* (Bloomington: Indiana University Press, 2005).

[127] In fact, Russian philosophy of the early nineteenth century mirrored intellectual developments in Poland. The failure of the Decembrist Uprising in 1825 against Nicholas I ushered in a new, more resigned era of philosophical Hegelianism, much as Polish Positivism later adopted aspects of Hegel's thought in Poland in its response to Romanticism. According to Andrzek Walicki, 'The impact of Hegelian philosophy in Russia, as well as in Poland, cannot be compared to that of any other Western thinker; its influence was both widespread and profound.' Walicki, *History of Russian Thought*, 115.

to be one of the Romantic set, addressed by fellow student Kostia as 'A man of ideas – and a man of action too' (*UWE*, 81). When he arrives in Geneva, Peter Ivanovitch receives Razumov as an emissary of such revolutionary action: 'Just now you are a man associated with a great deed' (*UWE*, 207). In Geneva, along with London the traditional European centre of exiled political dissidents such as Herzen and Bakunin in the nineteenth century, Razumov employs the language of the active struggle to convince the revolutionaries of his sincerity: 'I made my way here for my share of the action – action' (*UWE*, 226).

Natalia Haldin also believes in the necessity of action and that the nation is waiting to voice itself. The national 'will must be awakened, inspired, concentrated' (*UWE*, 133). In order to awaken this nation, Natalia believes that 'some great patriotic action' (*UWE*, 138) will be the catalyst, and she lives with the 'loftiest hope of action and faith in success' (*UWE*, 140). In her opposition to Positivist ideas, she maintains that 'One must look beyond the present' (*UWE*, 345). Victor Haldin is certain that his 'spirit shall go on warring in some Russian body till all falsehood is swept out of the world. [...] You are a sceptic. I respect your philosophical scepticism, Razumov, but don't touch the soul. The Russian soul that lives in all of us. It has a future. It has a mission' (*UWE*, 22). The messianism of Haldin's beliefs emerges when Sophia Antonovna says: 'The spirit of the heroic Haldin had passed through these dens of black wretchedness with a promise of universal redemption from all the miseries that oppress mankind' (*UWE*, 279). However, the portrayal of the drunken Ziemianitch, the 'bright Russian soul' (*UWE*, 30) representative of the people, proves Haldin's belief in the Russian people to be misguided. Conrad contrasts the radical language of national struggle with a mute and spiritless populace, suggesting that Russia possesses no equivalent of the 'constructive instinct of the people' that existed in Poland, no national foundation upon which to launch an effective insurrection. The ironic description of Peter Ivanovitch, a fictional relative of the exiled anarchists Mikhail Bakunin and Peter Kropotkin, as the 'Russian Mazzini' (*UWE*, 223) indicates that the major tenets of European cultural nationalism do not apply to Russia.

If Conrad's Russia does not possess the required national spirit to carry a revolution, it also lacks the values for a more mundane, positivistic struggle, represented by the position of Razumov. In 'Autocracy and War,' Conrad, echoing Herzen, compared Russia to 'A prisoner shut up in a noisome dungeon [who] concentrates all his hope and desire on the moment of stepping out beyond the gates. It appears to him pregnant with an immense and final importance; whereas what is important is the spirit in which he will draw the first breath of freedom, the counsels he will hear, the hands he may find extended' (*NLL*, 85). Russia is not prepared for 'the endless days of toil which must follow, wherein he will have to build his future with no other material but what he can find within himself' (*NLL*, 85). The aims of Polish Positivism, with its focus on the practical goals of economic betterment, equally cannot be applied to Russia, as, for Conrad, there is no historical tradition of cultural nationhood: 'To pronounce in the face of such a past the word evolution which is precisely the expression of the highest intellectual hope is a gruesome pleasantry. There can be no evolution out of a grave' (*NLL*, 83). Zdzisław Najder has written that a 'conservative philosopher who was greatly influential in Russia – Hegel – is echoed by Razumov,'[128] and the Hegelian aspects of Polish Positivism colour Conrad's representation of his protagonist. Razumov's 'main concern was with his work' (*UWE*, 10), while Haldin 'was not one of the industrious set' (*UWE*, 15). In polarising Romantic and Positivistic thought, Razumov claims his right as torchbearer of the nation: 'all this land is mine – or I have nothing. No doubt you shall be looked upon as a martyr some day – a sort of hero – a political saint. But I beg to be excused. I am content in fitting myself to be a worker' (*UWE*, 61).

Razumov's plans for the future are based on implementing gradual change for Russia in a process of 'logical, guided development' (*UWE*, 301). Just as the English liberal philosophy of Mill and Spencer influenced Polish Positivism, in *Under Western Eyes* those prepared to accept Hegelian theories of history are also deemed to be under the sway of Western thought. For revolutionists such as Peter Ivanovitch, the positivistic approach is tainted by foreign philosophical influences: 'Everything in a people that is not genuine, not its own by origin or development, is – well – dirt! Intelligence in the wrong place is that. Foreign-bred doctrines are that. Dirt! Dregs! [...] at this moment there yawns a chasm between the past and the future. It can never be bridged by foreign liberalism' (*UWE*, 211). Ivanovitch rejects Positivism and its basis on English Liberalism, and 'he

---

[128] Najder, 'Conrad and Rousseau,' 85.

added that whole cartloads of words and theories could never fill that chasm. No meditation was necessary. A sacrifice of many lives could alone –' (*UWE*, 212). Councillor Mikulin appeals to this philosophy in Razumov, aware that it constitutes the basis of his written creed: 'Don't forget that I have seen that interesting piece of paper. I understand your liberalism.' (*UWE*, 294). Nevertheless, Razumov maintains that his philosophy is based exclusively on Russian ideas and not on any Western tradition. He is not swayed by 'French or German thought – devil knows what foreign notions. But I am not an intellectual mongrel. I think like a Russian' (*UWE*, 90).

Although sceptical about philosophical systems, Conrad consistently unveils characters who set down in writing their views of knowledge and historical events, such as Decoud's letter, Marlow's written account of Jim's story, Don José Avellanoes *History*, Towson's *Inquiry*, and Razumov's diary. In his last diary entry, addressed to Natalia Haldin, Razumov treats the conflict between the activist and the positivist: 'I, too, had my guiding idea; and remember that, amongst us, it is more difficult to lead a life of toil and self-denial than to go out in the street and kill from conviction. But enough of that' (*UWE*, 358). The distinction between Romanticism and Positivism is clear: 'Visionaries work ever lasting evil on earth, Their Utopias inspires in the mass of mediocre minds a disgust of reality and a contempt for the secular logic of human development' (*UWE*, 95). Conrad's use of a Polish discourse in a Russian context communicates his belief in the mirage of Russian nationhood. The political rhetoric of both Razumov and the revolutionists is ironically contrasted with the novel's underlying belief in the absence of any spiritual nation upon which such political claims are founded. In 'Autocracy and War,' Conrad's Hegelian language challenged the politics of Herzen's *Russian People and Socialism*:

But under the shadow of Russian autocracy nothing could grow. Russian autocracy succeeded to nothing; it had no historical past, and it cannot hope for a historical future. It can only end. By no industry of investigation, by no fantastic stretch of benevolence, can it be presented as a phase of development through which a society, a state, must pass on the way to the full consciousness of its destiny. It lies outside the stream of progress. This despotism has been utterly un-European. (*NLL*, 81)

Conrad states that the Russian nation is 'autocracy and nothing else in the world' (*NLL*, 82), and the rulers of Russian autocracy have 'never risen to be the chiefs of a nation' (*NLL*, 84).

Conrad believed Poland was 'Western, with an absolute comprehension of all the Western modes of thought' (*NLL*, 109). *Under Western Eyes* also engages with a Western tradition of historical thought represented by Edmund Burke and Rousseau. The juxtaposition of the east of the story and the Western Eye of the narrator emphasises that Conrad's scrutiny of the Russian nation occurs through the lens of Western philosophy. Christopher GoGwilt has noted that 'there is something historically important in the success with which [Conrad] makes Rousseau stand for a contestation of claims to inheritance of "the West."'[129] In European political philosophy, Rousseau and Burke stand on opposite sides of the ideological divide that Razumov elucidates in his political confession. It is usually understood that 'Burke has a reverence for the past; Rousseau has a revolutionary's hatred of the present. Burke has a disposition to conserve; Rousseau, a rage to renovate or overturn.'[130] In *Under Western Eyes*, Haldin's philosophy echoes the received view of Rousseau, while Razumov's beliefs can be located in the Burkean political tradition. Alfred Cobban has written that the 'modern Western European conception of the nation has largely been a product of the fusion' of the thought of Rousseau and Burke.[131] In *Under Western Eyes*, Russia lacks the historical experience of nationhood of both these thinkers. For Rousseau, 'Patriotism specifically, but more broadly the whole range of emotional commitments a citizen may feel for the state, will help to make the public self predominate and thus assist in creating the conditions necessary for a stable and legitimate political order.'[132] For Burke, 'Society is indeed a contract [...] a partnership not only between those who are living, but between those who are living, those who are dead, and those who are to be born.'[133] In Conrad's Russia, no legitimate political order exists or can be estab-

---

[129] GoGwilt, *Invention of the West*, 150.

[130] David Cameron, *The Social Thought of Rousseau and Burke: A Comparative Study* (London: Weidenfeld & Nicholson, 1973), 5.

[131] Alfred Cobban, *The Nation State and National Self-Determination* (London: Collins, 1969), 121.

[132] Cameron, *Rousseau and Burke*, 130.

[133] Edmund Burke, *Reflections on the French Revolution* (London: Dent, 1910), 93.

lished, as Rousseau's patriotism and Burke's tradition have never emerged, thereby negating both Haldin's revolution and Razumov's evolution. Thus, while the teacher of languages ironically comments on Rousseau, *Under Western Eyes* shrewdly conceals salient aspects of his thought. In June 1907, Conrad wrote that government was 'the expression of a people's character or an illustrated commentary on the same' (*CL* 3, 454). Conrad espouses such a position in *Under Western Eyes*, engaging with European historical thought to dismiss Russia's claims to the inheritance of the West.

4

The World of Yesterday: Conrad, European History, and Napoleonic Legend

With 'Twixt Land and Sea (1912), Chance (1913), and Victory (1915), Conrad turned back to the established worlds of his earlier writing. 'Twixt Land and Sea reintroduced the scenes of his nineteenth-century maritime travels; Chance, consciously seeking a lucrative female readership, resurrected a usefully chauvinistic Marlow; and Victory, the tale of Axel Heyst, unveiled another Conrad character battling with his philosophical heritage in a tenebrous world. Heyst asserts that 'facts have a certain positive value' (V, 197). However, the volcanic imagery of Victory ensures that Heyst's Positivist exterior conceals a dormant Romanticism, with Heyst explaining that every rational philosophy inevitably accommodates an underlying Romantic temperament: 'the use of reason is to justify the obscure desires that move our conduct, impulses, passions, prejudices and follies, and also our fears' (V, 83). Victory's publication in Munsey's Magazine in February 1915 alongside an article entitled 'Belgium: The Story of the Brave Little State Famous as the Battle-ground of Europe,' by Richard Le Gallienne, ensured that Conrad's novel would raise expectations of war material amongst contemporary readers.[1] However, with Victory having been completed before the war, readers would not be granted any militaristic sensationalism, and the novel's unsettling nihilism sees Heyst, after rejecting his father's ascetic thought, cast adrift with a 'wrecked philosophy' (V, 185), capturing perfectly the worldview that emerged in the crisis of 1914–18.

---

[1] Munsey's Magazine, February 1915. 'Victory' took up pages 112–40.

ANGLO-GERMAN RIVALRY IN
'AUTOCRACY AND WAR'

During the First World War, Conrad believed himself peripheral to a transitional historical moment. In November 1914, he wrote: 'the thoughts of this war sit on one's chest like a nightmare. I am painfully aware of being crippled, of being idle, of being useless with a sort of absurd anxiety' (*CL* 5, 427). In August 1915, Conrad felt the 'world of 15 years ago is gone to pieces; what will come in its place God knows, but I imagine doesn't care' (*CL* 5, 503). The political forces of nineteenth-century Europe that had fashioned Conrad's literature, notably imperialism and nationalism, were undermined and unleashed anew by the violence of the Great War and the uncertain legacy of the conflict. Conrad closely observed Poland's fate during the war through his relationship with Polish activist Józef Retinger, which inspired 'A Note on the Polish Problem' (1916) and 'The Crime of Partition' (1919). While 1918 saw the political rebirth of an expansionist Poland under Marshall Józef Piłsudski, and its existence immediately tested in the Polish-Soviet War (1919–21), antagonisms provoked by the re-drawing of Europe's historical boundaries made Conrad uneasy. On Armistice Day, he wrote: 'The great sacrifice is consummated – and what will come of it to the nations of the earth the future will show. I can not confess to an easy mind. Great and very blind forces are set free catastrophically all over the world' (*CL* 6, 302).

H.G. Wells observed in *Mr. Britling Sees It Through* (1916) that 'the world-wide clash of British and German interests, had been facts in the consciousness of Englishmen for more than a quarter of a century. A whole generation had been born and brought up in the threat of this German war.'[2] From Erskine Childers's *The Riddle of the Sands* (1903) to William le Queux's *Invasion of 1910* (1906), the threat of Germany resonated throughout British society, and Michael Howard has written that if the youth of the rival countries howled for war in 1914, 'it was because for a generation or more they had been taught to howl.'[3]

---

[2] H.G. Wells, *Mr. Britling Sees it Through* (London: Cassell, 1916), 123.
[3] M.E. Howard, *Studies in War and Peace* (London: Temple Smith, 1970), 102. For an interesting 'mapping' of the genre of 'invasion literature' in Britain between

Awareness of pervasive anti-German writing appears in *The Secret Agent* (1907), as Winnie Verloc describes the pamphlets of the Future of the Proletariat, which related the story 'of a German soldier officer tearing half-off the ear of a recruit, and nothing was done to him for it. The brute! [...] The story was enough, too, to make one's blood boil. But what's the use of printing things like that? We aren't German slaves here, thank God' (*SA*, 60). *Victory* reveals Conrad's own engagement with anti-German sentiment prevalent in Britain. *Victory's* 'Note to the First Edition' explained that animosity towards the Teutonic Schomberg was part of Conrad's Polish cultural inheritance: 'far from being the incarnation of recent animosities, he is the creature of my old, deep-seated and, as it were, impartial conviction' (*V*, viii).[4] While antipathy to Germany had not prevented Conrad's sympathetic delineation of Stein in *Lord Jim*, it certainly informed 'Autocracy and War,' which appeared in *The Fortnightly Review* in July 1905.[5] Conrad wanted the piece to be a 'sensation' (*CL* 3, 272), and while he perceptively outlined recent trends in European history, he also orchestrated a crescendo of anti-Prussianism: 'The German eagle with a Prussian head looks all round the horizon not so much for something to do that would count for good in the records of the earth, as simply for something good to get. He gazes upon the land and upon the sea with the same covetous steadiness for he has become of late a maritime eagle' (*NLL*, 93). Conrad concluding with 'a warning that, so far as a future of liberty, concord, and justice is concerned: "*Le Prussianisme – voilà l'ennemi!*"' (*NLL*, 114). Conrad's essay formed part of a series of articles in the press dealing with British-German relations. 'Inflammatory articles in *Vanity Fair*, the *Army and Navy Gazette*, the *Spectator* and *National Review*

1871–1906, see Franco Moretti, *Atlas of the European Novel, 1800–1900* (London: Verso, 1999), 139.

[4] Wyndham Lewis offered a more disingenuous preface to *Tarr* in 1918: 'This book was begun eight years ago; so I have not produced this disagreeable German for the gratification of primitive partisanship aroused by the war. On the other hand, having had him up my sleeve for so long, I let him out at this moment in the undisguised belief that he is very apposite. I am incidentally glad to get rid of him.' Wyndham Lewis, *Tarr: The 1918 Version*, edited by Paul O'Keefe (Santa Rosa: Black Sparrow Press, 1990), 13.

[5] The essay was also published in the *North American Review* (33–55) in July 1905.

confirmed the impression that Germany was a dangerous rival.'[6] In the *Fortnightly Review* in November 1905, an essay entitled 'Great Britain and Germany,' by J.A. Spender, editor of *The Westminster Gazette*, sought to quieten the provocative atmosphere. Spender drew attention to the kind of writing represented in 'Autocracy and War,' noting that Anglo-German relations had descended into a 'quarrel about the future, a quarrel of conjectures, imputed motives and suspicions in which neither side can verify anything.'[7] In the *Review of Reviews* in July 1905, journalist W.T. Stead condemned Conrad, claiming he had the 'logic of the alarmist,'[8] while on its appearance in *Notes on Life and Letters* in 1921, the *Weekly Review* labelled the piece 'condemnation in the form of rhapsody.'[9]

'Autocracy and War' positions Conrad as a representative of the Edwardian generation that engendered the language of international rivalry before 1914. As Keith Carabine has noted, the 'ostensible stance of "Autocracy and War" is that of Joseph Conrad, the eminent English novelist, known to be of Polish origins, taking advantage of his unique position to warn his Edwardian public' of the threat posed by Germany.[10] Conrad prepared for hostilities at a time when journals 'exacerbated the existing tension' and only 'Germany had the capacity to upset the *status quo*; she alone, therefore, posed a threat to the peace of Europe.'[11] Conrad contributed to a European discourse of antagonism, and he would later sharply feel the accusation that such ideologies had encouraged war and sent youth off to fight and die.

[6] Zara S. Steiner and Keith Nelson eds., *Britain and the Origins of the First World War*, 2nd ed. (Basingstoke: Macmillan, 2003), 33.

[7] J.A. Spender, 'Great Britain and Germany,' *The Fortnightly Review* 467 (1905): 812.

[8] W.T. Stead, 'Russia: "Ghost, Ghoul, Djinn, Etc.": The Fantastic Rhetoric of Mr. Conrad,' *Review of Reviews* 33.187 (July 1905): 51–52.

[9] Quoted in J.H. Stape ed., introduction, Joseph Conrad, *Notes on Life and Letters* (Cambridge: Cambridge University Press, 2004), xlii.

[10] Keith Carabine, *The Life and the Art: A Study of Conrad's 'Under Western Eyes'* (Amsterdam: Rodopi, 1996), 84.

[11] Keith Nelson and Zara S. Steiner, *Britain and the Origins of the First World War*, 2nd edn (Basingstoke: Macmillan, 2003), 179, 189.

CONRAD AND THE FIRST WORLD WAR

Wyndham Lewis believed the 'curtain went down' on Conrad and Henry James in 1914.[12] Because he was in Poland between August and November 1914, Conrad was not summoned at the outbreak of the war by C.F.G. Masterman, head of the British War Propaganda Bureau, to a meeting of writers at Wellington House in London. Conrad may have been viewed as too much of an outsider at a time of intense national pride. As Zara Steiner and Keith Nelson note, in 1914 amongst the establishment, there 'was an excessive pride in being English and a contempt for foreigners which scarcely accords with the diplomatic profession.'[13] Nevertheless, Conrad's wartime work responds to the consequences of this literary meeting. According to Samuel Hynes, Masterman, in recruiting ageing war propagandists such as Hardy, Kipling, and Wells, initiated the concept of 'the Old Men, as the makers of the war and enemies of the young.'[14] The subsequent polarisation of home front and battlefield, the soldier and the home-front observer, saw Conrad accept the relative obsolescence of the writer during war: 'It seems almost criminal levity to talk at this time of books, stories, publication. This war attends my uneasy pillow like a nightmare' (*CL* 5, 439). Conrad's fatigue was revealed when 'Poland Revisited,' previously published in the *Daily News* and the *Boston Evening Transcript* in 1915, was routinely offered to Edith Wharton for *The Book of the Homeless* (1916), a volume of propaganda whose proceeds aided Belgian refugees.[15]

In 1916, J.M. Dent wrote to Conrad that 'we are witnessing the birth throes of a new world, and you of all men, it seems to me, should be the

---

[12] Wyndham Lewis, *Creatures of Habit and Creatures of Change: Essays on Art, Literature and Society 1914–1956*, Edited by Paul Edwards (Santa Rosa: Black Sparrow Press, 1989), 222.

[13] *Britain and the Origins of the First World War*, 185.

[14] Samuel Hynes, *A War Imagined: The First World War and English Culture* (London: Bodley Head, 1990), 26.

[15] The volume also featured W.B. Yeats's poem 'A Reason for Keeping Silent,' which echoed Conrad's sentiments. It was later published in *The Wild Swans at Coole* (1919) as 'On Being Asked for a War Poem': 'I think it better that in times like these/ A poet's mouth be silent, for in truth/ We have no gift to set a statesman right.' *Selected Poems of W.B. Yeats*, edited by M.L. Rosenthal (New York: Macmillan, 1962), 66.

prophet of its psychology' (*CL* 5, 681). 'Poland Revisited' recalls Conrad's 1914 journey to Poland in heightened Romantic language, featuring an elegiac representation of nineteenth century Poland and pre-war Britain.[16] Conrad idealises a pastoral England shattered by the onset of an industrialised war society. Remembering his departure from Kent for Poland, Conrad writes: 'All unconscious of going towards the very scenes of war I carried off in my eye this tiny fragment of Great Britain: a few fields, a wooded rise, a clump of trees or two, with a short stretch of road, and here and there a gleam of red wall and tiled roof above the darkening hedges wrapped up in a soft mist and peace' (*NLL*, 119). John Masefield's poem 'August 1914,' which appeared in the *English Review* in September, also observed the harmony of the English countryside in the gathering dusk of war: 'These homes, this valley spread below me here, / The rooks, the tilted stacks, the beasts in pen, / Have been the heartfelt things, past-speaking dear / To unknown generations of dead men.'[17] Turning to the continent, Conrad recognised 'the futilities of an individual past,' the traditional material for his fiction, instead noting the emergence of modern European history in 'the faint boom of the big guns at work on the coast of Flanders – shaping the future' (*NLL*, 173). History could be definitively observed *becoming* history, and Conrad's essay is an early example of the structuring of an ordered past before the disorder that accompanied the shaking of the European system. Geoff Dyer notes that: 'The past *as past* was preserved by the war that shattered it. By ushering in a future characterized by instability and uncertainty, it embalmed for ever a past characterized by stability and certainty.'[18]

In his post-war work *Disenchantment* (1922), C.E. Montague captured this still dominant view of European history, best represented by Joseph Roth's *The Radetzky March* (1932) and Stefan Zweig's *The World of Yesterday* (1943), which looked back to the pre-war days as a Golden Age. Zweig opened his autobiography with a chapter entitled

---

[16] The essay first appeared in the *Daily News* in four instalments, divided into such sections as: 'The March of Events,' 'The Fount of Memory,' 'Youth,' 'Memories,' 'Boyhood Days,' and 'Shaping the future.' See *Daily News and Leader*, March 29, 1915, March 31, 1915, April 6, 1915, and April 9, 1915.

[17] John Masefield, *Collected Poems* (London: Heinemann, 1924), 375. The same imagery appears in Wilfred Owen's 'The Send-Off.'

[18] Geoff Dyer, *The Missing of the Somme* (London: Phoenix Press, 1994), 5.

'The World of Security,'[19] and for Montague, 'A century of almost unbroken European peace – unbroken, that is, by wars hugely destructive – had built up insensibly in men's minds a consciousness of an unbounded general stability in the political as well as in the physical world.'[20] Conrad's 'London before the war' in 'Poland Revisited' engenders a retrospective idealisation of history, offering a 'Venice-like aspect of rainy evenings, the wet asphalted streets lying with the sheen of sleeping water in winding canals and the great houses of the city towering all dark like empty palaces above the reflected lights on the glistening roadway' (*NLL*, 120). Conrad here evokes the later, impressionistic pre-war world of Virginia Woolf's *Jacob's Room* (1922), offering an ordered past that basks innocently in 'the diminishing minutes of peace' (*NLL*, 120). Conrad's chronological shifts transport him further through history to a post-Napoleonic London rendered in a language of conscious historicism: In a 'Dickensian nook of London [. . .]. The dust of the Waterloo year lay on the panes and frames of its windows; early Georgian grime clung to its sombre wainscoting' (*NLL*, 122). The author embraces the security of the nineteenth century, and Conrad would later take refuge in the romance of the Napoleonic era. 'Poland Revisited' expresses Conrad's sense of history in flux: his journey to Poland, a 'journey in time, into the past' (*NLL*, 120), revisiting and symbolically entombing the world of the nineteenth century.

Once he engaged with the conflict, when his son Borys enlisted in the Army Service Corps, Conrad proposed to write an 'early personal experience thing' (*CL* 5, 441). This confirmed his position in 'Poland Revisited' that 'things acquire significance by the lapse of time' (*NLL*, 126). The renewed significance lay in Conrad's attempt to empathise with the experience of soldiers. Conrad insisted that there was 'no question here of any parallelism. That notion never entered my head. But there was a feeling of identity, though with an enormous difference of scale – as of one single drop measured against the bitter and stormy immensity of an ocean' (*SL*, vi–vii). Conrad's wartime fiction, *The Shadow-Line*, 'The Warrior's Soul,' and 'The Tale,' constitutes a dialogue with youth, one member of the older generation asking for

---

[19] Stefan Zweig, *The World of Yesterday* (London: University of Nebraska Press, 1964), 1–27.
[20] C.E. Montague, *Disenchantment* (London, 1922), 86.

understanding. Recalling the wartime composition of *The Arrow of Gold* (1919), Conrad wrote: 'If anything it is perhaps a little sympathy that the writer expects for his buried youth, as he lives it over again at the end of his insignificant course on this earth' (*AG*, 4–5). In this respect, the war influenced Conrad's posthumous reputation. In 1917, Conrad began producing 'Author's Notes,' stressing 'the authenticity of the stories as based on his personal experiences and observations; this was to become the dominant motif of his author's notes.'[21] Conrad alleviated his marginalisation by portraying his own youthful initiation into experience.

The Shadow-Line had 'a sort of spiritual meaning' (*CL* 5, 458). The story's dedication – 'To / Borys and all others / who like himself have crossed / in early youth the shadow-line / of their generation / With Love' – addresses the living and stands as a memorial to those already lost in the war. Conrad resurrected his characteristic literary voice, now endowed with a new importance, as the remembered younger self articulated Conrad's identification with youth at the Front while the controlling narrative voice, typically the ageing nostalgic, embodied Conrad's war-time position. *The Shadow-Line* aligns the experience of the soldier with the experience of the onlooker/artist. For the young captain facing the difficulties of his first command, the sense of stasis before the storm at sea corresponded to the anticipation of battle: 'In the tension of silence I was suffering from it seemed to me that the first crash must turn me into dust. And thunder was, most likely, what would happen next. Stiff all over and hardly breathing, I waited with a horribly strained expectation. Nothing happened. It was maddening' (*SL*, 113). *The Shadow-Line* saluted the youth of Europe (Conrad's dedication, notably, is not partisan) going through the fire of initiation to experience, while simultaneously portraying an ageing narrator sidelined by history. In 'The Warrior's Soul,' Conrad later wrote: 'And what more desolate prospect for a man with such a soul than to be imprisoned on the eve of war; to be cut off from his country in danger, from his family, from his duty, from honour, and – well – from glory, too' (*TH*, 16). *The Shadow-Line*, however, unites youth and age as Captain Giles collaborates with the young captain, and the denouement resolves the generational discord that began the work.[22]

As *The Shadow-Line* ran in the *English Review* and Conrad received favourable reviews of *Victory* and the collection of stories *Within the Tides*, Siegfried Sassoon's poetry was appearing in the *Cambridge Magazine*. Conrad was familiar with Sassoon's anti-war stance. Anticipating a visit from Sassoon in 1918, Conrad wrote: 'I know his verse only in extracts and I want to see it all before I meet the man' (*CL* 6, 310). Conrad's response to being on the fringes of the war forms part of a wider trend in the psyche of Britain between 1914–18. In *The Tatler* in October 1916, Richard King wrote that 'War – as we presently understand it – is the sacrifice of the young and the innocent on the altar erected by the old and middle-aged.'[23] In April 1916, the *Cambridge Magazine* had published 'The Betrayal of the Young,' which acknowledged that 'between the old and the young there is to-day a great gulf fixed.' A soldier noted that 'In the cavalry messes things are often said which wouldn't please Lord Northcliffe and the old men who made the war,' while a private about to return to France vehemently announced the soldier's alienation: 'You people at home are responsible for continuing this slaughter. Secretly you know it. Individually you mostly acknowledge it.'[24]

'The Warrior's Soul,' a tale of the Napoleonic Wars, appeared in *Land and Water* in March 1917, registering Conrad's continued response to generational conflict in English society.[25] The story opened

---

[22] In *All Quiet on the Western Front* (1929), Erich Maria Remarque remembered the trial of war: 'Perhaps it was only the privilege of our youth, but as yet we recognised no limits and saw nowhere an end. We had that thrill of expectation in the blood which united us with the course of our days.' Erich Maria Remarque, *All Quiet on the Western Front*, translated by A.W. Wheen (London: Putnam, 1929), 136–37. In *The Shadow-Line*, Conrad felt 'It is the privilege of early youth to live in advance of its days in all the beautiful continuity of hope which knows no pauses and no introspection' (*SL*, 3).

[23] Hynes, *A War Imagined*, 247.

[24] *Cambridge Magazine* 5.18 (1916), 407, 408.

[25] Conrad was not alone in his focus on the relevance of the Napoleonic campaigns and the figure of the French Emperor to the Great War. In 1915, *T.P.'s Weekly* featured regular articles comparing Napoleon's imprisonment on St. Helena with the expected fate of Kaiser Wilhelm II. Conrad's presentation of the Napoleonic Wars as the most important military event in European history contrasted with the views of those fighting between 1914–18, who regarded the First World War as superseding the past in its destructive force. T.E. Lawrence wrote of Thomas Hardy: 'Napoleon is a real man to

with a possible address to soldiers, as the 'old officer with long white moustaches gave rein to his indignation,' asking: 'Is it possible that you youngsters should have no more sense than that! Some of you had better wipe the milk off your upper lip before you start to pass judgement on the few poor stragglers of a generation which has done and suffered not a little in its time' (*TH*, 1). The veteran reminds the reader that 'we had our losses too' (*TH*, 5). 'The Warrior's Soul,' however, accepts misgivings about the old guard: 'the innocent [...] found himself in distinguished company there, amongst men of considerable position. And you know what that means: thick waists, bald heads, teeth that are not – as some satirist puts it. Imagine amongst them a nice boy, fresh and simple, like an apple just off the tree' (*TH*, 9). Conrad echoes Sassoon's 'The Fathers,' where old men sit at home in decaying complacency while the young soldier experiences battle. 'The Warrior's Soul' also treats perceived public enthusiasm for the war: 'People without compassion are the civilians, government officials, merchants and such like. As to the ferocious talk one hears from a lot of decent people in war time – well, the tongue is an unruly member at best, and when there is some excitement going there is no curbing its furious activity' (*TH*, 17). Most poignantly though, Conrad evoked a landscape disturbed by innumerable dead. In the 'general mourning I seemed to hear the sighs of mankind falling to die in the midst of a nature without life. [...] a pathetic multitude of small dark mounds stretching away under the moonlight in a clear, still, and pitiless atmosphere – a sort of horrible peace' (*TH*, 20).

Conrad's peripheral experience of the war was increased by his paternal anxiety about his son's safety (Borys Conrad survived the war), the loss of soldier friends such as Edward Thomas (1878–1917), but also because of his reputation as a writer of adventurous stories and his knowledge that soldiers read his work. Conrad's correspondence with press magnate Lord Northcliffe reinforced the public image of

---

him [...]. He lives in [t]his period, and thinks of it as the great war.' Lawrence, influenced by *Lord Jim* in the writing of *Seven Pillars of Wisdom* (1926), believed 'that nightmare through the fringe of which I passed has dwarfed all memories of other wars, so that they seem trivial, half-amusing incidents.' David Garnett ed., *The Letters of T.E. Lawrence* (London: Jonathan Cape, 1938), 429–30. For a study of the relationship between Conrad and Lawrence, see Ton Hoenselaars and Gene M. Moore, 'Conrad and T.E. Lawrence,' *Conradiana* 27.1 (1995): 3–20.

Conrad as a man who relished danger. Writing to Conrad after a visit to the Front, Northcliffe related: 'More than once have I found "Victory" being read by officers at the front. These men of action love your work.'[26] In February 1915, Jean Schlumberger, serving in France, and later co-founder of the *Nouvelle Revue Française*, wrote to Conrad of his delight in coming across a copy of 'The Secret Sharer.' Conrad expressed satisfaction that his work resonated with the experience of the soldier: 'Proud that my little tale can be read amidst the din of war' (*CL* 5, 443). Importantly, the outlets for Conrad's new fiction, *The English Review*, *Land and Water*, and *The Strand*, were all to be found at the Front, and Conrad initially published the essay 'First News,' an account of the outbreak of the war in Poland, in *Reveille: Devoted to the Disabled Sailor & Soldier* in August 1918. Conrad was therefore conscious that he had a contemporary audience amongst soldiers, as the 'reviews, especially *Blackwood's*, *The English Review*, and the *Cornhill* were much appreciated' by the military.[27] In these periodicals, soldiers could estimate the indifference of the home front to the fate of the soldier. According to Paul Fussell, the 'standard officers' dugout required [. . .] current copies of the *Bystander*, the *Tatler*, and *Punch*.'[28] In Theodore Wesley Koch's estimation, Conrad was popular in the trenches, and 'periodicals played a great part . . . with the wounded soldier, *The Strand*, *The Windsor*, *The Red*, *Pearson's*, *The Wide World*, and *John Bull*.'[29] In 1917, Conrad maintained *The Shadow-Line* was written for soldiers, not the general market for fiction: 'I did not like the idea of it being associated with fiction in a vol of stories. And this is also the reason I've inscribed it to Borys – and the others' (*CL* 6, 37). An article entitled the 'Effect of the War on Literature' in *The Scotsman* on 15 May 1916, announced that 'Joseph Conrad had come into his own' in popularity since August 1914.[30]

---

[26] J.H. Stape and Owen Knowles, eds, *A Portrait in Letters: Correspondence to and about Conrad* (Amsterdam: Rodopi, 1996), 108.

[27] Theodore Wesley Koch, *Books in the War: The Romance of Library War Service* (Cambridge: The Riverside Press, 1919), 182–83.

[28] Paul Fussell, *The Great War and Modern Memory* (London: Oxford University Press, 1975), 67.

[29] Koch, *Books in the War*, 258.

[30] 'Effect of the War on Literature,' *The Scotsman*, 15 May (1916): 7.

Published in *The Strand Magazine* in October 1917, 'The Tale' is infused with an 'infinite sadness,' capturing a society in mourning for soldiers from whom 'no answering murmur came' (*TH*, 59). Conrad's work resonates with later interpretations of the war, articulated in the outpouring of war memoirs in the 1920s. Securities and realities from the pre-war world are redundant. In 'The Tale' the writer has become irrelevant, and the woman in the story delivers judgement on those who held authority before the war: 'You used to tell – your – your simple and – and professional – tales very well at one time. [...] You had a – a sort of art – in the days – the days before the war' (*TH*, 60). The war has altered artistic representation. Previously, stories such as Conrad's could be written, but the war has shifted aesthetic and ideological presuppositions. According to Walter Benjamin, 'men returned from the battle-field grown silent – not richer but poorer in communicable experience,'[31] and Fussell notes that 'the presumed inadequacy of language itself to convey the facts about trench warfare is one of the motifs of all those who wrote about the war.'[32] Language is scrutinised in 'The Tale' as an Officer and his acquaintance discuss the meaning of the word 'duty.' The officer claims the word 'contains infinities,' but he is interrupted, his authority harshly undermined: 'What is this jargon?' (*TH*, 61).

'The Tale' resulted from Conrad's engagement in propaganda work, and from his correspondence with Ford Madox Ford, stationed in France in 1916, which discussed in detail the difficulties of artistically representing the war. In December 1916, from hospital in France, Ford wrote informing Conrad: 'I have been reading – rather deliriously – "Chance" since I have been in this nice kind place. [...] [E]ven in a comparatively loose work like "Chance" there is a sense of cavernous gloom, lit up by sparks from pickaxes.'[33] During the same period, Ford wrote that he would 'continue, "for yr information and necessary action" my notes upon sounds,' indicating here that Conrad had expressly asked Ford to relate the experience of the war. The letters

---

[31] Walter Benjamin, *Illuminations*, edited by Hannah Arendt (London: Pimlico, 1999), 84.
[32] Fussell, *Great War and Modern Memory*, 170.
[33] Ford Madox Ford, *Letters of Ford Madox Ford*, edited by Richard M. Ludwig (Princeton: Princeton University Press, 1965), 79.

are an intriguing account of someone trying to render the sounds and feelings of war to one desperate for information. Ford explained: 'Shells falling on a church: these make a huge "*corrump*" sound, followed by a noise like crockery falling of a tray – as the roof tiles fall off. [...] Emotions again: I saw two men and three mules (the first time I saw a casualty) killed by one shell. [...] These things gave me no *emotion* at all – they seemed *obvious*.'[34] Ford also believed that his recording of the war originated in 'the annalist's desire to help the historian – or, in a humble sort of way, my desire to help you, cher maître! – if you ever wanted to do anything in *"this line."* [...] And I, to that extent, shd. once more have collaborated.'[35] Conrad's only work 'in this line,' 'The Tale,' registers Ford's insistence on the impossibility of telling.

One vindication of Conrad's engagement with the war came in the *Westminster Gazette* in August 1917. In a prize-winning essay entitled 'The Tendency in English Fiction in 1917,' a prisoner of war named Karshish maintained that *The Shadow-Line* gave 'the impression of one who tells a tale while subjected to drawn-out mental or physical pain. The tale, it seems, would not be told were not the need to tell it imperative, and the pain is a spur hastening the action' (*CL* 6, 115).[36]

At the Admiralty's request, Conrad toured naval bases, went on a minesweeping expedition in the *Brigadier* in the North Sea, and tracked German submarines in the Q-ship *Ready* in autumn 1916. However, the importance of Conrad's propaganda activities should not be overstated. The short articles 'Flight' and 'The Unlighted Coast' 'contained no trace of propaganda and not even much optimism. This failure must have discouraged Conrad from further efforts, and, despite his own occasional mentions of projects, he did not write any more articles about the war.'[37] One reason for this can be found in Conrad's scepticism about official political and military doctrines in the Great War for Civilisation, which self-righteously resurrected the ancient dichotomy of civilisation and barbarism that Conrad had treated ironically in his writing. Despite his cordial relations with Lord Northcliffe, for whose *Daily Mail* Conrad wrote the article 'Tradition' in 1918, in a letter to

[34] Ford, *Letters*, 73–74.
[35] Ford, *Letters*, 75.
[36] See *Westminster Gazette*, 4 August 1917.
[37] Najder, *Conrad: A Chronicle*, 422.

John Quinn, Conrad expressed dissatisfaction with newspaper reporting of the war: 'A miserable affair no matter how much newspapers may try to write it up' (*CL* 5, 446).

Ford Madox Ford described the Armistice as a 'crack across the table of history,'[38] indicating the war had ruptured Europe's historical continuity. Despite his post-war observation of international politics, Conrad's Proustian engagement with the past meant the emerging legend of the *belle époque* held an easy fascination. While many post-war writers, such as Ford, Joseph Roth, and Thomas Mann, returned to pre-war culture in their work, Conrad looked further back, returning to his youth in Marseilles in *The Arrow of Gold* (1919), concluding former artistic ideas in *The Rescue* (1920), and visiting the formative points of nineteenth century history in *The Rover* (1923) and *Suspense* (1925). By placing himself in the nineteenth century and by employing conventional narrative methods, Conrad experienced the solace of memory and historical escapism, but, with the ascendancy of high-Modernist writers such as Joyce, Pound, Lewis, and later Faulkner and Céline, perhaps saw his worst wartime fears of artistic marginalisation ultimately realised.

EUROPEAN LITERATURE AND THE LEGEND OF NAPOLEON

The Rover (1923) and *Suspense* (1925) have been understood as 'the expiring gasp of a once-mighty intellect.'[39] Scholars cite creative exhaustion and Conrad's decision to write historical fiction as contributing factors to the weakness of his later work, with the writer criticised for exploring his interest in French history and culture.[40] While recent

---

[38] Ford Madox Ford, *A Man Could Stand Up* (London: Duckworth, 1926), 13.
[39] Review of *The Rover* by Frederick Van de Water, *New York Tribune* 16 (1923), reprinted in Sherry ed., *Critical Heritage*, 351.
[40] See Thomas Moser, *Joseph Conrad: Achievement and Decline* (Cambridge, MA: Harvard University Press, 1957); Albert Guerard, *Conrad the Novelist* (Cambridge, MA: Harvard University Press, 1958); and Eloise Knapp Hay, *The Political Novels of Joseph Conrad*. For sympathetic readings of Conrad's later works, see Ian Watt, *Essays on Conrad* (Cambridge: Cambridge University Press, 2000); Daniel Schwarz, *Conrad: The Later Fiction*; Daphna Erdinast-Vulcan, *Joseph Conrad and the Modern Temper* (Oxford: Clarendon Press, 1991); Robert Hampson, *Joseph Conrad: Betrayal and Identity* (Basingstoke: Macmillan, 1992); and Susan Jones, *Conrad and Women* (Oxford: Clarendon Press, 1999).

studies have challenged Thomas Moser's influential Achievement and Decline thesis, there has yet been a failure to examine critically the focus of Conrad's last works: Napoleon Bonaparte and his political and cultural significance.

In her study of Conrad's political novels, Eloise Knapp Hay gives a cursory analysis of *The Rover* and *Suspense*, insisting that what 'made Conrad and other Poles go on brooding over his [Napoleon's] career is hard to understand.'[41] Certainly, the 'nationality, the antecedents, made it impossible' (*PR*, 121) for Napoleon to be anything other than a major presence in Conrad's life and career. Napoleon and his legacy were a decisive political and cultural force in nineteenth-century Poland, and when Conrad moved to Adolphe Thiers and Marshall MacMahon's Third Republic France in the 1870s, he arrived in a country in which the political forces of right and left were still laying claim to the Emperor. Despite its ostensibly republican credentials, 'the pedagogues of the Third Republic did not hesitate to draw upon the imperial heritage: Napoleon, like Joan of Arc and Charlemagne, was a useful icon for a regime that sought to reconstruct the nation's collective identity on the ruins of the 1870–1871 defeat.'[42] Indeed, one of the chief figures in the Third Republic, Thiers, had, in his earlier *Histoire du Consulat et de l'Empire* (1845–62), written 'the first serious history of Napoleonic rule.'[43]

Conrad was by no means the first or most famous Pole to arrive in France shaped by the legend of Napoleon, and into a culture still negotiating its relationship with the Emperor. In the 1840s in Paris, Adam Mickiewicz had come under the influence of the mystic Andrzej Towiański (1779–1878), who introduced him to the 'romantic cult of Napoleon as a man of Destiny, [and] prepared in the poet the way for his mystic doctrine. He began in his course to teach this doctrine and to preach the cult of the Great Emperor.'[44] As Jean-Charles Gille-Maisani

---

[41] Knapp Hay, *Political Novels of Joseph Conrad*, 316–17.

[42] Sudhir Hazareesingh, *The Legend of Napoleon* (London: Granta, 2005), 265.

[43] Hazareesingh, *Legend of Napoleon*, 173.

[44] Wacław Lednicki, 'Mickiewicz at the Collège de France,' Mieczysław Giergielewicz ed., *Polish Civilisation: Essays and Studies* (New York: New York University Press, 1979), 197. Alexander Herzen gives an evocative critique of Mickiewicz's Napoleonic mysticism in *My Past and Thoughts* (Volume 3), recalling a meeting with the Polish poet in Paris in 1848 and his indoctrination by Towiański and the Polish mystic philosopher Józef

has remarked, 'Mickiewicz sees in Napoleon less a spiritual father than an ideal man, a man of destiny with supernatural attributes,' and Mickiewicz wrote that it was 'through Napoleon that the Polish people understand France.'[45] The return of Napoleon's remains from St. Helena to Paris in 1840 saw a heightened interest in the legacy of Napoleon in France. At this period, French literature was informing Polish culture, and the writing of Victor Hugo, a somewhat ambiguous proponent of the cult of Napoleon, was a major presence in Poland.[46] Apollo Korzeniowski's translations of Hugo's work ensured that Conrad was introduced to the legend of Napoleon and the battle over his memory from an early age. Napoleon surfaces intermittently throughout Conrad's literary career; he represents an historical reference point for Conrad in 'Autocracy and War'; the glamour and tragedy of the Napoleonic period appear in 'The Duel' (1908), *A Personal Record*, 'Prince Roman,' and 'The Warrior's Soul'; and as early as 1902, Conrad considered writing a Napoleonic novel.[47]

Before embarking on his artistic journey to Napoleonic France in his last works, Conrad recalled that 'The Duel' (1908) had captured the 'spirit' of the Napoleonic era. The legend of Napoleon was appealing to Conrad's creative imagination: 'The truth is that in my mind the story is nothing but a serious and even earnest attempt at a bit of historical fiction. I had heard in my boyhood a good deal of the great Napoleonic

Hoëne-Wroński (1778–1853): 'Messianism, that mania of Wronski's, that delirium of Tovjanski's, had turned the brains of hundreds of Poles, among them Mickiewicz himself. The worship of Napoleon had done nothing for them; he [Napoleon] had no love for Poland' (38). Herzen felt that 'Mickiewicz's private life was gloomy; there was something unfortunate about it, something dark, some "visitation of God"' (39).

[45] Jean-Charles Gille-Maisani, *Adam Mickiewicz, poète national de la Pologne: étude psychanalytique et caractérologique* (Paris: Belles Lettres, 1988), 658.

[46] Hugo championed the cause of an independent Polish state in his political writings and speeches. See the entry on Hugo in Jean Tulard ed., *Dictionnaire du Second Empire* (Paris: Fayard, 1995), 629.

[47] With the exception of a cameo appearance in *Suspense*, Napoleon does not feature in person in Conrad's writing. As early as 1913, in one of his periodic letters announcing plans for a Napoleonic novel, Conrad was aware he wanted Napoleon to be present in the novel in the tradition of nineteenth-century treatments of the Emperor, following Stendhal and Tolstoy. He envisaged a work that would reveal 'the shadow of the Emperor – for He will not appear, or only for a moment' (*CL* 5, 207). In 1922, as he worked on *Suspense*, Conrad avowed that it would be a work 'in which Napoleon 1st will have a speaking part of about twenty-two words' (*CL* 7, 491).

legend. I had a genuine feeling that I would find myself at home in it' (*SS*, viii). Conrad's treatment of Napoleon vacillated between the romantic and sceptical traditions of the 'great Napoleonic legend.' Two contrasting positions on Napoleon coloured nineteenth-century European literature, captured in the polarisation of the historical views of Stendhal in *Le Rouge et le Noir* (1830), *La Chartreuse de Parme* (1839), and his posthumously published *Vie de Napoléon* (1875), and those of Tolstoy in *War and Peace* (1865–69).[48] Stendhal submits to the idea of the great man in history, delineating the intensely romantic Julien Sorel, who falls under the spell of Napoleon through reading Emmanuel Las Cases's *Mémorial de Sainte Hélène* (1823). Tolstoy, although influenced by Stendhal, pronounces the impossibility of any individual controlling historical forces.[49] Conrad greatly admired Stendhal and Balzac, two writers whose works stoked the literary fire of the Napoleonic obsession.[50] Conrad's famously ambivalent relationship with Dostoevsky also has correspondences with the European fixation with Napoleon, as both writers engage with questions of men of genius and historical judgement.[51] In *Crime and Punishment*, Raskolnikov 'got terribly carried away with Napoleon – that is, essentially what carried him away was that a great many men of genius disregarded isolated evil and stepped over it without hesitation. He seems to have imagined that he, too, was a man of genius.'[52]

R.S. Alexander, Robert Gildea, and Sudhir Hazareesingh have detailed the simultaneous development of the Cult of Napoleon and the Black Legend; the Cult of Napoleon being the process whereby Napoleon emerged as representative of the ideals of the 1789 Revolution and symbolic of the French people, while the Black Legend demonised

---

[48] See Geoffrey Strickland, *Stendhal: The Education of a Novelist* (Cambridge: Cambridge University Press, 1974), 99–125.

[49] For an insightful treatment of Tolstoy's understanding of history, see Isaiah Berlin, *The Hedgehog and the Fox: An Essay on Tolstoy's View of History* (London: Weidenfeld & Nicholson, 1953).

[50] See J.H. Stape, 'One can learn something from Balzac: Conrad and Balzac,' *Conrad: Intertexts and Appropriations: Essays in Memory of Yves Hervouet*, edited by Gene M. Moore and J.H. Stape (Amsterdam and Atlanta, GA: Rodopi, 1997), 103–18.

[51] For a good an analysis of Conrad's relationship with Dostoevsky, see Carabine, *Life and the Art*, 64–96.

[52] Fyodor Dostoevsky, *Crime and Punishment*, translated by Richard Pevear and Larissa Volokhonsky (London: Vintage, 1993), 491.

Napoleon as a military dictator.[53] Conrad encountered such battles over Napoleon in Poland, France, and through his voracious reading of European literature. He recalled his ancestors' adventures in the Napoleonic armies in *A Personal Record*, and in *The Mirror of the Sea* Conrad remembered reading Balzac's *Histoire des Treize* (1833–35) (set in post-Napoleonic France) while in Marseilles. Conrad reveals his consciousness of the shifting reception of Napoleon's political ideology throughout nineteenth-century Europe. In England, Edmund Burke's *Reflections on the Revolution in France* (1791) stood opposed to the thought of William Hazlitt and William Godwin, who accepted Napoleon as a continuation of the French revolutionary spirit. Wordsworth, Coleridge, and Walter Savage Landor at first bowed to Napoleon's 'genius,' but later denounced him as a tyrant.[54] Conrad would echo these English responses to Napoleon in *Suspense*, with the attitudes of Burke, Coleridge, Walter Scott, Wordsworth, Byron, Robert Southey, Leigh Hunt, Landor, and Hazlitt all detectable in the novel, transmitted by the Englishman Cosmo Latham and the various political attitudes of his contemporaries in England. Cosmo's father is representative of the broad conservative English response to the Napoleonic wars: 'In politics he was a partisan of Mr. Pitt, rather than a downright Tory. He loved his country, believed in its greatness, in its superior virtue, in its irresistible power. Nothing could shake his fidelity to national prejudices of every sort. He had no great liking for grandees and mere aristocrats, despised the fashionable world, and would have nothing whatever to do with any kind of "upstart"' (*S*, 20). Conversely, the English Dr. Martel identifies Cosmo as a Hazlittean liberal: 'I know there are amongst us in England a good many young men who call themselves revolutionists and even republicans. Charming young men, generous and all that. Friends of Boney. You might be one of them' (*S*, 183).

---

[53] Hazareesingh, *Legend of Napoleon*, 2–3. For a study of the black legend of Napoleon see, Jean Tulard, *L'Anti-Napoléon: la légende noire de l'empereur* (Paris: Juillard, 1965); J. Lucas-Dubreton, *Le culte de Napoléon* (Paris: Albin Michel, 1960).

[54] For an excellent study of Napoleon's importance for English Romantic writers, see Simon Bainbridge, *Napoleon and English Romanticism* (Cambridge: Cambridge University Press, 1995).

In France, Napoleon evolved into a 'champion of French liberties because, in the popular mind, he had become (and perhaps had remained all the time) a powerful symbol of the Revolutionary era.'[55] Conrad's favourite French poet, Victor Hugo, captured the transformation of Napoleon in the popular imagination in 'Expiation,' from *Les Châtiments* (1853). Hugo's early hatred of Napoleon gradually dissipated, and the 1851 coup of Louis Napoleon that launched the French Second Empire forced Hugo to renegotiate his relationship with Napoleon the First. Hugo was critical of Napoleon's seizure of power of 1799, yet in the tradition of Marx's essay 'The Eighteenth Brumaire of Louis Bonaparte' (1852), which described Louis Bonaparte as a farcical descendant of the original Emperor, Hugo saw Napoleon now representing historical greatness compared to his nephew.[56] Hugo was 'divided against himself by the cult of Napoleon, seeing greatness on the one hand, despotism and militarism on the other. [...] The behaviour of Napoléon-le-Petit had a retrospective impact on perceptions of Napoléon-le-Grand. [...] And yet Hugo seemed able even then to keep separate the crimes of Napoleon from the "dazzling curtain of glory."'[57] In 'Expiation,' history constructed the reputation of its 'great' men: 'Napoleon went to sleep beneath his willow. / And then, from pole to pole, people forgot / The tyrant, and revered the hero. Poets/ Stamped the brows of the hangman kings, and thoughtfully/ Commiserated with his fallen glory.' For Hugo, time and popular culture were in the process of creating the Napoleon that would be handed down to posterity, overshadowing a just historical evaluation of the Emperor: 'Only one aspect of his age was noticed, / Only his days of brilliance were remembered; / It seemed the strange man had made history drunk.'[58] These competing claims to Napoleon colour Conrad's representation of the Emperor. In 'Autocracy and War,' Conrad viewed Napoleon as 'a personality without law or faith whom it has been the fashion to represent as an eagle, but was in truth much more like a sort

---

[55] Hazareesingh, *Legend of Napoleon*, 135.

[56] For a life of Hugo and his complex relationship with Napoleon, see Graham Robb, *Victor Hugo* (London: Picador, 1997).

[57] Robert Gildea, *The Past in French History* (New Haven and London: Yale University Press, 1996), 98.

[58] Victor Hugo, *Selected Poems of Victor Hugo*, translated by E.H. and A.M. Blackmore (London: University of Chicago Press, 2001), 141–43.

of vulture preying upon the body of a Europe which did indeed for some dozen of years resemble very much a corpse' (*NLL*, 73). Conrad condemns Napoleon's politics, but focuses on history and judgement, registering awareness of interpretations of Napoleon, the 'fashion to represent' the Emperor as either an eagle or vulture in the nineteenth century.

Nineteenth-century Poland first introduced Conrad to both the disappointing political legacy of Napoleon's failed campaigns and to the epic grandeur of the Napoleonic era. Conrad recalled encounters with his Uncle Nicholas B., a veteran of the Moscow campaign, and family stories that included accounts of Conrad's grandfather Teodor Korzeniowski, who had also participated in the Napoleonic campaigns. Conrad drew from these memories in *A Personal Record*. Nicholas B., with 'his worship for Napoleon the Great' (*PR*, 29), is introduced as 'Mr. Nicholas B., sub-lieutenant of 1808, lieutenant of 1813 in the French Army, and for a short time *Officier d'Ordonnance* of Marshal Marmont' (*PR*, 31). Conrad associated his earliest boyhood memories with this venerable family member and the knowledge that here was a warrior of the Napoleonic armies: 'But it is not by these fragmentary remains of perishable mortality that he lives in my memory. I knew, at a very early age, that my grand-uncle Nicholas B. was a Knight of the Legion of Honour and that he had also the Polish Cross for valour *Viruti Militari*. The knowledge of these glorious facts inspired in me an admiring veneration' (*PR*, 31–32). Conrad, however, in the Sternian mode of *A Personal Record*, and in a style representative of Conrad's treatment of Napoleon throughout his writing, undercuts this homage to 'the Great Napoleon' by recalling his other main memory of Nicholas B; the knowledge that his uncle 'once upon a time had eaten a dog' (*PR*, 32) in the service of the Emperor. In resurrecting Nicholas B., Conrad offers a memory of an illustrious predecessor under the spell of Napoleonic grandeur despite the sobering experience of Napoleon's campaigns.

Conrad indicates that this particular family rendering of Napoleonic myth introduced him to storytelling, associating Napoleon with his first initiation into the art of narrative: 'It is a good forty years since I heard the tale, and the effect has not worn off yet. I believe this is the very first, say, realistic, story I heard in my life; but, all the same, I don't know why I should have been so frightfully impressed' (*PR*, 32). Conrad then unveils the figure of Napoleon, responsible for this tragic family episode:

But upon the whole, and considering that this gastronomical degradation overtaking a gallant young officer lies really at the door of the Great Napoleon, I think that to cover it up by silence would be an exaggeration of literary restraint. Let the truth stand here. The responsibility rests with the Man of St. Helena, in view of his deplorable levity in the conduct of the Russian campaign. It was during the memorable retreat from Moscow that Mr. Nicholas B., in the company of two brother officers – as to whose morality and natural refinement I know nothing – bagged a dog on the outskirts of a village and subsequently devoured him. (*PR*, 32)

Nicholas B.'s implicit acceptance of Napoleonic splendour ('Great Napoleon,' 'memorable retreat') contrasted with the lightly treated, yet stark harshness of battle and the relegation of the ruler of Europe to the Man of St. Helena, reflects Conrad's paradoxical and pervasively ironic treatments of history. In *Suspense*, Napoleon is endowed with 'a mysterious complexity and a dual character' (*S*, 38), embodying the quintessential Conradian 'Homo duplex' (*CL* 3, 89).[59] Conrad's early interaction with ostensibly irreconcilable visions of Napoleon, the legend and reality of Bonaparte's actions in Poland, exposed him to two contradictory, yet mutually dependent methods of narrative, and this contrast between a romantic, subjective view of the past and a sceptical, objective investigation of history resonates throughout Conrad's work. *A Personal Record* explores Conrad's family connections with the Napoleonic campaigns, but Conrad comically deflates Napoleonic legend by aligning the historical experiences of Napoleon and Nicholas B. Nicholas B.'s wound to his heel elevates him in Conrad's ironic narrative to the pantheon of history's great men: 'In all the history of warfare there are, I believe, only three warriors publicly known to have been wounded in the heel – Achilles and Napoleon – demigods indeed – to

---

[59] The Napoleonic aspects of Conrad's most celebrated creations are evident. Kurtz, Jim, and Nostromo exhibit overreaching impulses on a Napoleonic scale, incorporating political ambition and personal vanity, while all three are endowed with an extraordinary individual prestige that masks a more mundane reality. In *Nostromo*, Decoud attributes Napoleonic qualities to Nostromo: 'Exceptional individualities always interest me,' and Nostromo has 'a sort of minor genius in his way' (*N*, 248), while Dr. Monygham realises that 'There was something in the genius of that Genoese seaman which dominated in the destinies of great enterprises and of many people' (*N*, 452). In *Progress and Other Sketches*, Graham wrote of the Napoleonic character of Latin American politics: 'Spanish-America has been so fertile in Napoleons.' R.B. Cunninghame Graham, *Progress and Other Sketches* (London: Duckworth, 1904), 66.

whom the familiar piety of an unworthy descendant adds the name of the simple mortal, Nicholas B.' (*PR*, 48–49). *A Personal Record* betrays Conrad's indebtedness to nineteenth-century estimations of the French Emperor, as Napoleon is intrinsically associated with contradictory modes of representation.

Despite Conrad's satirical handling of Nicholas B.'s gastronomical degradation, the story of the Napoleonic retreat from Moscow in *A Personal Record* also probes more seriously the intersections between Polish history and Napoleonic legend, speculating on Napoleon's sympathy for the Polish national cause. Napoleon betrayed Poland's 'unappeasable and patriotic desire,' encouraging 'a great illusion kindled like a false beacon by a great man to lead astray the effort of a brave nation' (*PR*, 35). The Polish national effort and its reliance on Napoleon in the early years of the nineteenth century ensured that Conrad's ambivalence towards Bonaparte was complex and multi-layered, encompassing questions of national identity, politics, and loyalty:

The devouring in a dismal forest of a luckless Lithuanian dog by my grand-uncle Nicholas B. in company of two other military and famished scarecrows, symbolised, to my childish imagination, the whole horror of the retreat from Moscow and the immorality of a conqueror's ambition. An extreme distaste for that objectionable episode has tinged the views I hold as to the character and achievement of Napoleon the Great. I need not say that these are unfavourable. It was morally reprehensible for that great captain to induce a simple-minded Polish gentleman to eat dog by raising in his breast a false hope of national independence. (*PR*, 46)

Conrad's considerations of Napoleon provoked immediate and divisive political and historical associations. In 1812, the Marquis de Caulaincourt (1773–1827), French ambassador to Russia, wrote that Napoleon 'had small regard for the Poles,' viewing Poland as 'a State difficult to shape to any useful purpose.'[60] Although Conrad stresses this version of Napoleon's manipulation of Poland, accusing Napoleon of raising the 'false hope of national independence' and leading 'astray the effort of a brave nation,' Conrad is largely silent, critical or otherwise, on the actual details and impact of Napoleon's brief stewardship of Poland. Studies have shown the

[60] Quoted in Christopher A. Blackburn, *Napoleon and the Szlachta* (Boulder: East European Monographs, 1998), 1.

imposition of Napoleonic rule in the short-lived Grand Duchy of Warsaw between 1807–15, despite the established reputation of the *Code Napoléon* for breaking down social boundaries and for modernising governmental practices, in fact strengthened the position of the intransigent ruling class, the *szlachta*. As Christopher Blackburn has pointed out:

> The 'political privileges' that once united the Polish elite into a 'single and indivisible legal corporation,' thus effectively creating a Polish nation based on the nobility, were salvaged and retrenched by the Polish implementation of Napoleonic reforms. Surprisingly, the duchy's charter singled out Poland's disproportionately large nobility for special treatment, thereby guaranteeing its continued prominence.[61]

Thus, for Conrad the ultimate defeat of the French army in Russia did not simply indicate levity on Napoleon's part about the rebirth of the Polish nation, it also saw Napoleon betray Conrad's own social class, the *szlachta*, which had seen its position improve during the period of the Duchy of Warsaw. Given Conrad's conservatism in *A Personal Record*, where he insisted that the 1863 revolt did not support the 'subversion of any social or political scheme of existence' (*PR*, vii–viii), it seems the success of the Napoleonic campaigns in Poland might have encompassed many of Conrad's conflicting and cherished views of the Polish nation.

While entrenching the position of the *szlachta*, Napoleonic rule also created the appearance of a Romantic and united Polish nation ready to expel oppressive Russian power. As Blackburn notes, 'the bulk of the Polish population saw Napoleon's destruction of the Prussian Army in 1806 as an excellent opportunity to avenge their fallen country and regain their lost independence.'[62] Napoleon observed that 'The Poles are exceedingly well disposed. They are forming corps of horse and foot with much activity. They show an eagerness to recover their independence: the nobility, clergy and peasants are all of the same mind.'[63] Napoleon's view of a cohesive Polish national spirit, embracing all strata of society and ethnicity, yet controlled by the hierarchical power of the *szlachta*, was something Conrad promoted. In March 1920, during the latest Polish struggle against Russia, Conrad wrote

---

[61] Blackburn, *Napoleon and the Szlachta*, 4.
[62] Blackburn, *Napoleon and the Szlachta*, 29.
[63] Quoted in Blackburn, *Napoleon and the Szlachta*, 30.

to John Quinn echoing Napoleon's view of the Polish spirit: 'the unbroken Polish front keeps Bolshevism off and . . . apparently the reborn State has one heart and soul, one indomitable will, from the poorest peasant to the highest magnate' (*CL* 7, 40).

Despite his criticism of Napoleon's political immorality, Conrad, understandably, draws more frequent attention to the greater crimes inflicted on Poland by Russia, Prussia, and Austria. It is worth mentioning that Conrad is never critical of what Napoleon offered to Poland, but of his failure to carry it through. The betrayal of Polish hopes with the treaty of Tilsit in 1807, in which Napoleon came to terms with Russia but failed to restore the pre-partition borders of Poland, and the ultimate destruction of Napoleon's forces by the Russian winter in 1812 ensured that Napoleon was destined to fulfil his role as a failed Messiah. However, despite 'its small size and its dependence on Napoleonic France, the Duchy of Warsaw was the greatest and longest-lasting success of the independence movement in the post- partition period.'[64] It supported Polish language and culture and was instrumental in resurrecting the type of mystical national consciousness Conrad frequently describes in his essays. For this reason, Poles looked back upon the period as one of great promise and betrayal, an era of hope that ended definitively when Napoleon's Polish legions, the comrades of Nicholas B., perished on the retreat from Moscow.

CONRAD, FRENCH ROMANTICISM, AND THE *GRANDE ARMÉE*

The 'whole horror of the retreat from Moscow' (*PR*, 46) had a powerful hold over Conrad's imagination. In his 'Preface' to *Tales of Hearsay* (1925), R.B. Cunninghame Graham wrote that Conrad had a mind 'steeped in the modern literature of Europe, especially in that of France' (*TH*, ix). Conrad draws most heavily on the French Romantic tradition in his depiction of the retreat from Moscow in 'The Duel,' *A Personal Record*, and 'The Warrior's Soul,' evoking the world captured by Balzac

---

[64] Jerzy Skowronek, 'The Direction of Political Change in the Era of National Insurrection, 1795–1864,' J. K. Fedowowicz ed., *A Republic of Nobles: Studies in Polish History to 1864* (Cambridge: Cambridge University Press, 1982), 268.

in *Le Médecin de campagne* (1833) and by Victor Hugo in 'Expiation.'
In *A Personal Record*, Conrad mentioned his father's translations of
Victor Hugo, saying: 'At ten years of age I had read much of Victor
Hugo and other romantics' (*PR*, 70). In her diary, Emilie Briquel,
whom Conrad met in Champel in 1895, noted that 'Like me he likes
Pierre Loti, [and] the poetry of Victor Hugo.'[65] Hugo's 'Expiation'
depicts the retreat from Moscow in all its tragic glory, with a vanquished
Emperor being punished for his 'conqueror's ambition,' yet one in the
course of being canonised, a process Hugo contributes to, as the
legendary figure of nineteenth-century European heritage:

> Snow. Their own victory had defeated them.
> The eagle hung its head for the first time.
> Wretched days! Slowly, then, the emperor
> Returned; Moscow was left in flames behind him.
> Snow The harsh winter thawed into an avalanche.
> One white plain on another. Neither leaders
> Now flag could be made out, what yesterday
> Had been the army was a flock of sheep.
> You couldn't tell the center from the flank.
> Snow. Wounded soldiers sheltered in dead horses'
> Bellies; by the deserted bivouacs
> Buglers were visible, still standing, frozen
> At their posts, silent, in the saddle, white
> With frost, bronze trumpets glued to stone lips. Cannonballs,
> Grapeshot, shrapnel, and snowflakes, dizzled down;
> Surprised at their own tremulousness, grenadiers
> Slunk deep in thought, with ice on their gray whiskers.
> Snow – and more snow! The chill wind howled; in unknown
> Places they went, through sleet, barefoot and breadless –
> No longer living souls or soldiers,
> Merely a dream roaming the mists, a mystery,
> A procession of shadows in the darkness.[66]

---

[65] Briquel quoted in Yves Hervoeut, *The French Face of Joseph Conrad* (Cambridge: Cambridge University Press, 1990), 9. See also Owen Knowles, 'Conrad, Anatole France, and the early French Romantic Tradition: some influences,' *Conradiana*, 11.1 (1979): 41–61.
[66] Hugo, *Selected Poems*, 129–31.

Hugo's focus on the grandeur of the imperial eagle forced to submit to the Russian winter and the judgement of history offers a vision of the disastrous campaign that glorifies the defeated splendour of the *Grande Armée*. Balzac's *Le Médecin de campagne* featured a personalised outline of Napoleon's career told by a veteran of the *Grande Armée*. As Graham Robb notes, this episode, 'from Corsica to Saint Helena in 7000 words,' was published separately and anonymously in June 1833 under the title 'The Life of Napoleon Told by a Soldier of the Imperial Guard to Peasants in a Barn,' and 'became instantly famous.'[67] It features the trademark features of subsequent accounts of the retreat from Moscow:

No longer an army, you understand? Neither generals nor even sergeants. It was a reign of misery and hunger, during which we were all reduced to equals! All we thought of was seeing France again, and we stopped for neither guns nor money; each of us went on ahead any way we liked without a thought of glory. Eventually the weather was so bad that the emperor lost sight of his guiding star. Something stood between him and the sky.[68]

In his writing on Napoleon and the exploits of the Napoleonic armies, Conrad is similarly preoccupied with the retreat from Moscow and with doing justice to the sacrifices and destruction of the French army. It begs the question whether Conrad's focus on the white plains of Russia, a vast expanse in the process of being marked by French and Polish dead, amongst others, may not in fact originate as much from the French Romantic tradition as from that of Mickiewicz, to which it is usually attributed. In *Under Western Eyes*, Conrad wrote that Russia is 'like a monstrous blank page awaiting the record of an inconceivable history' (*UWE*, 33). Conrad directly evokes Mickiewicz's lines from the poem *Digression*, in which the Polish poet wrote: 'This level plain lies open, waste, and white, / A wide-spread page prepared for God to write.'[69] Conrad's early letters to Marguerite Poradowska also illustrate the young author's interest in the bleak plains of Russia. As Susan Jones has noted, Conrad praised Poradowska's novel *Marylka* in 1895,

---

[67] See Graham Robb, *Balzac: A Biography* (London: Papermac, 1994), 236.
[68] Honoré de Balzac, *Le Médecin de campagne* (Paris: Gallimard, 1974), 235.
[69] Quoted in Carabine, *Life and the Art*, 88.

focusing particularly on her description of the frozen landscape.[70] The white plains of the Napoleonic retreat from Moscow are a recurring image in Conrad's writing, and to some extent Conrad's 'inconceivable history' is visualised through and written by the destruction of Napoleon's *Grande Armée*.

'The Duel' follows the continuing feud of two soldiers in Napoleon's forces whose enmity shadows their progress through the military ranks and across the Europe of Napoleon's conquests.[71] Conrad's Feraud and D'Hubert, despite their personal feud, which detracts from, or perhaps contributes to, the grandeur of the Napoleonic conquest, take part in the march to Moscow and the disastrous retreat. In his descriptions of the Moscow campaign, Conrad appropriates the imagery of Hugo's 'Expiation' to convey the magnitude of 'the greatest military disaster of modern history' (*PR*, 35):

> The retreat from Moscow submerged all private feelings in a sea of disaster and misery. [...] They plodded on, and their passage did not disturb the mortal silence of the plains, shining with the livid light of snows under a sky the colour of ashes. Whirlwinds ran along the fields, broke against the dark column, enveloped it in a turmoil of flying icicles, and subsided, disclosing it creeping on its tragic way without the swing and rhythm of the military pace. It struggled onwards, the men exchanging neither words nor looks; whole ranks marched touching elbow, day after day and never raising their eyes from the ground, as if lost in despairing reflections. [...] Then, with a cry or two of *vive l'Empereur!* it would resume its march, leaving behind a few lifeless bodies lying huddled up, tiny black specks on the white immensity of the snows.   (*SS*, 211–12)

In 'The Warrior's Soul,' Conrad charted the relationship between a French and Russian soldier, culminating in the retreat from Moscow. Here, through a Russian narrator, an explicit criticism of Napoleon is coupled with an implicit acceptance of the *post-factum* legend of the man and the tragedy of those who followed him. A consideration of

---

[70] Susan Jones, 'Conrad's Debt to Marguerite Porodowska,' *Conrad: Intertexts and Appropriations*, 13–14.

[71] For a discussion of the sources of 'The Duel,' see Michel Desforges, postface, Joseph Conrad, *Le Duel*, translated by Michel Desforges (Toulouse: Éditions Ombres, 1991), 127–38. J.H. Stape has considered the influence of Balzac's story *La Rabouilleuse* (1842) on 'The Duel' in 'One can learn something from Balzac: Conrad and Balzac.' See also, J.H. Stape, '"The End of the Tether" and Victor Hugo's *Les Travailleurs de la Mer*,' *The Conradian* 30.1 (2005): 71–80.

Napoleon's ambition leads to a simultaneous mythologising of his exploits and their incorporation into the canon of the European literary imagination:

He – the great Napoleon – started upon us to emulate the Macedonian Alexander, with a ruck of nations at his back. We opposed empty spaces to French impetuosity, then we offered them an interminable battle so that their army went at last to sleep in its positions lying down on the heaps of its own dead. Then came the wall of fire in Moscow. It toppled down on them.
     Then began the long rout of the Grand Army. I have seen it stream on, like the doomed flight of haggard, spectral sinners across the innermost frozen circle of Dante's Inferno, ever widening before their despairing eyes.   (*TH*, 1)

Conrad recalls some characteristic contemporary responses to Napoleon here by referencing Alexander the Great. Many early Romantic writers, such as Stendhal and Walter Savage Landor, saw Napoleon as the greatest historical figure since classical times.[72] However, reflecting its composition during the First World War, 'The Warrior's Soul' is also sceptical of the glory involved in warfare, employing a realist rhetoric to treat the physical and psychological degradation of war: 'I and my comrades had a close view of Napoleon's Grand Army. It was an amazing and terrible sight. I had heard of it from others; I had seen the stragglers from it: small bands of marauders, parties of prisoners in the distance. But this was the very column itself! A crawling, stumbling, starved, half-demented mob' (*TH*, 3).

     In addition to the catastrophic defeat of Napoleon's forces in 'The Warrior's Soul' and 'The Duel,' Conrad also delineated the post-Napoleonic culture that crystallised the legend of the Emperor. In 'The Warrior's Soul,' this is achieved by the controlling voice of the narrator who retrospectively embellishes his experiences during the Napoleonic campaigns. More overtly, 'The Duel' engages with the Napoleonic *culte de personnalité* sustained by the romantic, nostalgic *demi-soldes*, the retired Napoleonic Officers who looked back on the period of their campaigns with regret. Judging from his reading of Balzac, Conrad was interested in post-Napoleonic France, as Balzac's *Histoire des Treize* and *La Rabouilleuse* featured Napoleonic veterans active in Restoration society. As Hazareesingh has noted, veterans of

---

[72] See Bainbridge, *Napoleon and English Romanticism*, 1–17.

the Napoleonic campaigns were instrumental in keeping the flame of Napoleonic legend burning in nineteenth-century France. Upon Napoleon's journey to St. Helena, 'as their commander-in-chief was embarking on his final voyage, his valiant soldiers, discharged from the Army, began their own journey back to their native towns and villages, where many would in effect experience the torments of internal exile. These were the men who would become the high priests of the Napoleon cult.'[73] Conrad describes them thus:

The strangers wore civilian clothes. Lean and weather-beaten, lolling back in their chairs, they scowled at people with moody and defiant abstraction from under their hats pulled low over their eyes. It was not difficult to recognise them for two of the compulsorily retired officers of the Old Guard. [...] General D'Hubert's tender anticipations of a domestic future adorned with a woman's grace were traversed by the harsh regret of his warlike past, of that one long, intoxicating clash of arms, unique in the magnitude of its glory and disaster – the marvellous work and special possession of his own generation. (*SS*, 222–23)

The shift from the Napoleonic Wars to the Restoration, and the idea of these veterans being abandoned by history, is captured by Conrad: 'Only four and twenty months ago the masters of Europe, they had already the air of antique ghosts' (*SS*, 239). In *Suspense*, written in a post-First World War Europe uneasy with the presence of returned, mutilated soldiers, a subject strikingly represented in the paintings of German artists Max Beckmann and Otto Dix, Conrad again focused attention on the *demi-soldes* who would help create the legend of Napoleon: 'Their occupation is gone. Heroes are a thoughtless lot. Yet just look at that elderly lieutenant at the head of the table. Shabby coat. Old epaulette. He doesn't laugh. He will die a lieutenant – on half-pay. That's how heroic people end when the heroic times are over' (*S*, 67). The ending of 'The Duel' anticipates the battles that will be fought throughout France and Europe for Napoleon's memory in the nineteenth century. For the returned royalist émigré, the Chevalier de Valmassigue, Napoleon is indeed the self-made man of legend, but one who has usurped the natural order, merely 'a Corsican adventurer masquerading as an emperor' (*SS*, 244). However, for Feraud, Napoleon's fate is tragic: 'The thought of that sublime hero chained

---

[73] Hazareesingh, *Legend of Napoleon*, 37.

to a rock in the middle of a savage ocean makes life of so little value' (*SS*, 265). While sceptical of the French Emperor throughout his writing, Conrad nevertheless adopts the ambiguous language of legend that dominated European Romantic responses to Napoleon.[74] One need only consider Chateaubriand, Byron, Hazlitt, Scott, de Musset, Stendhal, Balzac, Dumas, Tolstoy, Dostoyevsky, Thackeray, and Hardy, to recognise that Napoleon was a central presence in European literary culture and an important informant of Conrad's consideration of history.

NAPOLEONIC LEGEND IN *THE ROVER*

Many of the objectionable certainties of Conrad's life were swept away by the Great War. Bolshevism replaced Russian autocracy in a revolution that, according to *Under Western Eyes* and 'Autocracy and War,' Conrad believed Russians were incapable of orchestrating, while the defeat of Germany and the break-up of the Austro-Hungarian Empire saw the demise of the historic dividers of Poland. While accepting the rebirth of Poland, Conrad realised that politically and culturally 'there was no possible return to the old order. The disruptions were too many and the effects too widespread. It was a changed world in which the rulers of Europe now operated.'[75] *Suspense* noted that 'Europe was aflame, and the blaze scorched and dazzled and filled one with awe and with forebodings; but then one always heard that fire purifies all which it cannot destroy. The world would perhaps come out better from it' (*S*, 143).

Observing the 1919 Peace Conference in Versailles, Conrad remarked there 'is an awful sense of unreality in all this babble of League of Nations and Reconstruction. [. . .] It is like people laying out a tennis court on a ground that is already moving under their feet. I ask myself who on earth is being deceived by all these ceremonies' (*CL* 6, 349–51). In *The Economic Consequences of the Peace* (1919), John Maynard

---

[74] For a discussion of Napoleon's shifting importance both left and right of the political spectrum, see R. S. Alexander, *Napoleon* (London: Arnold, 2001, and Gildea, *The Past in French History*).

[75] Steiner, *Lights that Failed*, 11.

Keynes described the settlement meetings, relating 'the futility and smallness of man before the great events confronting him; the mingled significance and unreality of the decisions.'[76] Amidst such unpredictability, Conrad registered his consciousness of a new era in European history in his post-war attitude to Poland. Conrad kept abreast of developments in Polish politics, but on being asked to become involved in the *Anglo-Polish Society* in 1920, he indicated that he was not 'in touch with the inner life of Poland, its problems and perplexities,' and as 'to the actual events of the last three years I am absolutely in the dark, not so much perhaps as to the facts themselves but as to their profounder significance' (*CL* 7, 29–30). In fact, Conrad's Polishness had always been anachronistic. 'Prince Roman' returned to the 1830 insurrection against Russian rule; Polish Romanticism and Positivism had an incalculable effect on Conrad's attitude to time and history; Conrad's vision of nationhood was rooted in Polish adaptations of Rousseau and Herder; and 'Poland Revisited,' had spoken less of a journey across space than through time.

While inspired by his own historical nostalgia, Conrad's historical fiction in *The Rover* and *Suspense* places him within wider contemporary debate about historical study in post-war England and Europe. The idea of a world gone wrong was perfectly captured with the publication of Oswald Spengler's *The Decline of the West* (1918–22). In Spengler's view, cultures went through prescribed stages, which he equated with the seasons of the year, and then declined. Spengler believed the age of history that had been reached and defined as 'Imperialism' was 'to be taken as a symbol of the end. Imperialism is civilisation unadulterated. In this phenomenal form the destiny of the West is now irrevocably set. The expansive tendency is a doom, something daemonic and immense.'[77] In 1920, H.G. Wells published his *Outline of History*, claiming:

The need for a common knowledge of the general facts of human history throughout the world has become very evident during the tragic happenings of

---

[76] John Maynard Keynes, *The Economic Consequences of the Peace* (London: Macmillan, 1920), 4.

[77] Oswald Spengler, *The Decline of the West*, an abridged edition by Helmut Werner. English abridged edition prepared by Arthur Helps from the translation by Charles Francis Atkinson (London: Allen & Unwin, 1961), 53. See also GoGwilt, *The Invention of the West*, 232–33.

the last few years. [...] But *there can be no common peace and prosperity without common historical ideas.* Without such ideas to hold them together in harmonious co-operation, with nothing but narrow, selfish, and conflicting nationalist traditions, races and peoples are bound to drift towards conflict and destruction.[78]

Wells's work, which lambasted patriotism and national loyalty, 'was immediately and overwhelmingly successful and ushered in a craze for "outlines" that was to last for over a decade.'[79] *The Outline of History* opened a discussion on the nature of the study of history in the pages of *History*, the journal of the Historical Association.[80] In 1924, G.M. Trevelyan argued that the 'object of the academic study both of history and of literature is to make the dead live, to record the manifold adventures of the spirit of man.'[81] Just as Conrad's consciousness of a female readership in *Chance* was contemporaneous with the rise of the women's suffrage movement,[82] in post-war England, as Trevelyan noted, there was a definite market for history: 'There is a public demand for historical literature, for the interpretation of the results of historical research thrown into a literary form.'[83] The subjects of history and memory informed a wide spectrum of literature after the First World War. Alongside the work of Wells, soldiers' accounts and regimental histories such as Rudyard Kipling's *The Irish Guards in the Great War* (1923) began the canonisation of the Great War, while Marcel Proust brought a new, exhaustive complexity to the investigation of the past. If 1922 was the year of high-Modernism, then according to Wyndham Lewis in *Time and Western Man* (1927), James Joyce's masterpiece *Ulysses* also represented historical fiction taken to extremes. For Lewis, Joyce 'collected like a cistern in his youth the last stagnant pumpings of victorian anglo-irish life. [...] Proust returned to the *temps perdu.* Joyce never left it.'[84]

[78] H.G. Wells, *The Outline of History* (London: Cassell, 1923), v.
[79] William T. Ross, *H.G. Wells's World Reborn: The Outline of History and its Companions* (London: Associated University Presses, 2002), 13.
[80] See Christopher Parker, *The English Historical Tradition Since 1850* (Edinburgh: John Donald, 1990).
[81] G. M. Trevelyan, 'History and Literature,' *History* 9 (1924–25): 82.
[82] See Jones, *Conrad and Women*, 99–133.
[83] Trevelyan, 'History and Literature,' 86.
[84] Wyndham Lewis, *Time and Western Man*, edited with Afterword and Notes by Paul Edwards (1927; Santa Rosa: Black Sparrow Press, 1993), 90–91.

E.F. Jacob explained in *History* in 1924 that Wells's *Outline of History* sought to 'bind men together and prevent both narrow and conflicting nationalist traditions and internal antagonisms.'[85] Conrad's treatment of Napoleon and dictatorship in his last works engaged with the form of political power that would dominate twentieth-century European politics. The subject of dictatorship went hand in hand with the question of nationalism in the early 1920s 'given the fate of the new states after the First World War such as Latvia, Estonia and Czechoslovakia, which failed to survive intact or became dictatorships, while many of the longer-established states came under Fascist control.'[86] The black legend of Napoleon vilified the French Emperor as an historical forerunner of modern dictators. Within his outline of history, Wells had labelled Napoleon 'one of the most illuminating figures in modern history.'[87] According to W.T. Ross, 'one of the most curious chapters in [*The Outline of History*] [was] devoted exclusively to deflating Napoleon.'[88] Wells elaborated on the transformation of Napoleon in the popular imagination during the nineteenth century: 'Many people in those hopeless days were disposed to regard even Napoleon with charity, and to accept his claim that in some inexplicable way he had, in asserting himself, been asserting the revolution and France. A cult of him as of something mystically heroic grew up after his death.'[89] Conrad's susceptibility to the cult of the French Emperor ensured that Napoleon emerged as an illuminating figure in *The Rover*. In the context of the troubled state of Europe in the 1920s, Conrad reassessed his perception of Napoleon's politics.

The Rover treats French history in the years following the Revolution and at the time of the rise of Napoleon. The final adventure and sacrifice of the old mariner Peyrol, who deceives the English fleet blockading Toulon, aids Napoleon in the launching of his expedition to Egypt. W. R. Martin sees *The Rover* as an allegory in which Peyrol 'represents the ancient, at first slumbering, but enduring finer spirit of France.'[90]

[85] E.F. Jacob, 'Recent World History and its Variety,' *History* 8 (1923–24): 243–44.
[86] Diarmaid Ferriter, *The Transformation of Ireland 1900–2000* (London: Profile, 2005), 297.
[87] Wells, *Outline of History*, 473.
[88] Ross, *H.G. Wells's World Reborn*, 60.
[89] Wells, *Outline of History*, 484.
[90] W.R. Martin, 'Allegory in Conrad's *The Rover*,' *English Studies in Africa* 10.2 (1967): 186.

Peyrol 'revives the true greatness of France after it has been temporarily obscured by the Revolution.'[91] In a letter to Sidney Colvin in 1917, Conrad expressed his respect for the inherent greatness of the French nation, stating that 'the greatest figure of the times through which we have lived was The People itself, *la Nation.* For 150 years the French people has been always greater (and better) than its leaders, masters and teachers' (*CL* 6, 73–74). Despite his faith in the French people, it is significant that in *The Rover,* Conrad, in light of the contemporary upheaval in Europe, is more forgiving of France's 'leaders, masters and teachers,' particularly Napoleon, than has been previously recognised. Conrad carefully portrays the period of the onset of Napoleonic rule as one that should be favourably contrasted with the days of the terror, with Citizen Scevola representing all the murderous excesses of that period.[92] As Hugh Epstein has pointed out, *The Rover* is 'a novel in which stilled lives mask a barely perceived hinterland of furious social and historical turmoil.'[93] The novel views the political changes in France from the detachment of the Escampobar farmhouse, reflecting Conrad's changing view of Napoleonic rule and his understanding of European politics observed from Kent after the First World War. With his focus on Napoleonic history, Conrad, like Peyrol in *The Rover,* 'was ready to appreciate contemporary history in his own particular way' (*R*, 25).

Peyrol is drawn as a quintessential Frenchman, characterised as authentically patriotic because he was absent from France through the vicissitudes of its recent history. Through his membership of the old Brotherhood of the Coast, a band of fellow sailors, Peyrol regards those who claim to represent a new republican form of politics as opportunists: 'we practised republican principles long before a republic was thought of; for the Brothers of the Coast were all equal and elected their own chiefs' (*R*, 5). For Peyrol, on his distant travels 'the words Republic, Nation, Tyranny, Liberty, Equality, and Fraternity, and the cult of the Supreme Being came floating on board ships from home, new cries and

---

[91] Martin, 'Allegory in Conrad's *The Rover,*' 191.

[92] See Balzac's short story 'Un épisode sous la Terreur' for the political loyalties of another Scevola in Revolutionary France.

[93] Hugh Epstein, '*The Rover:* A Post-Skeptical Novel,' *Conradiana* 27.1–2 (2005): 107.

new ideas which did not upset the slowly developed intelligence of the gunner Peyrol' (*R*, 8). Peyrol is connected to France through the mystical bonds of nationhood and by the patriotism of place that Conrad expounded on in his earlier writing. Conrad presents this Herderian and Rousseauvian patriotism as a constant in the midst of historical change: 'Every feature of the country with the darkly wooded rises, the barren flat expanse of stones and sombre bushes to his left, appealed to him with a sort of strange familiarity, because they had remained unchanged since the days of his boyhood' (*R*, 6).

The contrast in *The Rover* between the days of the Terror and the onset of Napoleon's rule is steadily stressed. The terror and the acts of Scevola are divulged thus: 'They had to kill traitors in the streets, in cellars, in their beds. The corpses of men and women were lying in heaps along the quays. There were a good many of his sort that got the name of drinkers of blood. Well, he was one of the best of them' (*R*, 20).[94] Scevola is symbolic of those former, blood-filled days: 'By himself he was nothing. He had never been anything but a creature of the universal bloodlust of the time' (*R*, 48). In a letter to Edward Garnett in December 1920, Conrad discussed *The Rover* and agreed with Garnett that Scevola 'was never formidable except as a creature of mob psychology. Away from the mob he is just a weak-minded creature' (*CL* 8, 238). Conrad's interest in mob psychology appears throughout the novel, and it can be interpreted as Conrad's response to the rise of Bolshevism in Russia and growing socialist activity in Europe in the wake of the First World War. As early as 1885, Conrad had written, rather infamously: 'Where's the man to stop the crashing avalanche?

---

[94] Conrad does not implicate Napoleon in the massacres at Toulon in December 1793, scene of Citizen Scevola's bloodiest excesses, where the Terror unleashed retribution on an estimated 800–2000 inhabitants of the royalist city for supporting the Anglo-Spanish fleet. Chateaubriand, in his *Mémoires d'outre tombe* (1848), noted that disseminators of the black legend of Napoleon found material here for castigating the crimes of the Emperor, insisting on Napoleon's presence at Toulon during the violence. According to Chateaubriand, 'It is something deplorable, but it must be recognised [...] part of Napoleon's power came from having immersed himself in the Terror.' Chateaubriand, *Vie de Napoléon* (Paris: Fallois, 1999), 87. Napoleon had made his name commanding the artillery that expelled the Anglo-Spanish forces from Toulon, but having been wounded, evidence indicates he left the city before the Jacobin reprisals. See B. Ireland, *The Fall of Toulon: The Last Opportunity to Defeat the French Revolution* (London: Weidenfeld and Nicholson, 2005).

Where's the man to stop the rush of social-democratic ideas? [...]
[T]he sun is set and the last barrier removed. England was the only
barrier to the pressure of infernal doctrines born in Continental back-
slums' (*CL* 1, 16). Analogous fears of social upheaval appear in *The
Rover*. In particular, Arlette's dream, concerning her anxiety about
Lieutenant Réal, exposes the traumatising forces of terror and Revolution that may rise again to challenge the new order that has descended
on France with the advent of Napoleon:

She had seen Réal set upon by a mob of men and women, all dripping with
blood, in a livid cold light, in front of a stretch of mere shells of houses
with cracked walls and broken windows, and going down in the midst of
a forest of raised arms brandishing sabres, clubs, knives, axes. There was also
a man flourishing a red rag on a stick, while another was beating a drum which
boomed above the sickening sound of broken glass falling like rain on the
pavement.   (*R*, 245–46)

As Andrzej Busza has written, '*The Rover*, in addition to its attractive
mix of adventure yarn, love-story, and nostalgic evocation of the Mediterranean littoral, offers reflections on the effects of political violence
and social upheaval on the individual and the community – a topic
obviously relevant in the years immediately following the First World
War and the Bolshevik Revolution.'[95]

The reinforced contrast of upheaval and relative stability sees *The Rover*
offer Conrad's least critical portrait of Napoleon's political influence, with
the uncertainty of contemporary Europe leading Conrad to demonstrate
Napoleon as representative of order, if not in fact 'the man' he called for in
his early letter to restore calm to Europe. Many aspects of the Napoleonic
cult resurface in *The Rover*. Lieutenant Réal has the positive virtues of
Napoleonic legend, for in 'the course of some eight years, suppressing his
faculties of love and hatred, he arrived at the rank of an officer by sheer
merit' (*R*, 70), thus playing on Napoleon's famously crafted reputation as
a self-made man. Conrad's understanding of Napoleon in *The Rover*
recalls Thomas Carlyle's interpretation in 'The Hero as King':

'*La carrière ouverte aux talents*, The implements to him who can handle them:' [sic]
this actually is the truth, and even the whole truth; it includes whatever the French

---

[95] Busza, '*The Rover*: Conrad's Nostos,' 39.

Revolution, or any Revolution, could mean. Napoleon, in his first period, was a true Democrat. And yet by the nature of him, fostered too by his military trade, he knew that Democracy, if it were a true thing at all, could not be anarchy: the man had a heart-hatred for anarchy. [...] Such faith in Democracy, yet hatred of anarchy, it is that carries Napoleon through all his great work.[96]

Peyrol possesses charismatic qualities of leadership, and the unfortunate Michel's philosophical acceptance of his lowly position in life as follower of Peyrol confirms the novel's acceptance of Napoleonic hierarchy and the right of the Man of Destiny, or any man of destiny, to fulfil his role. For Michel, 'Somebody must be last in this world' (*R*, 253). There is also an endorsement of Napoleon's authority in Peyrol's words: 'I have heard of and seen more gods than you could ever dream of in a long night's sleep, in every corner of the earth, in the very heart of forests, which is an inconceivable thing. Figures, stones, sticks. There must be something in the idea. [...] [T]heir republican god [...] has never given us seamen a chief like that one the soldiers have got ashore' (*R*, 76). Most convincing of all is Peyrol's Napoleonic panegyric, which dismisses rumours of the imperial black legend: 'I have heard no talk of an emperor. But what does it matter? Under one name or another a chief can be no more than a chief, and that general whom they have been calling consul is a good chief – nobody can deny that' (*R*, 77). *The Rover* thereby constitutes Conrad's most forgiving portrait of Napoleon's politics.

ALEXANDRE DUMAS AND FRENCH ROMANTIC ADVENTURE IN *SUSPENSE*

Set during Napoleon's imprisonment on Elba, a period when there was 'a fascination now about everything connected with that island' (*S*, 5), the unfinished *Suspense* borrowed heavily from the *Mémoires* of Adèle

---

[96] Thomas Carlyle, 'The Hero as King,' *On Heroes and Hero Worship and The Heroic in History* (London: Chapman & Hall, 1885), 196–97. According to Jonathan Mendilow, during 'the period when France was in danger of disintegration, Napoleon, Carlyle maintained, was a "missionary of order."' See Jonathan Mendilow, 'The Political Philosophy of Thomas Carlyle (1795–1881): Towards a Theory of Catch-All Extremism,' *Rediscoveries: Some Neglected Modern European Political Thinkers*, edited by John A. Hall (Oxford: Clarendon Press, 1986), 22.

d'Osmond, Comtesse de Boigne (1781–1866), amongst other works.[97]
Susan Jones has discussed *Suspense* in the context of sensation fiction in
England, drawing comparisons between the novel and M.E. Braddon's
Lady Audley's Secret (1862).[98] Conrad may also have had an earlier
sensational novel in mind, a landmark of European literature featuring
Napoleon's imprisonment on Elba. *Suspense* recalls Alexandre Dumas's
Le Comte de Monte-Cristo (1846), which opens with the docking of the
Pharaon at Marseilles on 24 February 1815, carrying the young sailor
Edmond Dantès.[99] Dantès's decision to stop off at Elba to deliver a
message from his dying captain instigates this epic tale of revenge.
Dumas incorporates political discussions of Napoleon's position off
the coast of France. According to *procureur* of Marseilles, M. de Ville-
fort, 'Napoleon is close to France on Elba; his presence in sight of our
coast gives hope to his partisans. Marseilles is filled with demi-solde
officers, who, everyday, under some frivolous pretext, look for trouble
with Royalists, leading to duels amongst the higher classes and mur-
ders amongst the people.'[100] *Suspense* opens with conspirators sending
covert messages to Elba, and the 'suspsense' of the novel arises from the
expectation of Napoleon's imminent escape and the crystalisation of
his legend before his final military defeat at Waterloo. As with *Le Comte
de Monte-Cristo*, which follows the imprisonment of Edmond Dantès
into the depths of the Château d'If off the coast of Marseilles, thereby
upsetting readers' anticipations of actually witnessing the dramatic
departure from Elba, Napoleon's heroic return is absent from *Suspense*

---

[97] See Hans Van Marle and Gene M. Moore, 'The Sources of *Suspense*,' *Conrad:
Intertexts and Appropriations*, 141–63.
[98] Jones, '*Suspense* and the Novel of Sensation,' *Conrad and Women*, 192–220.
[99] Given the setting of *The Rover* and *Le Comte de Monte-Cristo* in the south of
France, parallels could be drawn between the Mediterranean homecomings of Peyrol and
Edmond Dantès. Further, in *The Arrow of Gold*, set in Marseilles in the 1870s, Conrad
wrote: 'Certain streets have an atmosphere of their own, a sort of universal fame and the
particular affection of their citizens. One of such streets is the Cannebière, and the jest:
"If Paris had a Cannebière it would be a little Marseilles" is the jocular expression of
municipal pride. I, too, have been under its spell' (*AG*, 7). In *Le Comte de Monte-Cristo*,
Dumas noted: 'the famous Cannebière, of which the modern Phoceans are so proud that
they say with the utmost seriousness and in an accent that gives so much character to
their utterances: "If Paris had a Cannebière, Paris would be a little Marseilles.' Alexandre
Dumas, *Le Comte de Monte-Cristo* (1846; Paris: Gallimard, 1981), 12.
[100] Dumas, *Comte de Monte-Cristo*, 57.

owing to its unfinished state, leading the *Saturday Review* in 1925 to place Conrad's novel 'among the greatest preludes in our literature.'[101] Contemporary reviews identified Conrad's final artistic statement with traditional adventure literature. In the *Nation and Athenaeum* Leonard Woolf asserted that *Suspense* was an 'historical novel of the classic type,' while in the *Revue des Deux Mondes* Louis Gillet praised Conrad's portrait of the Napoleonic era.[102] In his classic study *The Historical Novel* (1937), Georg Lukács traced the origins of modern historical fiction to Walter Scott and 'the beginning of the nineteenth century at about the time of Napoleon's collapse.'[103] While Scott's fiction projected its gaze towards British history and legend, Dumas, heavily influenced by Shakespeare, Scott, Byron, and English Romanticism, turned frequently in works such as *Napoléon* (1830) and *Joseph Balsamo* (1848) to French Revolutionary politics and Napoleonic intrigue to evoke the grandeur and intensity of a former age.[104] Conrad had evaluated the appeal of Dumas in the essay 'Books' (1905), which also drew attention to the other major exponents of French Romanticism: Stendhal and Balzac. However, Conrad reserved a special mention for Dumas and his famously dynamic literary reputation: 'At the heart of fiction, even the least worthy of the name, some sort of truth can be found – if only the truth of a childish theatrical ardour in the game of life, as in the novels of Dumas' (*NLL*, 11).[105] Notably, *A Personal Record* concludes with the young Conrad in Marseilles and a description

---

[101] 'New Fiction: *Suspense*,' *The Saturday Review* (3 October, 1925): 373.

[102] Leonard Woolf, 'The Last Conrad,' *Nation and Athenaeum* 38 (3 October, 1925): 18; and Louis Gillet, 'Le dernier roman de Conrad,' *Revue des Deux Mondes*, 7ième série, XCV (Nov–Dec 1925): 931–42.

[103] Georg Lukács, *The Historical Novel* (1937; London: Merlin Press, 1989), 19.

[104] See Daniel Zimmermann, *Alexandre Dumas le Grand* (Paris: Phébus, 2002) for the most authoritative biography of Dumas. That Dumas's work constitutes merely boys-own literature is an issue that has marginalised his position in modern literary histories. Respected critics of Dumas in France return frequently to the subject. Along with numerous other introductions and prefaces for Gallimard, see Claude Schopp ed., Alexandre Dumas, *Joseph Balsamo: mémoires d'un médecin* (Paris: Robert Laffont, 1990).

[105] In 1898, W.E. Henley had written to Conrad about his collaboration with Ford Madox Ford on *Romance* (1903), an adventurous tale of piracy in the Caribbean. Conrad responded to W.E. Henley, 18 October 1898, addressing Henley's comparison of the adventure tale and the collaboration to the works of Stevenson and Dumas: 'The line of your argument has surprised me. R.L.S. – Dumas – these are big names and I assure You it had never occurred to me they could be pronounced in connection with my plan to work with Hueffer' (*CL* 2, 107). Citing Dumas's famous literary and culinary reputa-

of his first encounter with the English language and a British ship. Conrad's initiation in the handling of a boat's tiller off the coast of Marseilles is connected to the adventurous spirit of childhood literature, as Conrad enters the scenes of *Le Comte de Monte-Cristo*: 'There was a great solitude around us; the islets ahead, Monte Cristo and the Château d'If in full light, seemed to float towards us – so steady, so imperceptible was the progress of our boat' (*PR*, 130). Conrad's later narrative methods and Romantic historical subject matter attempt to emulate the literary qualities that Conrad attributed to the author of *Les Trois Mousquetaires*. However, illustrating his late-career transition from experimental to conventional literary modes, Conrad's early work had juxtaposed adventurous Romanticism with an innovative modernism. *Nostromo*, for example, offers a modern vision of a failed Edmond Dantès, with its eponymous hero unable to exploit his buried island wealth in the Romantic tradition of *Le Comte de Monte-Cristo*, thereby upsetting the traditional adventure resolution that Conrad sceptically adopts in the closing scenes of the novel. Nostromo 'had kept the treasure for purposes of revenge; but now he cared nothing for it' (*N*, 541).

Linda Dryden and Andrea White have discussed Conrad in the context of British imperial adventure literature and travel writing.[106] However, while both critics treat Conrad's ambivalent attitude to Stevenson's work (*CL* 2, 371), neither gives any attention to Dumas, one of the most celebrated travel writers of the nineteenth-century, and whose popular literature is clearly discernible in the classics of the British imperial literary tradition. Dumas's writing was a major influence and lifelong passion for Stevenson, and in H. Rider Haggard's *King Solomon's Mines* (1885) the discovery of Solomon's treasure provokes immediate associations with Dumas's work for the hero Allan Quatermain: 'We are the richest men in the world . . . Monte Cristo is a fool to us.'[107] In *Memories and Portraits* (1887), Stevenson discussed his love of *Le Vicomte de Bragelonne*, citing it as his most frequently read book: 'I

---

tion, Conrad joked: 'Were I a Dumas I would eat up Hueffer without compunction. Was it you who called the old man "a natural force"? He was *that*' (*CL* 2, 108).

[106] Linda Dryden, *Joseph Conrad and the Imperial Romance* (Basingstoke: Macmillan, 2000), and Andrea White, *Joseph Conrad and the Adventure Tradition: Constructing and Deconstructing the Imperial Subject* (Cambridge: Cambridge University Press, 1993).

[107] H. Rider Haggard, *King Solomon's Mines* (1885; London: Penguin, 1963), 224.

may be said to have passed the best years of my life in these six volumes' (234). In 'A Gossip on Romance,' Stevenson wrote of the adventure tradition: 'The early part of *Monte Cristo*, down to the finding of the treasure, is a piece of perfect story-telling; the man never breathed who shared these moving incidents without a tremor; and yet Faria is a thing of packthread and Dantès little more than a name. [...] I do not believe there is another volume extant where you can breathe the same un-mingled atmosphere of romance.'[108] In 1922, Conrad wrote to Dumas expert Robert Garnett, Edward's elder brother, claiming that he had 'read with the greatest interest your communications to the *Times* in the Dumas-Maquet affair' (*CL* 7, 517). Garnett's letter had discussed at length the legal disputes between the heirs of Dumas and those of his collaborator Auguste Maquet (1813–88) over publishing rights. Noting the popularity of Dumas in Britain and his importance to British literature, Garnett stressed: 'In no country is Dumas more read than here – owing in some measure, no doubt, to the tributes paid to his talent by such critics as Robert Louis Stevenson, Andrew Lang, and William Ernest Henley.'[109] Arguably, Conrad's borrowing from adven-ture literature originates as much in the energetic respect he held for Dumas and the grand European tradition of Romantic literature as from the immediate contextual setting of the British Imperial Romance.

Suspense excavates the nineteenth-century obsession with the Napoleonic period, an era that Dumas's generation consistently exam-ined in order to scrutinise and simultaneously reinforce the legend of Napoleon. Conrad's susceptibility to the romantic view of Bonaparte emerges in his fascination with the extraordinary circumstances of the escape from Elba on 26 February 1815, the event that elevated Napoleon to the realm of myth in the European historical imagination. Earlier, in 'The Duel,' Conrad had expressed a sense of wonder at 'The triumphant return from Elba, a historical fact as marvellous and incred-

---

[108] Robert Louis Stevenson, *Memories & Portraits* (1887; London: Chatto & Windus, 1900), 262–63.
[109] 'The Maquet-Dumas Case,' *Times Literary Supplement* (22 June, 1922): 412; and 'Dumas and Maquet' (20 July, 1922): 476. Auguste Maquet supplied Dumas with material for numerous of his historical novels and wrote substantial parts of them, something openly acknowledged by Dumas but kept secret by publishers and with Maquet's consent. Maquet's tomb at Père-Lachaise Cemetery has the titles of these many works proudly engraved on its façade.

ible as the exploits of some mythological demi-god' (*SS*, 220). Conrad's awe at Napoleon's veritable resurrection matches some contemporaries of Bonaparte later capable of more sober judgement, such as the young historian Thomas Babington Macaulay. Macaulay wrote: 'All my detestation of his crimes, all my horror at his conduct is completely swallowed up in astonishment, awe, and admiration, at the more than human boldness of his present attempt.'[110] In *Le Comte de Monte-Cristo*, Dumas reflected on the escape from Elba and the ensuing Hundred Days, the period between 20 March 1815, when Napoleon arrived in Paris, until the restoration of Louis XVIII after Napoleon's defeat at Waterloo: 'Everyone knows about this return from the island of Elba, a strange, miraculous return, which was without precedent in the past and which will probably remain unmatched in the future.'[111] In *Suspense*, Cosmo Latham's journey to Genoa, within sight of Elba, finds him 'looking across the water in the direction of that crumb of land that is the last refuge of your greatest enemy' (*S*, 4), and in the Europe of the Elba period Napoleon is always 'an unseen presence' (*S*, 93).

In addition to Dumas, Conrad's praise of Stendhal in 'Books' singled out *La Chartreuse de Parme*, one of Stendhal's 'two great novels' written in a 'spirit of fearless liberty' (*NLL*, 12).[112] *La Chartreuse de Parme* opens with Napoleon's return from Elba and the decision of Stendhal's hero Fabrice del Dongo to make a pilgrimage to join his illustrious hero at the Battle of Waterloo. As Italo Calvino notes, Stendhal portrays Napoleonic history 'side by side with and at the same pace as the rhythm of the individual life.'[113] *Suspense* also sees Conrad situate his protagonist in the midst of unfolding history and legend, with the novel concentrating on the charismatic individual in history and the French Emperor's popular appeal. Carlyle's work on this subject, which had influenced Conrad in his presentation of Kurtz in 'Heart of Darkness,'

---

[110] Quoted in Stuart Semmel, *Napoleon and the British* (New Haven: Yale University Press, 2004), 161.

[111] Dumas, *Comte de Monte-Cristo*, 119.

[112] A letter by Ralph Block to the *Saturday Review* noted similarities between the plots and historical settings of *Suspense* and *La Chartreuse de Parme*. *Saturday Review* (12 September, 1925): 130.

[113] Italo Calvino, *Why Read the Classics*, translated by Martin McLaughlin (London: Vintage, 2000), 132.

resurfaces. According to Carlyle, in 'The Hero as Poet,' the 'grand fundamental character is that of Great Man; that the man be great. Napoleon has words in him which are like Austerlitz Battles.'[114] In *Suspense*, Napoleon's appeal lies in his chameleon identity. When the Italian conspirator Cantelucci is asked 'what is it that makes you people love this man?' he responds: 'Signore, it is the idea' (*S*, 182). However, for the Englishman Dr. Martel, Napoleon embodies political manipulation and deception: 'Devil only knows what that idea is, but I suspect it's vague enough to include every illusion that ever fooled mankind. There must be some charm in that grey coat and that old three-cornered hat of his, for the man himself has betrayed every hatred and every hope that have helped him on his way' (*S*, 182–83). However, echoing 'The Hero as King,' in which Carlyle conceded that 'Napoleon *had* a sincerity,'[115] *Suspense* refuses an outright dehumanisation of Bonaparte. Dr. Martel realises that 'A man who would really be a monster would arouse nothing but loathing and hatred. But this man has been loved by an army, by a people. For years his soldiers died for him with joy' (*S*, 181).

Conrad's delineation of Europe on the eve of the Hundred Days relied on the contemporary English response to Napoleon. Stuart Semmel has examined the hundreds of popular anti-Napoleon broadsides and pamphlets published in England in the early years of the nineteenth century, showing England was inundated with images of the 'Corsican upstart' and the fear of Napoleonic invasion.[116] Cosmo Latham's sister Henrietta is one of those English fascinated by Napoleon. In her correspondence with Cosmo, she 'solemnly charged him to write everything he could find out, hear, or even guess about Napoleon' (*S*, 72). *Suspense* reproduces the views of William Cobbett, Leigh Hunt, and William Hazlitt, who examined British claims to freedom and justice in the face of accusations of Napoleonic tyranny. In his weekly *Examiner*, between 1808 and 1821, Hunt levelled criticism at Napoleon

---

[114] Carlyle, 'The Hero as Poet,' *On Heroes and Hero Worship and The Heroic in History*, 65–66.
[115] Carlyle, 'The Hero as King,' *On Heroes and Hero Worship and The Heroic in History*, 195.
[116] Semmel, *Napoleon and the British*, 38–71. In addition to exploring the individual character of Napoleon, Thomas Hardy's epic-drama *The Dynasts* (1904, 1906, 1908) treats English fears of a Napoleonic invasion.

but also noted that 'the destruction of one tyrant is not the destruction of all.'[117] An increasingly radicalised William Cobbett asked whether British Rule in India and recent territorial acquisitions in Java were not as despotic as Napoleon's military gains.[118] *Suspense* questions British claims to freedom and political righteousness when the young Italian conspirator insists to the English youth Cosmo: 'And yet all the tyrants of the world are your allies' (*S*, 11). Conrad again echoed Stefan Buszczyński's *La Décadence de l'Europe*, which had sceptically questioned English political liberties in light of the growth of its expansive empire during the nineteenth century. Cosmo Latham is a Hazlitt or Hunt-like figure; fascinated by the deeds of Napoleon, but like Conrad, wavering in his final judgement of the Emperor. Latham observes the 'intense drama of contemporary history, dominated by one enormously vital, and in its greatness, immensely mysterious individuality – the only man of his time' (*S*, 37). Yet, Cosmo 'had adopted neither of the contrasted views of the Emperor Napoleon entertained by his contemporaries' (*S*, 38), and Cosmo is dazzled by the 'moving force in his genius' (*S*, 38). When asked what Napoleon stands for, Cosmo responds: 'Many things, and some of them too obvious to mention. But I can't help thinking that there are some which cannot be seen yet' (*S*, 38). Like Victor Hugo's 'Expiation,' *Suspense* indicates that Napoleon's place in European history has yet to be determined. That would be left to those born later, such as Conrad, who, whether drawn to the defeated prisoner of St. Helena or the victor of Austerlitz, yielded to the spell of the Man of Destiny.

Conrad's late focus on Napoleon invites a circular interpretation to his life and career, with his last works confronting subjects that had inspired the tales of his childhood and shaped the political realities into which he was born. If one examines Conrad's reading at the time, this is not surprising. In a letter to Christopher Sandeman in November 1922, Conrad wrote: 'I've lately read nothing but Marcel Proust. But I share your opinion of the historians who have treated of the Second Empire. What an astonishing atmosphere that time had!' (*CL* 7, 599). The combination of a Proustian journey into the past and an appetite for

[117] Hunt quoted in Semmel, *Napoleon and the British*, 135.
[118] Semmel, *Napoleon and the British*, 144.

the atmosphere of a distant period of history, in this case the France of Napoléon-le-Petit, encouraged Conrad, like Victor Hugo before him, to engage with Napoléon-le-Grand, the figure representative of the shifting and subjective power of history throughout Conrad's life and writing.

Conclusion

Artists in general, (poor devils!) I am afraid, are not a long-lived race. They break up commonly about forty, their spirits giving way with the disappointment of their hopes of excellence, or the want of encouragement for that which they have attained – their plans disconcerted, and their affairs irretrievable; and in this state of mortification and embarrassment (more or less prolonged and aggravated) they are either starved, or else drink themselves to death.[1]

Conrad's life and career did not end with the disastrous prospect envisaged by William Hazlitt. The popular success of *Chance* (1913), and Conrad's critical reputation, bolstered by book-length studies of his work by Richard Curle in 1914 and Wilson Follett in 1915, ensured that the author could settle debts to his agent J.B. Pinker and look back on many examples of his own literary 'excellence.' Indeed, Conrad expended much of his energy in his last years doing just this, with concern over his 'Author's Notes,' Collected Editions, and the sale of any last remaining scrap of manuscript occupying much of his time.

On 3 August 1924, G. Jean-Aubry wrote from Canterbury to Konstanty Skirmunt, the Polish chargé d'affaires in London: 'I arrived in Canterbury this morning to learn that Mr. Joseph Conrad died suddenly at 8.30. I hasten to inform you because he was a Pole not only by birth but in his sentiments. In him we lose one of the greatest minds of our time, and your country can claim his memory.'[2] The Polish claim to

---

[1] William Hazlitt, 'On the Old Age of Artists,' *The Plain Speaker: Opinions on Books, Men, and Things*, edited by William Carew Hazlitt (London: George Bell & Sons, 1903), 122.

[2] Letter from G. Jean-Aubry to Konstanty Skirmunt, 3 August 1924, Stape and Knowles eds., *A Portrait in Letters*, 245.

Conrad was facilitated by Virginia Woolf's elegiac tribute, written later that August, which set Conrad beyond the pale of English tradition, attributing his unique character largely to his Polish inheritance:

Suddenly, without giving us time to arrange our thoughts or prepare our phrases, our guest has left us; and with his withdrawal without farewell or ceremony is in keeping with his mysterious arrival, long years ago, to take up his lodging in this country. For there was always an air of mystery about him. It was partly his Polish birth, partly his memorable appearance, partly his preference for living in the depths of the country, out of earshot of gossip, beyond reach of hostesses so that for news of him one had to depend upon the evidence of simple visitors with a habit of ringing door-bells who reported of their un-known host that he had the most perfect manners, the brightest eyes, and spoke English with a strong foreign accent.[3]

By 1948, Conrad had been placed within the 'Great Tradition' of English novelists by the prominent critic F.R. Leavis, who noted that Conrad 'has, of course, long been generally held to be among the English masters.'[4] Leavis's reading of Conrad as a bearer of the literary flame reaching back to George Eliot and Henry James ensured that Conrad was perceived as an English writer, one who, if his literary influences pointed anywhere other than England, directed his gaze west as a response to Henry James. According to Raymond Williams, a propos of *The Great Tradition*, by the 1970s Leavis had 'completely won. I mean if you talked to anyone about [it], including people who were hostile to Leavis, they were in fact reproducing his sense of the shape of its history.'[5]

In 1933, however, a French survey of the history of English literature had elucidated the impact of Conrad's Polish and French heritage, arguing that Conrad had enriched English letters through his diverse cultural and linguistic experience, producing a 'new literary cosmopolitanism' for the twentieth century:

No one before him had so clearly broken the narrow-minded link that binds the artistic handling of a language to the exclusive possession of a national intellect.

---

[3] Virginia Woolf, *Collected Essays*, vol. 1 (London: Hogarth Press, 1968), 302.
[4] F.R. Leavis, *The Great Tradition* (London: Penguin, 1980), 200.
[5] Quoted in Raman Selden, Peter Widdowson and Peter Brooker, *A Reader's Guide to Contemporary Literary Theory*, 4th ed. (London: Harvester Wheatsheaf, 1997), 23.

The language of his childhood and youth was Polish; as it was the language of his inner voice. He was strongly influenced by French literature, and his technique derives from the teaching of our realists. English, first studied in books, then adopted fully by his adult personality, became his means of reflective and creative expression.[6]

The flood of academic criticism since the 1970s on all aspects of Conrad's life and writing has accepted the view forwarded by the French Academy in 1933, with awareness of Conrad's tri-national and tri-linguistic past now essential for an appreciation of his achievement. Yet, questions originating from Conrad's European background continue to arise, particularly those addressing Romanticism, Positivism, nationalism, and narratological authority; issues paramount individually to Poland, France, and Britain, but also subjects unbound by the geographical frontiers of Conrad's heritage. This book has aimed to uncover fresh contexts for Conrad's work. Firstly, an understanding of August Cieszkowski and Polish Romantic thought may illuminate the wider culture into which Conrad was born and first exposed to literature, philosophy, and history. Secondly, while scholars have recently sought to locate Conrad's work within British popular culture at the turn of the twentieth century, the importance of the contemporary philosophical milieu of Britain and Europe to Conrad's literature should not be eclipsed. Conrad undoubtedly remains a major writer through his engagement with profound concerns of time, history, and identity, thereby contributing to an immemorial spirit of philosophical reflection. While the bonds of nationhood constrained many Europeans in the divisive nineteenth and early twentieth centuries, Conrad emerged from a traditionally patriotic homeland to produce a literature that can be regarded with an assured idealism as belonging to all nations and to none.

Alongside a re-examination of Conrad's Polish past and an assessment of the nation in his major works, it is hoped this study will instigate future discussion of the connections between Conrad, French Romanticism, and French history. These correspondences offer a fruitful means of redeeming Conrad's later output, but also of discerning continuity across his career. Conrad's fiction incorporated a wealth of historical,

---

[6] E. Legouis and L. Cazamian, *Histoire de la littérature anglaise* (Paris: Hachette, 1933), 1254.

philosophical, and aesthetic ideas, and the literary import of Conrad's work, while principally emanating from the artist's intrinsic genius, owes a debt to Conrad's dialogue with European philosophy and history of the nineteenth century. The thought of Rousseau, Herder, Hegel, and the Polish Romantics represents the backdrop to Conrad's explorations of individual and communal identity, and the major problems, figures, and turning points of modern Europe, such as nationalism, Napoleon, and the Great War, fill the pages of Conrad's writing as a testament to the unfolding narrative of human history.

The popular image of Conrad as a man inclined to hazy-eyed contemplation of history, captured in his portrait by Walter Tittle in the National Portrait Gallery in London, shows an author conditioned by time, but also transcending it with an Olympian detachment. The representation of time and transience inspired Conrad's art, from the nostalgia of 'Youth' to Conrad's captivation with the romance of the Napoleonic era. In *Chance*, Conrad's Marlow felt the 'dead stillness of your present where nothing moves except the irrecoverable minutes of your life' (C, 354–55). Conrad's conception of time reflects that described by Oswald Spengler in *The Decline of the West*. For Spengler, time was 'something beyond comprehension, this transformation of future into past, and thus time, in its contrast with space, has always a [...] baffling, oppressive ambiguity from which no serious man can wholly protect himself.'[7] Conrad ceaselessly meditated on history, committing himself to a creative enterprise that would always remain highly subjective. He recognised that the work he set before the public could never convey everything he had invested in it. In November 1919, recalling his early letter to W.E. Henley on *The Nigger of the 'Narcissus'* in which he stressed the impossibility of fully unveiling his experiences, Conrad wrote to William Reno Kane of *The Editor*, who had asked for a brief account of Conrad's experiences as a writer:

Oh, yes, it can be made brief enough. Years of unremitting concentration upon the task, hours of meditation, days in which one didn't know whether the sun shone or not – not one man in a million would understand and take to heart the truth that lies under those words. The majority would smile. What a fuss

---

[7] Spengler, *Decline of the West*, 78.

over a mere story! A story which, when it is done, does not seem so very extraordinary after all! How ridiculous!... Here and there some reader gifted with a little imagination and humanity would comment to himself: 'Poor devil!'... Hardly worth while to lay one's heart bare to all mankind for that. (CL 6, 522)

Bibliography

Achebe, Chinua. *Hopes and Impediments: Selected Essays 1965–87.* Oxford: Oxford University Press, 1988.

Acton, Lord. *Essays on Freedom and Power.* Edited with an Introduction by Gertrude Himmelfarb. London: Thames, 1956.

Alexander, R.S. *Napoleon.* London: Arnold, 2001.

Allen, James Smith. *Popular French Romanticism: Authors, Readers, and Books in the 19th Century.* New York: Syracuse University Press, 1991.

Ambrosini, Paul. *Conrad's Fiction as Critical Discourse.* Cambridge: Cambridge University Press, 1991.

Amiel, Henri-Frédéric. *Amiel's Journal.* Trans. Mrs. Humphrey Ward. 2 vols. London: Macmillan, 1885.

Anderson, Benedict. *Imagined Communities.* London: Verso, 1991.

Archer, R.L., ed. *Rousseau on Education.* London: Edward Arnold, 1912.

Arendt, Hannah. *The Origins of Totalitarianism.* London: Allen & Unwin, 1967.

Ashton, Rosemary. *The German Idea: Four English Writers and the Reception of German Thought, 1800–1860.* Cambridge: Cambridge University Press, 1980.

Avineri, Shlomo. *The Social and Political Thought of Karl Marx.* Cambridge: Cambridge University Press, 1968.

Baehr, Peter and Melvin Richter, eds. *Dictatorship in History and Theory: Bonapartism, Caesarism, and Totalitarianism.* Cambridge: Cambridge University Press, 2004.

Baillie, J.M. 'Truth and History.' *Mind* 7 (1898): 506–22.

Bainbridge, Simon. *Napoleon and English Romanticism.* Cambridge: Cambridge University Press, 1995.

Baines, Jocelyn. *Joseph Conrad: A Critical Biography.* London: Weidenfeld & Nicholson, 1960.

Barbusse, Henri. *Under Fire.* Trans. Fitzwater Wray. 1916. London: Dent, 1933.

Barnard, F.M., ed. *Herder on Social and Political Culture.* Cambridge: Cambridge University Press, 1969.

——. 'National Culture and Political Legitimacy: Herder and Rousseau.' *Journal of the History of Ideas* 44.2 (1983): 231–53.

———. *Herder on Nationality, Humanity, and History.* London: McGill-Queen's University Press, 2003.

Batchelor, John. *The Life of Joseph Conrad: A Critical Biography.* Oxford: Blackwell, 1994.

———. *'Lord Jim.'* London: Unwin, 1988.

Benjamin, Walter. *Illuminations.* Edited with an Introduction by Hannah Arendt. London: Pimlico, 1999.

Berlin, Isaiah. *The Hedgehog and the Fox: An Essay on Tolstoy's View of History.* London: Weidenfeld & Nicholson, 1953.

———. *Vico and Herder: Two Studies in the History of Ideas.* London: Hogarth Press, 1992.

———. *The Proper Study of Mankind: An Anthology of Essays.* Edited by Henry Hardy and Roger Hausheer. London: Pimlico, 1998.

Berthoud, Jacques. *Joseph Conrad: The Major Phase.* Cambridge: Cambridge University Press, 1978.

———, ed. *The Shadow-Line.* London: Penguin, 1986.

———. 'Conrad the Englishman: The Case of *Chance*.' *Conrad's Century: The Past and Future Splendour.* Ed. Laura L. Davis. Conrad: Eastern and Western Perspectives 7. Lublin: Marie Curie-Skłodowska University; Boulder, CO: East European Monographs, 1998. 133–48.

Bevan, Ernest. 'Marlow and Jim: The Reconstructed Past.' *Conradiana* 15.3 (1983): 191–202.

Bjorkman, E.A. 'Joseph Conrad: A Master of Literary Color.' *American Review of Reviews* 45 (1912): 557–60.

———. *Blackwood's Magazine* 164 (August 1898): 283–95.

———. *Blue Peter* 10 (1930): 638–40.

———. *The Bookman* 46 (1918).

Blackburn, Christopher A. *Napoleon and the Szlachta.* Boulder, CO: East European Monographs, 1998.

Borges, Jorge Luis. *Collected Fictions.* Translated by Andrew Hurley. London: Allen Lane, 1998.

Bradley, F.H. 'On Memory and Judgement.' *Mind* 17 (1908): 153–74.

———. *Collected Essays.* Oxford: Clarendon Press, 1935.

Breckman, Warren. *Marx, the Young Hegelians, and the Origins of Radical Social Theory: Dethroning of the Self.* Cambridge: Cambridge University Press, 1999.

Brodsky, Stephen G.W. 'Conrad's Two Polish Pasts: A History of Thirty Years of Critical Misrule.' *Conrad and Poland.* Ed. Alex S. Kurczaba. Conrad: Eastern and Western Perspectives 5. Lublin: Marie Curie-Skłodowska University; Boulder, CO: East European Monographs, 1996. 9–31.

Brooks, Peter. "An Unreadable Report: Conrad's 'Heart of Darkness.' " *New Casebooks: Joseph Conrad.* Ed. Elaine Jordan. London: Macmillan, 1996. 67–86.

Bronowski, J. and Bruce Mazlish. *The Western Intellectual Tradition.* Harmondsworth: Pelican Books, 1963.

Bross, Addison. 'Apollo Korzeniowski's Mythic Vision: *Poland and Muscovy,* "Note A." ' *The Conradian* 20.1 (1995): 77–102.

——. 'The January Rising and Its Aftermath: The Missing Theme in Conrad's Political Consciousness.' *Conrad and Poland.* Ed. Alex S. Kurczaba. Conrad: Eastern and Western Perspectives 5. Lublin: Marie Curie-Skłodowska University; Boulder, CO: East European Monographs, 1996. 61–87.

——. '*Almayer's Folly* and the Polish Debate about Materialism.' *Conrad's Century: The Past and Future Splendour.* Ed. Laura L. Davis. Conrad: Eastern and Western Perspectives 7. Lublin: Marie Curie-Skłodowska University; Boulder, CO: East European Monographs, 1998. 29–45.

Buitenhaus, Peter. *The Great War of Words: Literature as Propaganda 1914–1918 and After.* London: Batsford, 1989.

Bullen, J.B., ed. *Writing and Victorians.* Harlow: Longman, 1997.

Burke, Edmund. *Reflections on the French Revolution.* 1790. London: Dent, 1910.

Burrow, J.A. *The Ages of Man: A Study in Medieval Writing and Thought.* Oxford: Clarendon Press, 1986.

Burrow, John. *A History of Histories: Epics, Chronicles, Romances and Inquiries from Herodotus and Thucydides to the Twentieth Century.* London: Allen Lane, 2007.

Busza, Andrzej. 'Conrad's Polish Literary Background and Some Illustrations of the Influence of Polish Literature on his Work.' *Antemurale* 10 (1966): 109–255.

——. 'Rhetoric and Ideology in *Under Western Eyes.' Joseph Conrad: A Commemoration.* Ed. Norman Sherry. Basingstoke: Macmillan, 1976. 105–18.

——. '*The Rover*: Conrad's Nostos.' *The Ugo Mursia Memorial Lectures: Second Series.* Ed. Mario Curreli Pisa: Edizioni ETS, 2005. 31–41.

Buszczyński, Stefan. *La Décadence de l'Europe.* Paris, 1867.

——. *La Décadence de l'Europe.* Deuxieme Édition. 2 vols. Réimprimé 1916 «Hallwag» S.A. Berne: Haller & Édition Wagner, 1916.

Butler, Robert N. 'The Life Review: An Interpretation of Reminiscence in the Aged.' *Psychiatry* 26 (1963): 65–76.

Butterwick, Richard. *Poland's Last King and English Culture: Stanislaw August Poniatowski 1732–1798.* Oxford: Clarendon Press, 1998.

Cambridge Magazine. 5.18 (1916); 7.1 (1917).

Cameron, David. *The Social Thought of Rousseau and Burke: A Comparative Study.* London: Weidenfeld & Nicholson, 1973.

Canovan, Margaret. 'Hannah Arendt on Totalitarianism and Dictatorship.' *Dictatorship in History and Theory: Bonapartism, Caesarism, and Totalitarianism.* Ed. Peter Baehr and Melvin Richter. Cambridge: Cambridge University Press, 2004. 241–60.

Carabine, Keith, ed. *Joseph Conrad: Critical Assessments.* 4 vols. Robertsbridge: Helm Information, 1992.

———. *The Life and the Art: A Study of Conrad's 'Under Western Eyes.'* Amsterdam: Rodopi, 1996.

Carey, John. *The Intellectuals and the Masses: Pride and Prejudice among the Literary Intelligentsia, 1880–1939.* London: Faber, 1992.

Carlyle, Thomas. *On Heroes and Hero Worship and The Heroic in History.* London: Chapman & Hall, 1885.

———. *Critical and Miscellaneous Essays.* London: Chapman & Hall, 1887.

———. *Sartor Resartus.* 1838. Oxford: Oxford University Press, 1987.

Carr, David. *Time, Narrative, and History.* Indianapolis: Indianapolis University Press, 1986.

Carr, E.H. *What is History?* London: Macmillan, 1962.

Cavanaugh, Jan. *Out Looking In: Early Modern Polish Art, 1890–1918.* London: University of California Press, 2000.

Cecil, Hugh, and Peter H. Liddle, eds. *Facing Armageddon: The First World War Experienced.* London: Leo Cooper, 1996.

Chateaubriand, François-René. *Vie de Napoléon.* Paris: Éditions de Fallois, 1999.

Chew, Samuel C. *The Pilgrimage of Life.* London: Kennikat Press, 1973.

Cieszkowski, August. *Selected Writings of August Cieszkowski.* Edited and Translated with an Introductory Essay by André Liebach. Cambridge: Cambridge University Press, 1979.

Clark, Christopher. *Iron Kingdom: The Rise and Downfall of Prussia 1600–1947.* London: Penguin, 2007.

Cobban, Alfred. *The Nation State and National Self-Determination.* London: Collins, 1969.

Conrad, Borys. *My Father Joseph Conrad.* London: Caldar & Boyars, 1970.

Conrad, Joseph, and Ford Madox Hueffer. *The Inheritors: An Extravagant Story.* New York: Doubleday, Page, 1925.

———. *The Collected Edition of the Works.* London: Dent, 1946–55.

———. *The Cambridge Edition of the Works of Joseph Conrad.* Cambridge: Cambridge University Press, 1994.

———. *The Collected Letters of Joseph Conrad.* 9 vols. Ed. Frederick R. Karl and Laurence Davies. Cambridge: Cambridge University Press, 1983–2008.

Conrad, Joseph, *Selected Short Stories*. Ed. Keith Carabine. Ware: Wordsworth, 1997.

Cottom, Daniel. '*Lord Jim*: Destruction through Time.' *The Centennial Review* 27.1 (1983): 10–29.

Crankshaw, Edward. 'Conrad and Russia.' *Joseph Conrad: A Commemoration.* Ed. Norman Sherry. Basingstoke: Macmillan, 1976. 91–104.

Cunninghame Graham, G. & R. B. *Father Archangel of Scotland and Other Essays.* London: Adam and Charles Black, 1896.

Cunninghame Graham, R. B. *Thirteen Stories.* London: Heinemann, 1900.

———. *Progress and Other Sketches.* London: Duckworth, 1904.

Curreli, Mario. 'Napoleone all'Elba in Conrad e Hardy.' *Revisita Italiana di Studi Napoleonici* 27.1 (1980): 63–77.

———, ed. *The Ugo Mursia Memorial Lectures: Second Series.* Pisa: Edizioni ETS, 2005.

Curle, Richard, ed. *Conrad to a Friend: 150 Selected Letters from Joseph Conrad to Richard Curle.* London: Sampson Low, Marston, 1928.

Czartoryski, Adam. *Essai sur la diplomatie.* Paris, 1830.

Dale, Patricia. 'Conrad: A Borrowing from Hazlitt's Father.' *Notes and Queries* ns 10 (1963): 146.

Darío, Rubén. *Selected Poems of Rubén Darío.* Translated by Lysander Kemp. Austin: University of Texas Press, 1988.

Davies, Laurence and Cedric Watts. *Cunninghame Graham: A Critical Biography.* Cambridge: Cambridge University Press, 1979.

Davies, Norman. *God's Playground: A History of Poland.* 2 vols. Oxford: Clarendon Press, 1981.

Davis, Laura L., ed. *Conrad's Century: The Past and Future Splendour.* Conrad: Eastern and Western Perspectives 7. Lublin: Marie Curie-Skłodowska University; Boulder, CO: East European Monographs, 1998.

Davis, Rupert Hart. *Hugh Walpole: A Biography.* London: Macmillan, 1952.

Descotes, Maurice. *La légende de Napoléon et les écrivains français du XIXe siècle.* Paris: Lettres Modernes Minard, 1967.

Desforges, Michel, ed. *Le Duel.* Toulouse: Éditions Ombres, 1991.

Deutsch, Karl. *Nationalism and Social Communication: An Inquiry into the Foundations of Nationality.* London: Chapman & Hall, 1953.

———. 'The Growth of Nations: Some Recurrent Patterns of Political and Social Integration.' *World Politics* 5.2 (1953): 168–95.

Donovan, Stephen. *Joseph Conrad and Popular Culture.* London: Palgrave, 2005.

Dostoevsky, Fyodor. *Notes From Underground/The Double.* Trans. Jessie Coulson. London: Penguin, 1972.

——. *Crime and Punishment*. Trans. Richard Pevear and Larissa Volokhonsky. London: Vintage, 1993.

Dryden, Linda. *Joseph Conrad and the Imperial Romance*. Basingstoke: Macmillan, 2000.

Dumas, Alexandre. *Le Comte de Monte-Cristo*. 1846. Paris: Gallimard, 1981.

——. *Joseph Balsamo: mémoires d'un médecin*. Edited by Claude Schopp. Paris: Robert Laffont, 1990.

——. *Pauline*. Ed. Anne-Marie Callet-Bianco. 1838. Paris: Gallimard, 2002.

Eile, Stanisław. *Literature and Nationalism in Partitioned Poland, 1795–1918*. Basingstoke: Macmillan, 2000.

Eksteins, Modris. *Rites of Spring: The Great War and the Birth of the Modern Age*. London: Papermac, 2000.

Emmett, V.J. 'Carlyle, Conrad, and the Politics of Charisma: Another Perspective on "Heart of Darkness."' *Conradiana* 7.2 (1975): 145–55.

Epstein, Hugh. 'A Pier-Glass in the Cavern: London in *The Secret Agent*.' *Conrad's Cities: Essays for Hans van Marle*. Ed. Gene M. Moore. Amsterdam: Rodopi, 1992. 175–96.

——. 'The Duality of "Youth": Some Literary Contexts.' *The Conradian* 21.2 (1996): 1–14.

——. '*The Rover*: A Post-Skeptical Novel.' *Conradiana* 37.1–2 (2005): 101–18.

Erdnast-Vulcan, Daphna. *Joseph Conrad and the Modern Temper*. Oxford: Clarendon Press, 1991.

——. '"Sudden Holes in Space and Time": Conrad's Anarchist Aesthetics in *The Secret Agent*.' *Conrad's Cities: Essays for Hans van Marle*. Ed. Gene M. Moore. Amsterdam: Rodopi, 1992. 207–21.

——. *The Strange Short Fiction of Joseph Conrad*. Oxford: Oxford University Press, 1999.

Erikson, E.H. *Insight and Responsibility*. London: Faber, 1964.

Featherstone, Mike and Andrew Wernick, eds. *Images of Aging: Cultural Representations of Later Life*. London: Routledge, 1995.

Fedowowicz, J.K., ed. *A Republic of Nobles: Studies in Polish History to 1864*. Cambridge: Cambridge University Press, 1982.

Ferriter, Diarmaid. *The Transformation of Ireland 1900–2000*. London: Profile, 2005.

Fleishman, Avrom. *Conrad's Politics: Community and Anarchy in the Fiction of Joseph Conrad*. Chicago: University of Chicago Press, 1967.

Follett, Wilson. *Joseph Conrad: A Short Study of his Intellectual and Emotional Attitude Toward His Work and of the Chief Characteristics of His Work*. Garden City, NY: Doubleday, Page, 1915.

Ford, Ford Madox. *A Little Less Than Gods.* London: Duckworth, 1928.

——. *A Man Could Stand Up.* London: Duckworth, 1926.

——. *War Prose.* Ed. Max Saunders. Manchester: Carcanet Press, 1999.

Ford, Jane. 'James Joyce and the Conrad Connection: The Anxiety of Influence.' *Conradiana* 17.1 (1985): 3–18.

Forster, E. M. *Abinger Harvest.* London: Edward Arnold, 1936.

Fortnightly Review 463 and 467 (1905).

Foulke, Robert. "Life in the Dying World of Sail, 1870–1910." *The Journal of British Studies* 3 (1963): 105–36.

France, Anatole. *Oeuvres.* Vol. 2. Ed. Marie-Claire Bancquart. Paris: Gallimard, 1987.

Freud, Sigmund. *The Standard Edition of the Complete Psychological Works of Sigmund Freud.* Translated and Edited by James Strachey. 24 vols. London: Hogarth and Institute of Psycho-analysis, 1953–74.

Furet, Francois. *Interpreting the French Revolution.* Trans. Elborg Forster. Cambridge: Cambridge University Press, 1981.

——. *The French Revolution 1770–1814.* Trans. Antonia Nevill. Oxford: Blackwell, 1998.

Fussell, Paul. *The Great War and Modern Memory.* London: Oxford University Press, 1975.

Garnett, David, ed. *The Letters of T.E. Lawrence.* London: Cape, 1938.

Garnett, Edward, ed. *Letters From Conrad.* London: Nonesuch, 1928.

Gaskell, H.M. *British Red Cross Society and Order of St. John War Library, Surrey House, Marble Arch, London, For the FREE supply of Books and Magazines to Sick and Wounded Soldiers and Sailors in Hospitals and Hospital Ships at Home and Abroad,* 1918.

Gekoski, R.A. *Conrad: The Moral World of the Novelist.* London: Elek, 1978.

Gellner, Ernest. *Thought and Change.* London: Weidenfeld & Nicholson, 1972.

Gibaldi, Joseph. *MLA Handbook for Writers of Research Papers.* 5th Ed. New York: MLA, 1999.

Gildea, Robert. *The Past in French History.* London: Yale University Press, 1996.

Gille-Maisani, Jean-Charles. *Adam Mickiewicz, poéte national de la Pologne: étude psychanalytique et caractérologique.* Paris: Belles Lettres, 1988.

Gillet, Louis. 'Le dernier roman de Conrad.' *Revue des Deux Mondes.* 7ième série. XCV (Nov-Dec 1925): 931–42.

Gillon, Adam. *The Eternal Solitary: A Study of Joseph Conrad.* New York: Bookman Associates, 1960.

——. 'Conrad in Poland.' *Polish Review* 19.3–4 (1974): 3–28.

GoGwilt, Christopher. *The Invention of the West: Joseph Conrad and the Double-Mapping of Europe and Empire*. Stanford, CA: Stanford University Press, 1995.

Gooch, G.P. *History and Historians in the Nineteenth Century*. London: Longman, 1928.

Goodrich, Diana S. *Facundo and the Construction of Argentine Culture*. Austin: University of Texas Press, 1996.

Goody, Jack. *The Domestication of the Savage Mind*. Cambridge: Cambridge University Press, 1977.

Graham, Stephen. *A Private in the Guards*. London: Macmillan, 1919.

Grayling, A.C., ed. *Philosophy 1: A Guide Through the Subject*. Oxford: Oxford University Press, 2001.

Greaney, Michael. *Conrad, Language, and Narrative*. Cambridge: Cambridge University Press, 2002.

Griffiths, John W. *Joseph Conrad and the Anthropological Dilemma*. Oxford: Clarendon Press, 1995.

Grottger, Artur. *Warszawa, Polonia, Lituania, Wojna*. Warsaw: Wydawnictwo & Bellona, 1994.

Guerard, Albert. *Conrad the Novelist*. Cambridge, MA: Harvard University Press, 1958.

Güiraldes, Ricardo. *Don Segundo Sombra*. 1926; Buenos Aires: Agebe, n.d.

Haggard, H. Rider. *King Solomon's Mines*. 1885. London: Penguin, 1963.

Halicz, Emanuel. *Polish National Liberation Struggles and the Genesis of the Modern Nation*. Odense: Odense University Press, 1982.

Hall, John A., ed. *Rediscoveries: Some Neglected Modern European Political Thinkers*. Oxford: Clarendon Press, 1986.

Hampson, Robert, ed. *Lord Jim*. London: Penguin, 1989.

——. *Joseph Conrad: Betrayal and Identity*. Basingstoke: Macmillan, 1992.

——. '"Topographical Mysteries": Conrad and London.' *Conrad's Cities: Essays for Hans van Marle*. Ed. Gene M. Moore. Amsterdam: Rodopi, 1992. 154–74.

——. 'Conrad and the Rossettis: "A Casual Conversation about Anarchists."' *The Ugo Mursia Memorial Lectures: Second Series*. Ed. Mario Curreli. Pisa: Edizioni ETS, 2005. 289–304.

Hansford, James. 'Reflection and Self Consumption in "Youth."' *The Conradian* 12. 2 (1987): 150–65.

Hardy, Thomas. *The Dynasts*. Edited by Harold Orel. London: Macmillan, 1978.

——. *The Trumpet-Major: A Tale*. 1880. London: Penguin, 1997.

Hastings, Adrian. *The Construction of Nationhood: Ethnicity, Religion, and Nationalism*. Cambridge: Cambridge University Press, 1997.

Hawkins, Hunt. 'Conrad's *Heart of Darkness*: Politics and History.' *Conradiana* 24.3 (1992): 207–17.

Hawthorn, Jeremy. *Joseph Conrad: Narrative Technique and Ideological Commitment.* London: Edward Arnold, 1990.

Hay, Eloise Knapp. *The Political Novels of Joseph Conrad.* Chicago: University of Chicago Press, 1972.

——. 'Nostromo.' *The Cambridge Companion to Joseph Conrad.* Ed. J.H. Stape. Cambridge: Cambridge University Press, 1996. 81–99.

Hayes, Carlton J.H. *Essays on Nationalism and the Historical Evolution of Modern Nationalism.* New York: Macmillan, 1931.

——. *The Historical Evolution of Modern Nationalism.* New York: Macmillan, 1949.

Hazareesingh, Sudhir. *The Legend of Napoleon.* London: Granta, 2005.

Hazlitt, William. *Life of Napoleon Buonaparte.* London, 1830.

——. *The Plain Speaker: Opinions on Books, Men, and Things.* Ed. William Carew Hazlitt. London: George Bell & Sons, 1903.

——. *Table Talk or Original Essays.* London: Dent, 1908.

——. *Sketches and Essays/Winterslow.* London: George Bell & Sons, 1909.

Hearder, Harry. *Italy in the Age of Risorgimento.* London: Longman, 1983.

Hegel, G.W.F. *The Phenomenology of Mind.* Trans. J.B. Baillie. 2nd Edition. London: Allen & Unwin, 1961.

——. *Philosophy of Nature.* Ed. A.V. Miller. Oxford: Clarendon Press, 1970.

——. *Introduction to the Philosophy of History.* Trans. Leo Rauch. Indianapolis: Hackett, 1988.

——. *On Art, Religion, and the History of Philosophy: Introductory Lectures.* Indianapolis: Hackett, 1997.

Hepner, Benoit P. 'History and the Future: The Vision of August Cieszkowski.' *The Review of Politics* 15.3 (1953): 328–49.

Hernández, José. *Martín Fierro.* Buenos Aires: Losada, 2005.

Herodotus. *The Histories.* Ed. John M. Marincola. London: Penguin, 1996.

Hervouet, Yves. *The French Face of Joseph Conrad.* Cambridge: Cambridge University Press, 1990.

Herzen, Alexander. *My Past and Thoughts.* 6 Volumes. Translated by Constance Garnett. London: Chatto & Windus, 1924–26.

——. *From the Other Shore and The Russian People and Socialism: An Open Letter to Jules Michelet.* Translated by Richard Wollheim. London: Weidenfeld & Nicholson, 1956.

Higdon, David Leon. 'The Text and Context of Conrad's First Critical Essay.' *The Polish Review* 20 (1975): 97–105.

Hobson, J.A. *Imperialism: A Study.* London: James Nisbet, 1902.

Hobsbawm Eric and Terence Ranger, eds. *The Invention of Tradition.* Cambridge: Cambridge University Press, 1983.

——. *Nations and Nationalism since 1780: Programme, Myth, Reality.* Cambridge: Cambridge University Press, 1990.

——. *The Age of Extremes: 1914–1991.* London: Abacus, 2004.

Hochschild, Adam. *King Leopold's Ghost: A Story of Greed, Terror, and Heroism in Colonial Africa.* London: Pan, 2006.

Hoenselaars, Ton and Gene M. Moore. 'Conrad and T.E. Lawrence.' *Conradiana* 27.1 (1995): 3–20.

Homer. *The Odyssey.* Ed. Peter V. Jones. London: Penguin, 1991.

Hopwood, Alison L. 'Carlyle and Conrad: Past and Present and "Heart of Darkness."' *Review of English Studies* 23 (1972): 162–72.

Howard, M.E. *Studies in War and Peace.* London: Temple Smith, 1970.

Hugo, Victor. *Les Châtiments.* 1853. Paris: Pocket, 1998.

——. *Selected Poems of Victor Hugo.* Translated by E.H. and A.M. Blackmore. London: University of Chicago Press, 2001.

Hutchinson, John and Anthony D. Smith, eds. *Nationalism.* Oxford: Oxford University Press, 1994.

Hynes, Samuel. *A War Imagined: The First World War and English Culture.* London: Bodley Head, 1990.

Ireland, B. *The Fall of Toulon: The Last Opportunity to Defeat the French Revolution.* London: Weidenfeld & Nicholson, 2005.

Jacob, E.F. 'Recent World History and its Variety.' *History* 8 (1923–24): 241–55.

Jakubowski, Marek. N. 'On August Cieszkowski's "Philosophy of Action."' *Dialectics and Humanism* 4 (1977): 95–104.

——. 'The Meaning of History in August Cieszkowski: Between Hegel and Romantic Historiography.' *Dialectics and Humanism* 3 (1981): 145–55.

James, William. *Principles of Psychology* (1890). 2 vols. Cambridge, MA: Harvard University Press, 1981.

Jameson, Frederic. *The Political Unconscious: Narrative as Socially Symbolic Act.* London: Routledge, 2002.

Jameson, John Franklin. 'The Development of Modern European Historiography.' *Atlantic Monthly* 66 (1890): 322–33.

Jean-Aubry, G., ed. *Joseph Conrad: Life and Letters.* 2 vols. London: Heinemann, 1927.

Jenkins, Keith. *On 'What is History?' From Carr and Elton to Rorty and White.* London: Routledge, 1995.

Jones, Stanley. *Hazlitt: A Life: From Winterslow to Frith Street.* Oxford: Clarendon Press, 1989.

Jones, Susan. 'Conrad's Debt to Marguerite Porodowska.' *Conrad: Intertexts and Appropriations: Essays in Memory of Yves Hervouet.* Ed. Gene M. Moore and J.H. Stape. Amsterdam and Atlanta, GA: Rodopi, 1997. 7–27.

——. *Conrad and Women.* Oxford: Clarendon Press, 1999.

Jordan, Elaine, ed. *New Casebooks: Joseph Conrad.* London: Macmillan, 1996.

Joyce, James. *Ulysses.* Ed. Jeri Johnson. Oxford: Oxford University Press, 1993.

Jünger Ernst. *Storm of Steel.* Trans. Michael Hofmann. London: Allen Lane, 2003.

Kaplan, Carola M. 'Conrad's Narrative Occupation of/by Russia in *Under Western Eyes.*' *Conradiana* 27.2 (1995): 97–114.

——, Peter Mallios, and Andrea White eds. *Conrad in the Twenty-First Century: Contemporary Approaches and Perspectives.* London: Routledge, 2005.

Karl, F.R. *Joseph Conrad: The Three Lives.* London: Faber, 1979.

Kedourie, Elie. *Nationalism.* 1960. Oxford: Blackwell, 1993.

Kenyon, John. *The History Men: The Historical Profession in England since the Renaissance.* London: Weidenfeld & Nicholson, 1983.

Keynes, John Maynard. *The Economic Consequences of the Peace.* London: Macmillan, 1920.

Kipling, Rudyard. *Many Inventions.* 1893. London: Macmillan, 1949.

Kirschner, Paul. *Conrad: The Psychologist as Artist.* Edinburgh: Oliver & Boyd, 1968.

——, ed. *Under Western Eyes.* London: Penguin, 1997.

Klein, Herbert G. 'Charting the Unknown: Conrad, Marlow, and the World of Women.' *Conradiana* 20.2 (1988): 147–57.

Kliszczewski, Władysław Spiridion. 'A Short Account of My Early Life.' *The Conradian* 34.1 (2009): 5–37.

Knowles, Owen. 'Conrad, Anatole France, and the Early French Romantic Tradition: Some Influences.' *Conradiana* 11.1 (1979): 41–61.

——. *A Conrad Chronology.* Basingstoke: Macmillan, 1989.

——, ed. *Almayer's Folly.* London: Dent, 1995.

——, and Gene M. Moore, eds. *The Oxford Reader's Companion to Conrad.* Oxford: Oxford University Press, 2001.

Koch, Theodore Wesley. *Books in Camp, Trench and Hospital.* London: Dent, 1917.

——. *War Libraries and Allied Studies.* New York: G.E. Stechert & Co., 1918.

——. *Books in the War: The Romance of Library War Service.* Boston and New York: Houghton; Cambridge: The Riverside Press, 1919.

Kramer, Lloyd and Sarah Maza, eds. *A Companion to Western Historical Thought.* Oxford: Blackwell, 2002.

Kristeva, Julia. *Nations without Nationalism.* Trans. Leon S. Roudiez. New York: Columbia University Press, 1993.

Kukiel, M. *Czartoryski and European Unity 1770–1861.* Princeton: Princeton University Press, 1955.

Kurczaba, Alex S., ed. *Conrad and Poland.* Conrad: Eastern and Western Perspectives 5. Lublin: Marie Curie-Skłodowska University; Boulder, CO: East European Monographs, 1996.

Lacey, A. R. *Bergson.* London: Routledge, 1993.

Lankester, Ray E. *Degeneration: A Chapter in Darwinism.* London: Macmillan, 1880.

Lawrence, Paul. *Nationalism: History and Theory.* London: Longman, 2005.

Lawrence, T.E. *Seven Pillars of Wisdom.* London: Penguin, 1976.

Le Poidevin, Robin, and Murray MacBeath, eds. *Oxford Readings in Philosophy: The Philosophy of Time.* Oxford: Oxford University Press, 1993.

Leavis, F.R. *The Great Tradition.* Harmondsworth: Penguin, 1980.

Lemon, M.C. *Philosophy of History: A Guide for Students.* London: Routledge, 2003.

Lednicki, Wacław. 'Mickiewicz at the Collège de France.' *Polish Civilisation: Essays and Studies.* Ed. Mieczysław Giergielewicz. New York: New York University Press, 1979. 182–97.

Legouis, E. and L. Cazamian. *Histoire de la littérature anglaise.* Paris: Hachette, 1933.

Lenker, Lagrette Tallent, and Sara Munson Deats, eds. *Ageing and Identity: A Humanities Perspective.* London: Praeger, 1999.

Leslie, R.F. *Reform and Insurrection in Russian Poland 1856–1865.* London: The Athlone Press, 1963.

Lester, John. *Conrad and Religion.* Basingstoke: Macmillan, 1988.

Lewis, Wyndham. *Creatures of Habit and Creatures of Change: Essays on Art, Literature and Society 1914–1956.* Ed. Paul Edwards. Santa Rosa: Black Sparrow Press, 1989.

——. *Tarr: The 1918 Version.* Ed. Paul O' Keefe. Santa Rosa: Black Sparrow Press, 1990.

——. *Time and Western Man.* Ed. Paul Edwards. 1927. Santa Rosa: Black Sparrow Press, 1993.

Liebach, André. *Between Ideology and Utopia: The Politics and Philosophy of August Cieszkowski.* Dordrecht: Reidel, 1979.

Llobera, Josep R. *The God of Modernity: The Development of Nationalism in Western Europe.* Oxford: Berg, 1994.

Lobkowicz, Nikolaus. 'Eschatology and the Young Hegelians.' *Review of Politics* 27.3 (1965): 434–39.

López, Lucio V. *La gran aldea.* Buenos Aires: Kapeleusz, 1965.

Lothe, Jakob. *Conrad's Narrative Method*. Oxford: Clarendon Press, 1989.

——, Jeremy Hawthorn, and James Phelan, eds. *Joseph Conrad: Voice, Sequence, History, Genre*. Columbus: Ohio State University Press, 2008.

Lucas-Dubreton, J. *Le culte de Napoléon*. Paris: Albin Michel, 1960.

Ludwig, Richard M., ed. *Letters of Ford Madox Ford*. Princeton: Princeton University Press, 1965.

Ludwikowski Rett R. *Continuity and Change in Poland: Conservatism in Polish Political Thought*. Washington: Catholic University of America Press, 1991.

Lukács, Georg. *Goethe and his Age*. Trans. Robert Anchor. London: Merlin Press, 1968.

——. *The Historical Novel*. Translated by Hannah and Stanley Mitchell. London: Merlin Press, 1989.

Lukowski, Jerzy and Hubert Zawadzki. *A Concise History of Poland*. Cambridge: Cambridge University Press, 2001.

Luna, Félix. *A Short History of the Argentinians*. Translated by Cynthia Mansfield and Ian Barnett. Buenos Aires: Booket, 2000.

Lutosławski, Wincenty. *The Polish Nation*. Paris: Boyveau et Chevillet, 1917.

McDonald, Peter D. *British Literary Culture and Publishing Practice, 1880–1914*. Cambridge: Cambridge University Press, 1997.

McLynn, Frank. *Stanley: Dark Genius of African Exploration*. London: Pimlico, 2004.

McTaggart, J.M. 'The Unreality of Time.' *Mind* 17 (1908): 457–74.

Mallios, Peter. 'Undiscovering the Country: Conrad, Fitzgerald, and Meta-National Form.' *Modern Fiction Studies* 47.2 (2001): 356–90.

Marcus, Miriam. 'Monsieur Rousseau, I Presume!: Jean-Jacques Rousseau's *The Government of Poland* and Joseph Conrad's "Prince Roman."' *Conradiana* 31.3 (1999): 199–211.

Martin, W.R. 'Allegory in Conrad's *The Rover*.' *English Studies in Africa* 10.2 (1967): 186–94.

Martineau, Harriet. *Society in America*. Ed. Seymour Martin Lipset. New York: Anchor-Doubleday, 1962.

Masefield, John. *The Collected Poems of John Masefield*. London: Heinemann, 1924.

Masterman, George Frederick. *Seven Eventful Years in Paraguay: A Narrative of Personal Experience Amongst the Paraguayans*. London, 1869.

Mazzini, Giuseppe. *The Duties of Man*. London: Dent, 1907.

Melchiori, Barbara Arnett. *Terrorism in the Late Victorian Novel*. London: Verso, 1985.

Mendilow, Jonathan. 'The Political Philosophy of Thomas Carlyle (1795–1881): Towards a Theory of Catch-All Extremism.' *Rediscoveries:*

Some Neglected Modern European Political Thinkers. Edited by John A. Hall. Oxford: Clarendon Press, 1986. 7–26.

Messinger, Gary. S. *British Propaganda and the State in the First World War.* Manchester: Manchester University Press, 1992.

Michelet, Jules. *Pologne et Russie: légende de Kosciusko.* Paris, 1852.

Mickiewicz, Adam. *The Books and the Pilgrimage of the Polish Nation.* London: James Ridgeway, 1833.

——. *Selected Poetry and Prose.* Edited with an Introduction by Stanisław Helsztynski. Warsaw: Polonia Publishing House, 1955.

——. *Selected Poems.* Edited by Clark Mills. New York: Noonday Press, 1956.

——. *Forefathers.* Trans. Count Potocki of Montalk. Draguignan: The Royal Polish Cultural Foundation, 1968.

Miller, J.H. *Fiction and Repetition: Seven English Novels.* Cambridge, MA: Harvard University Press, 1982.

Miller, Nicholas Andrew. *Modernism, Ireland and the Erotics of Memory.* Cambridge: Cambridge University Press, 2002.

Miłosz, Czesław. 'Joseph Conrad in Polish Eyes.' *Atlantic Monthly* 200:5 (1957): 219–28.

——. *The History of Polish Literature.* London: Macmillan, 1969.

Mind 6 (1897): 228–40.

Monod, Sylvère, ed. *Conrad: Oeuvres V.* Paris: Gallimard, 1992.

Montague, C.E. *Disenchantment.* London: Chatto & Windus, 1922.

Moorcroft Wilson, Jean. *Siegfried Sassoon: The Making of a War Poet, A Biography (1886–1918).* London: Duckworth, 1998.

Moore, Gene M., ed. *Conrad's Cities: Essays for Hans van Marle.* Amsterdam: Rodopi, 1992.

——, and J.H. Stape, eds. *Conrad: Intertexts and Appropriations: Essays in Memory of Yves Hervouet.* Amsterdam and Atlanta, GA: Rodopi, 1997.

Morawski, Stefan. 'Polish Theories of Art Between 1830 and 1850.' *The Journal of Aesthetics and Art Criticism* 16.2 (1957): 217–36.

Moret, Eugène. 'An Anarchist.' *The Strand Magazine* 8 (Jan-June, 1894): 339–47.

Moretti, Franco. *Atlas of the European Novel, 1800–1900.* London: Verso, 1999.

Morf, Gustav. *The Polish Heritage of Joseph Conrad.* London: Sampson, Low, Marston, 1930.

——. *The Polish Shades and Ghosts of Joseph Conrad.* New York: Astra Books, 1976.

Morfill, W.R. *A Simplified Grammar of the Polish Language.* London: Trübner & Co., 1884.

Morfill, W.R. *An Essay on the Importance of the Study of Slavonic Languages.* London: Henry Frowde, 1890.

Moser, Thomas. *Joseph Conrad: Achievement and Decline.* Cambridge, MA: Harvard University Press, 1957.

Munsey's Magazine (1915).

Murray, Oswyn. 'Herodotus and Oral History.' *Achaemenid History: Proceedings of the Groningen Achaemenid History Workship II. The Greek Sources.* Ed. Heleen Sancisi-Weerdenburg and Amúlie. Kuhrt. Leiden: Nederlands Instituut voor het Nabije Oosten, 1987. 93–115.

Nadelhaft, Ruth L. *Joseph Conrad.* Hemel Hempstead: Harvester Wheatsheaf, 1991.

Najder, Zdzisław, ed. *Conrad's Polish Background: Letters to and From Polish Friends.* Trans. Halina Carroll. London: Oxford University Press, 1964.

——. 'Conrad and Rousseau: Concepts of Man and Society.' *Joseph Conrad: A Commemoration.* Ed. Norman Sherry. Basingstoke: Macmillan, 1976. 77–90.

——, ed. *Congo Diary and Other Uncollected Pieces.* New York: Doubleday, 1978.

——, ed. *Conrad Under Familial Eyes.* Trans. Halina Carroll-Najder. Cambridge: Cambridge University Press, 1983.

——. *Joseph Conrad: A Chronicle.* Cambridge: Cambridge University Press, 1983.

——. *Conrad in Perspective: Essays on Art and Fidelity.* Cambridge: Cambridge University Press, 1997.

——. 'Fidelity and Art: Joseph Conrad's Cultural Heritage and Literary Program.' *Conrad's Century: The Past and Future Splendour.* Ed. Laura L. Davis. Conrad: Eastern and Western Perspectives 7. Lublin: Marie Curie-Skłodowska University; Boulder, CO: East European Monographs, 1998. 11–27.

——. 'Polish Inheritance.' *Oxford Reader's Companion to Conrad.* Ed. Owen Knowles and Gene M. Moore. Oxford: Oxford University Press, 2000. 319–21.

——. 'Joseph Conrad and the Classical World: A Sketch of an Outline.' *The Ugo Mursia Memorial Lectures: Second Series.* Ed. Mario Curreli. Pisa: Edizioni ETS, 2005. 19–30.

Nelson, Keith, and Zara S. Steiner, eds. *Britain and the Origins of the First World War.* 2nd Edition. Basingstoke: Macmillan, 2003.

Nicholson, Peter P. *The Political Philosophy of the British Idealists: Selected Studies.* Cambridge: Cambridge University Press, 1990.

Nietzsche, Friedrich. *On the Advantages and Disadvantages of History for Life.* Indianapolis: Hackett, 1980.

Niland, Richard. '"Who's that Fellow Lynn?": Conrad and Robert Lynd.' *The Conradian* 33.1 (2008): 130–44.

Nordau, Max. *Degeneration*. London: Heinemann, 1895.

Norman, Richard J. *Hegel's Phenomenology: A Philosophical Introduction*. Aldershot: Gregg, 1991.

O'Leary, Brendan. 'On the Nature of Nationalism: An Appraisal of Ernest Gellner's Writings on Nationalism.' *British Journal of Political Science* 27.2 (1997): 191–222.

Orel, Harold. *Popular Fiction in England 1914–1918*. Lexington: University Press of Kentucky, 1992.

Owen, Wilfred. *The Collected Poems of Wilfred Owen*. Edited with an Introduction by C. Day Lewis. London: Chatto & Windus, 1968.

Parker, Christopher. *The English Historical Tradition Since 1850*. Edinburgh: John Donald, 1990.

Peacock, Noel. '"Undefaced Image": Autobiography and Vision in *A Personal Record*.' *Conrad's Century: The Past and Future Splendour*. Ed. Laura L. Davis. Conrad: Eastern and Western Perspectives 7. Lublin: Marie Curie-Skłodowska University; Boulder, CO: East European Monographs, 1998. 151–65.

Pegum, J.M.C. and R. Niland eds. *Carnage, Casualties, and Catharsis: The Great War Statistics Correspondence*. Cambridge: Reinhardt-Cash, 2003.

Petterson, Torrsten. *Consciousness and Time*. Abo: Abo Akademi, 1982.

Porter, Brian. *When Nationalism Began to Hate: Imagining Modern Politics in Nineteenth-Century Poland*. Oxford: Oxford University Press, 2000.

Proust, Marcel. *Remembrance of Things Past*. Trans. C.K. Scott Moncrieff and Terence Kilmartin. London: Penguin, 1985.

Ransel, David L., and Bozena Shallcross, eds. *Polish Encounters, Russian Identity*. Bloomington: Indiana University Press, 2005.

Raval, Suresh. *The Art of Failure: Conrad's Fiction*. Boston: Allen & Unwin, 1986.

Ray, Martin. 'The Landscape of *The Secret Agent*.' *Conrad's Cities: Essays for Hans van Marle*. Ed. Gene M. Moore. Amsterdam: Rodopi, 1992. 197–206.

Read, Herbert. *Annals of Innocence and Experience*. London: Faber, 1940.

Red Cross: The Official Journal of The British Red Cross Society 3.6 (1916).

Reilly, Jim. *Shadowtime: History and Representation in Hardy, Conrad, and George Eliot*. London: Routledge, 1993.

Remarque, Erich Maria. *All Quiet on the Western Front*. Trans. A.W. Wheen. London: Putnam, 1929.

Renner, Stanley. '"Youth" and the Sinking Ship of Faith: Conrad's Mature Nineteenth Century Epic.' *Ball State University Forum* 28 (1987): 57–73.

Ressler, Steve. *Joseph Conrad: Consciousness and Integrity.* New York: New York University Press, 1988.

Ricoeur, Paul. *Time and Narrative.* Vol. 1. Trans. Kathleen McLaughlin and David Pellauer. Chicago: University of Chicago Press, 1984.

Ritchie, David G. *Darwin and Hegel, with Other Philosophical Writings.* London: Swan Sonnenschein & Co., 1893.

Robb, Graham. *Balzac: A Biography.* London: Papermac, 1994.

———. *Victor Hugo.* London: Picador, 1997.

———. *Rimbaud.* London: Picador, 2000.

Roberts, Andrew Michael. *Conrad and Masculinity.* Basingstoke: Macmillan, 2000.

Rodó, José E. *Ariel.* Edited by Gordon Brotherston. Cambridge: Cambridge University Press, 1967.

———. *Ariel.* Translated by Margaret Sayers Peden. Prologue by Carlos Fuentes. Austin: University of Texas Press, 1988.

———. *Ariel.* Buenos Aires: Losada, 2007.

Rogers, R. *A Psychoanalytic Study of the Double in Literature.* Detroit: Wayne State University Press, 1970.

Ross, William T. *H.G. Wells's World Reborn: The Outline of History and its Companions.* London: Associated University Presses, 2002.

Rossen, Janice and Anne M. Wyatt-Brown, eds. *Aging and Gender in Literature: Studies in Creativity.* London: University Press of Virginia, 1993.

Roth, Joseph. *La Marche de Radetzsky.* Paris: Éditions du Seuil, 1982.

Rousseau, Jean-Jacques. *The Social Contract and Discourses.* Trans. G.D.H. Cole. London: Dent, 1963.

Ruppel, Richard. 'Yanko Gooral in the Heart of Darkness: "Amy Foster" as Colonialist Text.' *Conradiana* 28.2 (1996): 126–32.

Russell, Bertrand. *Portraits From Memory.* London: Allen & Unwin, 1956.

Rylance, Rick. 'Twisting: Memory from Eliot to Eliot.' *Memory and Memorials, 1789–1914: Literary and Cultural Perspectives.* Ed. Matthew Campbell, Jacqueline M. Labbe, and Sally Shuttleworth. London: Routledge, 2000. 98–116.

———. *Victorian Psychology and British Culture 1850–1880.* Oxford: Oxford University Press, 2000.

Said, Edward. *Joseph Conrad and the Fiction of Autobiography.* Cambridge, MA: Harvard University Press, 1966.

———. *Culture and Imperialism.* London: Vintage, 1994.

Sarmiento, Domingo F. *Facundo, or Civilization and Barbarism.* Introduction by Ilan Stavans. Translated by Mary Peabody Mann. London: Penguin, 1998.

———. *Facundo.* Buenos Aires: Terramar, n.d.

———. *Recuerdos de provincia.* Buenos Aires: Gradifco, 2006.

Sartre, Jean-Paul. *Being and Nothingness*. Trans. Hazel. E. Barnes. London: Methuen, 1957.

Sassoon, Siegfried. *Memoirs of an Infantry Officer*. London: Faber, 1930.

——. *Diaries 1915–1918*. Ed. Rupert Hart-Davis. London: Faber, 1983.

Schiller, Friedrich. *On the Aesthetic Education of Man*. Trans. Reginald Snell. New York: Dover, 2004.

Schwarz, Daniel R. *Conrad: The Later Fiction*. London: Macmillan, 1982.

Schivelbusch, Wolfgang. *The Culture of Defeat: On National Trauma. Mourning and Recovery*. Trans. Jefferson Chase. London: Granta Books, 2003.

Selden, Raman, Peter Widdowson, and Peter Brooker. *A Reader's Guide to Contemporary Literary Theory*. 4th Edition. London: Harvester Wheatsheaf, 1997.

Semmel, Stuart. *Napoleon and the British*. New Haven: Yale University Press, 2004.

Sherry, Norman. *Conrad and His World*. London: Thames & Hudson, 1972.

——, ed. *Conrad: The Critical Heritage*. London: Routledge & Kegan Paul, 1973.

——, ed. *Joseph Conrad: A Commemoration*. London: Macmillan, 1976.

Shuttleworth, Sally, Jacqueline Cabbe, and Matthew Campbell, eds. *Memory and Memorials, 1789–1914: Literary and Cultural Perspectives*. London: Routledge, 2000.

Siegle, Robert. 'The Two Texts of *Chance*.' *Conradiana* 16.2 (1984): 83–101.

Simmons, Allan H. *Critical Issues: Joseph Conrad*. London: Palgrave, 2006.

——. '*The Nigger of the "Narcissus"*: History, Narrative, and Nationalism.' *Joseph Conrad: Voice, Sequence, History, Genre*. Edited by Jakob Lothe, Jeremy Hawthorn, and James Phelan. Columbus: Ohio State University Press, 2008. 141–59.

Skowronek, Jerzy. 'The Direction of Political Change in the Era of National Insurrection, 1795–1864.' *A Republic of Nobles: Studies in Polish History to 1864*. Ed. J.K. Fedowowicz. Cambridge: Cambridge University Press, 1982. 258–81.

Słowacki, Juliusz. *Genesis from the Spirit*. Trans. Col. K. Chodkiewicz. 1844. London: Col. K. Chodkiewicz, 1966.

Spender, J.A. 'Great Britain and Germany.' *The Fortnightly Review* 467 (1905): 811–28.

Spengler, Oswald. *The Decline of the West*. Ed. Helmut Werner. English abridged edition prepared by Arthur Helps from the translation by Charles Francis Atkinson. London: Allen & Unwin, 1961.

Stadter, Philip A. 'Historical Thought in Ancient Greece.' *A Companion to Western Historical Thought*. Ed. Lloyd Kramer and Sarah Maza. Oxford: Blackwell, 2002. 35–59.

Stanley, Henry Morton. *In Darkest Africa.* 2 Vols. London, 1890.

Stape, J.H. '"The Crime of Partition"': Conrad's Sources.' *Conradiana* 15 (1983): 219–26.

——. and Owen Knowles, eds. *A Portrait in Letters: Correspondence to and about Conrad.* Amsterdam: Rodopi, 1996.

——, ed. *The Cambridge Companion to Joseph Conrad.* Cambridge: Cambridge University Press, 1996.

——. 'One can learn something from Balzac: Conrad and Balzac.' *Conrad: Intertexts and Appropriations: Essays in Memory of Yves Hervouet.* Ed. Gene M. Moore and J.H. Stape. Amsterdam and Atlanta, GA: Rodopi, 1997. 103–18.

——, ed. *Notes on Life and Letters.* Cambridge: Cambridge University Press, 2004.

——. '"The End of the Tether" and Victor Hugo's *Les Travailleurs de la Mer.*' *The Conradian* 30.1 (2005): 71–80.

——. 'The Kliszczewski Document.' *The Conradian* 34.1 (2009): 1–4.

Stead, W.T. 'Russia: "Ghost, Ghoul, Djinn, Etc.": The Fantastic Rhetoric of Mr. Conrad.' *Review of Reviews* 33.187 (July 1905): 51–52.

Steiner, Zara. *The Lights that Failed: European International History, 1919–1933.* Oxford: Oxford University Press, 2005.

Stendhal. *Napoléon.* Ed. Catherine Mariette. Paris: Stock, 1998.

——. *La Chartreuse de Parme.* 1839. Paris: Gallimard, 2003.

Stephenson, R.H. *Goethe's Conception of Knowledge and Science.* Edinburgh: Edinburgh University Press, 1995.

Stevenson, Robert Louis. *Memories & Portraits.* London: Chatto & Windus, 1900.

Strand Magazine. January-June (1894) and October (1917).

Strickland, Geoffrey. *Stendhal: The Education of a Novelist.* Cambridge: Cambridge University Press, 1974.

Sun Lee, Yoon. *Nationalism and Irony: Burke, Scott, Carlyle.* Oxford: Oxford University Press, 2004.

Sutherland, J.G. *At Sea with Joseph Conrad.* London: Grant Richards, 1922.

Swisher, Clarice, ed. *Readings on 'Heart of Darkness.'* San Diego CA: Greenhaven Press, 1999.

Tadié, Alexis. 'Perceptions of Language in *Lord Jim.*' *The Conradian* 31.1 (2006): 16–36.

Talmon, J.L. *Political Messianism: The Romantic Phase.* New York: Praeger, 1960.

Tangye Lean, E. *The Napoleonists: A Study in Political Disaffection 1760–1960.* London: Oxford University Press, 1970.

Tanner, Tony. *Conrad: 'Lord Jim.'* London: Arnold, 1963.

———. ' "Gnawed Bones" and "Artless Tales" – Eating and Narrative in Conrad.' *Joseph Conrad: A Commemoration.* Ed. Norman Sherry. London: Macmillan, 1976. 17–36.

Thackeray, William. *Vanity Fair.* 1848. London: Penguin, 1972.

Thane, Pat, and Paul Johnson, eds. *Old Age from Antiquity to Post-Modernity.* London: Routledge, 1998.

———. *Old Age in English History: Past Experiences, Present Issues.* Oxford: Oxford University Press, 2000.

Thomas, Brook. 'Preserving and Keeping Order by Killing Time in *Heart of Darkness.*' *Joseph Conrad, 'Heart of Darkness:' A Case Study in Contemporary Criticism.* Ed. Ross C. Murfin. New York: St. Martin's Press, 1989. 239–57.

Thomas, Mark Ellis. 'Doubling and Difference in Conrad: "The Secret Sharer," *Lord Jim* and *The Shadow Line.*' *Conradiana* 27.3 (1995): 222–33.

Thomson, Paul. *The Edwardians: The Remaking of British Society.* London: Weidenfeld & Nicholson, 1984.

Toews, John. *Hegelianism: The Path Towards Dialectical Humanism, 1805–1841.* Cambridge: Cambridge University Press, 1980.

Tolstoï, Léon. *La Guerre et la Paix.* Traduction par Henri Mongault. Paris: Gallimard, 1952.

T.P's Weekly (1914–1918).

Trevelyan, G.M. 'History and Literature.' *History* 9 (1924–25): 81–91.

Tuchman, Barbara W. *The Proud Tower: A Portrait of the World before the War 1890–1914.* New York: Ballantine, 1996.

Tulard, Jean. *L'Anti-Napoléon: la légende noire de l'empereur.* Paris: Juillard, 1965.

———. *Le mythe de Napoléon.* Paris: Armand Colin, 1971.

———, ed. *Dictionnaire du Second Empire.* Paris: Fayard, 1995.

———, ed. *Dictionnaire Napoléon.* Paris: Fayard, 1989.

Turgenev, Ivan. *Fathers and Children.* Trans. Constance Garnett. London: Heinemann, 1895.

———. *On the Eve.* Trans. Constance Garnett. 1895. London: Heinemann, 1928.

Turner, Bryan S. 'Aging and Identity: Some Reflections on the Somatization of the Self.' *Images of Aging: Cultural Representations of Later Life.* Ed. Mike Featherstone and Andrew Wernick. London: Routledge, 1995. 245–60.

van Ghent, Dorothy. *The English Novel: Form and Function.* Holt, Reinhart & Winston, 1953.

van Marle, Hans. 'A Novelist's Dukedom: From Joseph Conrad's Library.' *The Conradian* 16.2 (1991): 55–78.

van Marle, Hans. and Gene M. Moore. 'The Sources of *Suspense.*' *Conrad: Intertexts and Appropriations: Essays in Memory of Yves Hervouet.* Ed. Gene M. Moore and J.H. Stape. Amsterdam and Atlanta, GA: Rodopi, 1997. 141–63.

Vansina, Jan. *Oral Tradition: A Study in Historical Methodology.* Trans. H.M. Wright. London: Routledge & Kegan Paul, 1973.

———. *Oral Tradition as History.* London: James Currey, 1985.

Varouxakis, Georgias. ' "Patriotism," "Cosmopolitanism," and "Humanity" in Victorian Political Thought.' *European Journal of Political Theory* 5.1 (2006): 100–18.

Verleun, Jan. 'The Changing Face of Charlie Marlow, 1.' *The Conradian* 8.2 (1983): 21–27.

———. 'The Changing Face of Charlie Marlow, 2.' *The Conradian* 9.1 (1984): 15–24.

Walicki, Andrzej. *The Slavophile Controversy: History of a Conservative Utopia in Nineteenth-Century Russian Thought.* Trans. Hilda Andrews-Rusiecka. Oxford: Clarendon Press, 1975.

———. *Philosophy and Romantic Nationalism: The Case of Poland.* Oxford: Clarendon Press, 1982.

———. *A History of Russian Thought from the Enlightenment to Marxism.* Oxford: Clarendon Press, 1988.

———. *The Enlightenment and the Birth of Modern Nationhood: Polish Political Thought from Noble Republicanism to Tadeusz Kościuszko.* Notre Dame: University of Notre Dame Press, 1989.

Walsh, W.H. 'Bradley and Critical History.' *The Philosophy of F.H. Bradley.* Ed. Anthony Manser and Guy Stock. Oxford: Clarendon Press, 1984. 33–51.

Watson, John. 'The Problem of Hegel.' *The Philosophical Review* 3.5 (1894): 546–67.

Watt, Ian, ed. *Conrad, The Secret Agent: A Casebook.* Basingstoke: Macmillan, 1973.

———. *Conrad in the Nineteenth Century.* London: Chatto & Windus, 1980.

———. *Essays on Conrad.* Cambridge: Cambridge University Press, 2000.

———. 'Ideological Perspectives: Kurtz and the Fate of Victorian Progress.' *New Casebooks: Joseph Conrad.* Ed. Elaine Jordan. Basingstoke: Macmillan, 1996. 32–47.

———. *Joseph Conrad 'Nostromo.'* Cambridge: Cambridge University Press, 1988.

Watts Cedric, and Laurence Davies. *Cunninghame Graham: A Critical Biography.* Cambridge: Cambridge University Press, 1979.

Watts, Cedric. *The Deceptive Text: An Introduction to Covert Plots.* Brighton: Harvester, 1984.

——, ed. *The Nigger of the 'Narcissus.'* London: Penguin, 1989.

——. *Joseph Conrad: Nostromo.* London: Penguin, 1990.

——. 'Conrad and the Myth of the Monstrous Town.' *Conrad's Cities: Essays for Hans van Marle.* Ed. Gene M. Moore. Amsterdam: Rodopi, 1992. 17–30.

——. *A Preface to Conrad.* 2nd Ed. London: Longman, 1993.

——. 'Jews and Degenerates in *The Secret Agent.*' *The Conradian* 32.1 (2008): 70–82.

Wells, H.G. *Mr Britling Sees it Through.* London: Cassell, 1916.

——. *The Outline of History.* London: Cassell, 1923.

Wharton, Edith, ed. *The Book of the Homeless.* London: Macmillan, 1916.

White, Andrea. *Joseph Conrad and the Adventure Tradition.* Cambridge: Cambridge University Press, 1993.

White, Hayden. *Metahistory: The Historical Imagination in Nineteenth-Century Europe.* London: Johns Hopkins University Press, 1973.

Whitworth, Michael H. *Einstein's Wake: Relativity, Metaphor, and Modernist Literature.* Oxford: Oxford University Press, 2001.

Williamson, Edwin. *The Penguin History of Latin America.* London: Penguin, 1992.

Winter, J.M. 'Britain's "Lost Generation" of the First World War.' *Population Studies* 31 (1977): 449–66.

Wollaeger, M. *Joseph Conrad and the Fictions of Skepticism.* Stanford, CT: Stanford University Press, 1990.

Woodcock, George. *Anarchism: A History of Libertarian Ideas and Movements.* Harmondsworth: Penguin, 1986.

Woodward, Kathleen. *Aging and its Discontents: Freud and other Fictions.* Indianapolis: Indianapolis University Press, 1991.

Woolf, Leonard. 'The Last Conrad.' *Nation and Athenaeum* 38 (3 October, 1925): 18.

Woolf, Virginia. *Collected Essays.* London: Hogarth Press, 1968.

Yeats, W.B. *Selected Poems of William Butler Yeats.* Ed. M.L. Rosenthal. New York: Macmillan, 1962.

Zawadski, W.H. *A Man of Honour: Adam Czartoryski as a Statesman of Russia and Poland 1795–1831.* Oxford: Clarendon Press, 1993.

Zimmermann, Daniel. *Alexandre Dumas le Grand: biographie.* Paris: Phébus, 2002.

Zweig, Stefan. *The World of Yesterday.* Lincoln: University of Nebraska Press, 1964.

Index